Contents

Readings in the History of Christian Theology

Volume 2

Books by William C. Placher
Published by The Westminster Press

Readings in the History of Christian Theology, Volume 1:
From Its Beginnings to the Eve of the Reformation

Readings in the History of Christian Theology, Volume 2:
From the Reformation to the Present

A History of Christian Theology: An Introduction

Readings in the History of Christian Theology

Volume 2

From the Reformation
to the Present

William C. Placher

The Westminster Press
Philadelphia

© 1988 William C. Placher

All rights reserved—no part of this book may be reproduced in any form without permission in writing from the publisher, except by a reviewer who wishes to quote brief passages in connection with a review in magazine or newspaper.

Scripture quotations from the Revised Standard Version of the Bible, copyrighted 1946, 1952, © 1971, 1973 by the Division of Christian Education of the National Council of the Churches of Christ in the U.S.A., are used by permission.

Scripture quotations marked NEB are from *The New English Bible.* © The Delegates of the Oxford University Press and the Syndics of the Cambridge University Press 1961, 1970. Used by permission.

Book design by Gene Harris

First edition

Published by The Westminster Press®
Philadelphia, Pennsylvania

PRINTED IN THE UNITED STATES OF AMERICA

9 8 7 6 5

*These volumes are dedicated
to my mother,
in gratitude for a lifetime
of friendship, understanding,
and love*

Library of Congress Cataloging-in-Publication Data

Readings in the history of Christian theology / [edited by] William C. Placher. — 1st ed.
    p.   cm.
  Bibliography: p.
  Contents: v. 1. From its beginnings to the eve of the Reformation — v. 2. From the Reformation to the present.
  ISBN 0-664-24057-7 (pbk. : v. 1).
  ISBN 0-664-24058-5 (pbk. : v. 2)

  1. Theology. I. Placher, William C. (William Carl), 1948–
BT80.R35 1988
230—dc19   87-29540
                                                           CIP

Preface

In 1983 The Westminster Press published a book I had written called *A History of Christian Theology*. The book's reviewers have been kind, and sales have been good. I have been particularly pleased by the teachers and students who have thanked me for the help it gave them in teaching and learning theology's history.

That earlier book, however, had an obvious limitation: it presented its story primarily in my words, with my interpretations. As soon as possible, students of any kind of history should be reading primary texts for themselves and reaching their own interpretations. But that isn't always easy. One of the themes of my earlier book was that Christian theology has always been a pluralistic affair, but with the escalating price of books, it is difficult to put together an affordable collection of readings that captures that diversity. I hope these two volumes will help.

To cast modesty aside, I think I have succeeded beyond my expectations. I had expected to put together a book of readings that would need to function as a supplement to a narrative history—my own or someone else's. That certainly remains one possible use. But, rather to my surprise, I found it possible to put together excerpts that, with brief introductions, form a roughly coherent narrative and stand on their own as a history of Christian theology. Keeping in mind that they might be used independently, I have repeated some material from my earlier book in introductions and suggestions for further reading.

These volumes share some of the features of my earlier book: an ecumenical perspective, a commitment to representing the tradition's diversity, a focus on the history of ideas rather than institutional history. I have tried to choose selections long enough to give a sense of the writer's style and to make it clear that theology does not consist simply of unsupported assertions but involves arguments. I have sought to keep my own introductions and notes to a minimum, to make room for as much of the primary texts as possible. Occasionally I have substituted U.S. spellings for British. Teachers are sometimes tempted to leave out things that have become, for them, overly familiar—but even the most familiar texts are often new to a student. Therefore, while I hope that even those expert in the field will find a few unfamiliar passages here, I have tried not to leave out the obvious ones.

No anthology is ever really satisfactory. If I were more learned or more imaginative, I am sure this one would be better. We keep learning more about the past, and we keep asking new questions of it as new issues arise in the present. So history keeps going out of date. In compiling this anthology, I was particularly conscious that new insights in feminist scholarship raise questions about both the selection and the translation of texts. I wish I had been able to take them more into account.

I am grateful to James Heaney, a committed and courageous editor who encouraged and supported my earlier book, and to Cynthia Thompson, my helpful editor for these volumes. The Lilly Library of Wabash College and the Regenstein Library of the University of Chicago and their staffs helped me at many points. My emeritus colleague John Charles answered questions over coffee about everything from medieval history to Greek grammar. I am also grateful to James McCord and the Center of Theological Inquiry for providing me with a wonderful "home away from home" for a year during which the final stages of this project were completed. My colleagues, students, and friends at Wabash continue to be a community that nurtures me in many ways. Wabash faculty development funds and money from the Eric Dean Fund helped support my research. I am above all grateful to my two research assistants: for over a year, David Schulz did everything from typing to tracking down publishers, and David Kirtley provided invaluable assistance in the project's final stages. Without them, I am not sure either I or the book would have made it.

W.C.P.

CHAPTER 1

Luther
and the Radical Reformation

The history of Christian theology forms a connected story; it allows for no clean divisions. Recent scholarship concerning the Reformation, for instance, has often emphasized its roots in the late Middle Ages. Still, if one has to divide Christian theology's history in half, the Reformation of the sixteenth century does mark a decisive watershed. The same story continues, but here a dramatically new chapter begins.

That chapter opened modestly enough. In 1517 a German monk named Martin Luther wrote ninety-five theses criticizing abuses in the selling of indulgences. According to late-medieval theology, anyone who had sinned, even once forgiven, owed a penance. But those who repented and contributed money to the church could receive an indulgence that let them off the penance. In the hands of unscrupulous popular preachers, all this could sound like buying permission to sin. As Luther thought about indulgences, however, he realized that his real objection was not just to such popular abuses but to a whole theology that seemed to suppose one could earn or deserve God's grace. Luther read in Paul's letter to the Romans that the just shall live by faith, and he concluded that those who have faith are justified by God's unmerited grace alone, without regard for their good works.

At first, Luther thought he was only clarifying the true teaching of the church. But in 1519 the Catholic theologian Johannes Eck challenged Luther to a public debate and convinced him that he was in disagreement with official statements of popes and councils. Called in 1521 before the assembled nobility of Germany to recant, Luther insisted, "Unless I am convinced by the testimony of Scripture or by clear reason, for I do not trust either in Pope or in councils alone, since it is well known that they have often erred and contradicted themselves . . . I cannot and will not retract anything."

The Protestant Reformation began with that challenge to traditional authority. The newly invented printing press spread Luther's message of

11

"justification by faith" and "the authority of Scripture alone" through Germany and the rest of Europe. Others, such as Ulrich Zwingli in the Swiss city of Zurich, were arriving independently at conclusions like those of Luther and were beginning "reformations" of their own. The "reformers" soon began to disagree among themselves. Luther and Zwingli debated a number of issues, especially the nature of the Lord's Supper, and followers of Zwingli and other Swiss Reformers grew into the family of "Reformed" Protestants, to be distinguished from "Lutherans."

As the Reformation spread, it inevitably divided the Christian community, but both Luther and Zwingli tried to keep all Christians within a given territory together in one church, even at the cost of making some compromises. Others, however, felt that true reform meant creating a purified church of the truly committed, even if that meant founding small separated communities. They often took willingness to be rebaptized as an adult as the necessary sign of membership in such communities and were therefore called Anabaptists ("rebaptizers").

Many Anabaptists suffered persecution. Some, like the leaders of the city of Münster in the 1530s, tried to impose their own beliefs by force. A young preacher named Thomas Müntzer did not advocate rebaptizing but is often classified with the Anabaptists as part of the "Radical Reformation." A widespread revolt among German peasants in 1525 appealed to Luther for support, but he refused to challenge secular authority as he had that of the church. Müntzer, however, denounced everything he considered a form of oppressive authority and joined the peasants, only to be killed by their opponents as he fled after the defeat of the peasant army.

Associations with violence were giving the "Radical Reformation" a bad name. In the later 1500s a Dutchman named Menno Simons and others regrouped the surviving Anabaptists into withdrawn, disciplined, pacifist communities, which survive as the Amish and Mennonites. While Menno Simons was uniting divided Anabaptists, Lutheran theologians were dividing over such issues as the role of human freedom in salvation, divisions settled only with the Formula of Concord in 1577. Reforming Christian theology was proving to be a complicated and controversial task.

Martin Luther (1483–1546)

From *The Freedom of a Christian*

In 1520 Pope Leo X required Luther to retract his views and submit to papal authority. Luther wrote this treatise within weeks of having received the papal demand. About the time he finished it, the emperor summoned him to the imperial Diet that would meet at Worms the following year. Luther burned the papal demand and at the Diet refused to recant his position. The Reformation had begun, and this treatise, as much as any other, summarized its basic principles— justification by faith, the authority of scripture, and the priesthood of all believers.

To make the way smoother for the unlearned—for only them do I serve—I shall set down the following two propositions concerning the freedom and the bondage of the spirit:

A Christian is a perfectly free lord of all, subject to none.

A Christian is a perfectly dutiful servant of all, subject to all.

These two theses seem to contradict each other. If, however, they should be found to fit together they would serve our purpose beautifully. Both are Paul's own statements, who says in 1 Cor. 9 [:19], "For though I am free from all men, I have made myself a slave to all," and in Rom. 13 [:8], "Owe no one anything, except to love one another." Love by its very nature is ready to serve and be subject to him who is loved. So Christ, although he was Lord of all, was "born of woman, born under the law" [Gal. 4:4] and therefore was at the same time a free man and a servant, "in the form of God" and "of a servant" [Phil. 2:6–7].

Let us start, however, with something more remote from our subject, but more obvious. Man has a twofold nature, a spiritual and a bodily one. According to the spiritual nature, which men refer to as the soul, he is called a spiritual, inner, or new man. According to the bodily nature, which men refer to as flesh, he is called a carnal, outward, or old man, of whom the Apostle writes in 2 Cor. 4 [:16], "Though our outer nature is wasting away, our inner nature is being renewed every day." Because of this diversity of nature the Scriptures assert contradictory things concerning the same man, since these two men in the same man contradict each other, "for the desires of the flesh are against the Spirit, and the desires of the Spirit are against the flesh," according to Gal. 5 [:17].

First, let us consider the inner man to see how a righteous, free, and pious Christian, that is, a spiritual, new, and inner man, becomes what he is. It is evident that no external thing has any influence in producing Christian righteousness or freedom, or in producing unrighteousness or servitude. . . .

One thing, and only one thing, is necessary for Christian life, righteousness, and freedom. That one thing is the most holy Word of God, the gospel of Christ, as Christ says, John 11 [:25], "I am the resurrection and the life; he who believes in me, though he die, yet shall he live"; and John 8 [:36], "So if the Son makes you free, you will be free indeed"; and Matt. 4 [:4], "Man shall not live by bread alone, but by every word that proceeds from the mouth of God." Let us then consider it certain and firmly established that the soul can do without anything except the Word of God and that where the Word of God is missing there is no help at all for the soul. If it has the Word of God it is rich and lacks nothing, since it is the Word of life, truth, light, peace, righteousness, salvation, joy, liberty, wisdom, power, grace, glory, and of every incalculable blessing. This is why the prophet in the entire Psalm [119] and in many other places yearns and sighs for the Word of God and uses so many names to describe it. . . .

You may ask, "What then is the Word of God, and how shall it be used, since there are so many words of God?" I answer: The Apostle explains this in Romans 1. The Word is the gospel of God concerning his Son, who was made flesh, suffered, rose from the dead, and was glorified through the Spirit who sanctifies. To preach Christ means to feed the soul, make it righteous, set it free, and save it, provided it believes the preaching. Faith alone is the saving and efficacious use of the Word of God, according to Rom. 10 [:9]: "If you confess with your lips that Jesus is Lord and believe in your heart that God raised him from the dead, you will be saved." Furthermore, "Christ is the end of the law, that every one who has faith may be justified" [Rom. 10:4]. Again, in Rom. 1 [:17], "He who through faith is righteous shall live." The Word of God cannot be received and cherished by any works whatever but only by faith. Therefore it is clear that, as the soul needs only the Word of God for its life and righteousness, so it is justified by faith alone and not any works; for if it could be justified by anything else, it would not need the Word, and consequently it would not need faith.

This faith cannot exist in connection with works—that is to say, if you at the same time claim to be justified by works, whatever their character—for that would be the same as "limping with two different opinions" [1 Kings 18:21], as worshiping Baal and kissing one's own hand [Job 31:27–28], which, as Job says, is a very great iniquity. Therefore the moment you begin to have faith you learn that all things in you are altogether blameworthy, sinful, and damnable, as the Apostle says in Rom. 3 [:23], "Since all have sinned and fall short of the glory of God," and, "None is righteous, no, not one; . . . all have turned aside, together they have gone wrong" (Rom. 3:10–12). When you have learned this you will know that you need Christ, who suffered and rose again for you so that, if you believe in him, you may through this faith become a new man in so far as your sins are forgiven and you are justified by the merits of another, namely, of Christ alone.

Since, therefore, this faith can rule only in the inner man, as Rom. 10 [:10] says, "For man believes with his heart and so is justified," and since faith alone justifies, it is clear that the inner man cannot be justified, freed, or saved by any outer work or action at all, and that these works, whatever their character, have nothing to do with this inner man. . . .

When, however, God sees that we consider him truthful and by the faith of our heart pay him the great honor which is due him, he does us that great honor of considering us truthful and righteous for the sake of our faith. Faith works truth and righteousness by giving God what belongs to him. Therefore God in turn glorifies our righteousness. It is true and just that God is truthful and just, and to consider and confess him to be so is the same as being truthful and just. Accordingly he says in 1 Sam. 2 [:30], "Those who honor me I will honor, and those who despise me shall be lightly esteemed." So Paul says in Rom. 4 [:3] that Abraham's faith "was reckoned to him as righteousness" because by it he gave glory most perfectly to God, and that for the same reason our faith shall be reckoned to us as righteousness if we believe.

The third incomparable benefit of faith* is that it unites the soul with Christ as a bride is united with her bridegroom. By this mystery, as the Apostle teaches, Christ and the soul become one flesh [Eph. 5:31–32]. And if they are one flesh and there is between them a true marriage—indeed the most perfect of all marriages, since human marriages are but poor examples of this one true marriage—it follows that everything they have they hold in common, the good as well as the evil. Accordingly the believing soul can boast of and glory in whatever Christ has as though it were its own, and whatever the soul has Christ claims as his own. Let us compare these and we shall see inestimable benefits. Christ is full of grace, life, and salvation. The soul is full of sins, death, and damnation. Now let faith come between them and sins, death, and damnation will be Christ's, while grace, life, and salvation will be the soul's; for if Christ is a bridegroom, he must take upon himself the things which are his bride's and bestow

---

*The first was that faith "makes the law and works unnecessary for any man's righteousness and salvation"; the second was that "it honors him whom it trusts [God] with the most reverent and high regard."

upon her the things that are his. If he gives her his body and very self, how shall he not give her all that is his? And if he takes the body of the bride, how shall he not take all that is hers?

Here we have a most pleasing vision not only of communion but of a blessed struggle and victory and salvation and redemption. Christ is God and man in one person. He has neither sinned nor died, and is not condemned, and he cannot sin, die, or be condemned; his righteousness, life, and salvation are unconquerable, eternal, omnipotent. By the wedding ring of faith he shares in the sins, death, and pains of hell which are his bride's. As a matter of fact, he makes them his own acts as if they were his own and as if he himself had sinned; he suffered, died, and descended into hell that he might overcome them all. . . .

From this you once more see that much is ascribed to faith, namely, that it alone can fulfill the law and justify without works. You see that the First Commandment, which says, "You shall worship one God," is fulfilled by faith alone. Though you were nothing but good works from the soles of your feet to the crown of your head, you would still not be righteous or worship God or fulfill the First Commandment, since God cannot be worshiped unless you ascribe to him the glory of truthfulness and all goodness which is due him. This cannot be done by works but only by the faith of the heart. Not by the doing of works but by believing do we glorify God and acknowledge that he is truthful. Therefore faith alone is the righteousness of a Christian and the fulfilling of all commandments, for he who fulfills the First Commandment has no difficulty in fulfilling all the rest.

But works, being inanimate things, cannot glorify God, although they can, if faith is present, be done to the glory of God. . . .

That we may examine more profoundly that grace which our inner man has in Christ, we must realize that in the Old Testament God consecrated to himself all first-born males. The birthright was highly prized for it involved a twofold honor, that of priesthood and that of kingship. The first-born brother was priest and lord over all the others and a type of Christ. . . .

Injustice is done those words "priest," "cleric," "spiritual," "ecclesiastic," when they are transferred from all Christians to those few who are now by a mischievous usage called "ecclesiastics." Holy Scripture makes no distinction between them, although it gives the name "ministers," "servants," "stewards" to those who are now proudly called popes, bishops, and lords and who should according to the ministry of the Word serve others and teach them the faith of Christ and the freedom of believers. Although we are all equally priests, we cannot all publicly minister and teach. We ought not do so even if we could. Paul writes accordingly in 1 Cor. 4 [:1]: "This is how one should regard us, as servants of Christ and stewards of the mysteries of God."

That stewardship, however, has now been developed into so great a display of power and so terrible a tyranny that no heathen empire or other earthly power can be compared with it, just as if laymen were not also Christians. Through this perversion the knowledge of Christian grace, faith, liberty, and of Christ himself has altogether perished, and its place has been taken by an unbearable bondage of human works and laws until we have become, as the Lamentations of Jeremiah [1] say, servants of the vilest men on earth who abuse our misfortune to serve only their base and shameless will. . . .

Rather ought Christ to be preached to the end that faith in him may be established that he may not only be Christ, but be Christ for you and me, and that what is said of him and is denoted in his name may be effectual in us. Such faith is produced and preserved in us by preaching why Christ came, what he brought and bestowed, what benefit it is to us to accept him. This is done when that Christian liberty which he bestows is rightly taught and we are told in what way we Christians are all kings and priests and therefore lords of all and may firmly believe that whatever we have done is pleasing and acceptable in the sight of God, as I have already said. . . .

Now let us turn to the second part, the outer man. . . .

Although, as I have said, a man is abundantly and sufficiently justified by faith inwardly, in his spirit, and so has all that he needs, except insofar as this faith and these riches must grow from day to day even to the future life; yet he remains in this mortal life on earth. In this life he must control his own body and have dealings with men. Here the works begin; here a man cannot enjoy leisure; here he must indeed take care to discipline his body by fastings, watchings, labors, and other reasonable discipline and to subject it to the Spirit so that it will obey and conform to the inner man and faith and not revolt against faith and hinder the inner man, as it is the nature of the body to do if it is not held in check. The inner man, who by faith is created in the image of God, is both joyful and happy because of Christ in whom so many benefits are conferred upon him; and therefore it is his one occupation to serve God joyfully and without thought of gain, in love that is not constrained.

While he is doing this, behold, he meets a contrary will in his own flesh which strives to serve the world and seeks its own advantage.

This the spirit of faith cannot tolerate, but with joyful zeal it attempts to put the body under control and hold it in check. . . .

In doing these works, however, we must not think that a man is justified before God by them, for faith, which alone is righteousness before God, cannot endure that erroneous opinion. . . .

We should think of the works of a Christian who is justified and saved by faith because of the pure and free mercy of God, just as we would think of the works which Adam and Eve did in Paradise, and all their children would have done if they had not sinned. We read in Gen. 2 [:15] that "The Lord God took the man and put him in the garden of Eden to till it and keep it." Now Adam was created righteous and upright and without sin by God so that he had no need of being justified and made upright through his tilling and keeping the garden; but, that he might not be idle, the Lord gave him a task to do, to cultivate and protect the garden. This task would truly have been the freest of works, done only to please God and not to obtain righteousness, which Adam already had in full measure and which would have been the birthright of us all.

The works of a believer are like this. Through his faith he has been restored to Paradise and created anew, has no need of works that he may become or be righteous; but that he may not be idle and may provide for and keep his body, he must do such works freely only to please God. Since, however, we are not wholly recreated, and our faith and love are not yet perfect, these are to be increased, not by external works, however, but of themselves. . . .

We do not, therefore, reject good works; on the contrary, we cherish and teach them as much as possible. We do not condemn them for their own sake but on account of this godless addition to them and the perverse idea that righteousness is to be sought through them; for that makes them appear good outwardly, when in truth they are not good. They deceive men and lead them to deceive one another like ravening wolves in sheep's clothing [Matt. 7:15]. . . .

Let this suffice concerning works in general and at the same time concerning the works which a Christian does for himself. Lastly, we shall also speak of the things which he does toward his neighbor. A man does not live for himself alone in this mortal body to work for it alone, but he lives also for all men on earth; rather, he lives only for others and not for himself. To this end he brings his body into subjection that he may the more sincerely and freely serve others. . . .

Behold, from faith thus flow forth love and joy in the Lord, and from love a joyful, willing, and free mind that serves one's neighbor willingly and takes no account of gratitude or ingratitude, of praise or blame, of gain or loss. For a man does not serve that he may put men under obligations. He does not distinguish between friends and enemies or anticipate their thankfulness or unthankfulness, but he most freely and most willingly spends himself and all that he has, whether he wastes all on the thankless or whether he gains a reward. As his Father does, distributing all things to all men richly and freely, making "his sun rise on the evil and on the good" [Matt. 5:45], so also the son does all things and suffers all things with that freely bestowing joy which is his delight when through Christ he sees it in God, the dispenser of such great benefits. . . .

We conclude, therefore, that a Christian lives not in himself, but in Christ and in his neighbor. Otherwise he is not a Christian. He lives in Christ through faith, in his neighbor through love. By faith he is caught up beyond himself into God. By love he descends beneath himself into his neighbor. Yet he always remains in God and in his love, as Christ says in John 1 [:51], "Truly, truly, I say to you, you will see heaven opened, and the angels of God ascending and descending upon the Son of man."

Translated by W. A. Lambert. From "The Freedom of a Christian," in *Martin Luther, Three Treatises,* Second Revised Edition, pages 277–281, 285–288, 291–296, 300–301, 304, 309. Copyright © 1970 by Fortress Press. Used by permission of the publisher.

Ulrich Zwingli (1484–1531)

From *An Account of the Faith of Zwingli*

Zwingli began his career as a priest, a humanist scholar, and a Swiss patriot. He came to Reformation, he always insisted, quite independently of Luther, and, beginning in 1519, led the Reformation of the Swiss city of Zurich. The authority of scripture and the need to purify Christian worship played particularly important roles in his version of the Reformation. In some ways Zwingli very much inherited the attitudes of Renaissance humanism—in his emphasis on careful study of the biblical text and, as this selection mentions, his reluctance to treat the inheritance of original sin as really a sin. He fought a series of debates with Luther that centered on interpretations of the Lord's Supper and with the early Anabaptists over the question of infant baptism. Zwingli wrote this summary of his faith for presentation to the Emperor Charles V at the Diet of Augsburg in 1530.

First of all, I both believe and know that God is one and He alone is God, and that He is by nature good, true, powerful, just, wise, the Creator and Preserver of all things, visible and invisible; that Father, Son and Holy Spirit are indeed three persons, but that their essence is one and single. And I think altogether in accordance with the Creed, the Nicene and also the Athanasian, in all their details concerning the Godhead himself, the names or the three persons. . . .

Secondly—I know that this supreme Deity, which is my God, freely determines all things, so that His counsel does not depend upon the contingency of any creature. For it is peculiar to defective human wisdom to reach a decision because of preceding discussion or example. God, however, who from eternity to eternity surveys the universe with a single, simple look, has no need of any reasoning process or waiting for events; but being equally wise, prudent, good, etc., He freely determines and disposes of all things, for whatever is, is His. Hence it is that, although having knowledge and wisdom, He in the beginning formed man who should fall, but at the same time determined to clothe in human nature His Son, who should restore him when fallen. For by this means His goodness was in every way manifested. . . .

Fourthly—I know that our primeval ancestor and first parent, through self-love, at the pernicious advice suggested to him by the malice of Satan, was induced to desire equality with God. When he had determined upon this crime, he took of the forbidden and fatal fruit, whereby he incurred the guilt of the sentence of death, having become an enemy and a foe of his God. Although He could therefore have destroyed him, as justice demanded, nevertheless, being better disposed, God so changed the penalty as to make a slave of him whom He could have punished with death. This condition neither Adam himself nor anyone born of him could remove, for a slave can beget nothing but a slave. Thus through his fatal tasting of the fruit he cast all of his posterity into slavery.

Hence I think of original sin as follows: An act is called sin when it is committed against the law; for where there is no law there is no transgression, and where there is no transgression there is no sin in the proper sense, since sin is plainly an offense, a crime, a misdeed or guilt. I confess, therefore, that our father [Adam] committed what was truly a sin, namely an atrocious deed, a crime, an impiety. But his descendants have not sinned in this manner, for who among us crushed with his teeth the forbidden apple in Paradise? Hence, willing or unwilling, we are forced to admit that original sin, as it is in the children of Adam, is not properly sin, as has been explained; for it is not a misdeed contrary to law. It is, therefore, properly a disease and condition—a disease, because just as he fell through self-love, so do we also; a condition, because just as he became a slave and liable to death, so also are we born slaves and children of wrath [Eph. 2:3] and liable to death. However, I have no objection to this disease and condition being called, after the habit of Paul, a sin; indeed it is a sin inasmuch as those born therein are God's enemies and opponents, for they are drawn into it by the condition of birth, not by the perpetration of a definite crime, except as far as their first parent has committed one. . . .

I believe that there is one Church of those who have the same Spirit, through whom they are made certain that they are the true children of the family of God; and this is the first fruits of the Church. I believe that this Church does not err in regard to truth, namely in those fundamental matters of faith upon which everything depends. I believe also that the universal, visible Church is one, while it maintains that true confession, of which we have already spoken. I believe also that all belong to this Church who give their adherence to it according to the rule and promise of God's Word. I believe that to this Church belong Isaac, Jacob, Judah and all who were of the seed of Abraham, and also those infants whose parents in the first beginnings of the Christian Church, through the preaching of the apostles, were won to the cause of Christ. For if Isaac and the rest of the ancients had not belonged to the Church, they would not have received the Church's token, circumcision. Since these, then, were members of the Church, infants and children belonged to the primitive Church. Therefore I believe and know that they were sealed by the sacrament of baptism. For children also make a confession, when they are offered by their parents to the Church, especially since the promise offers them to God, which is made to our infants no less, but even far more amply and abundantly, than formerly to the children of the Hebrews.

These are the grounds for baptizing and commending infants to the Church, against which all the weapons and war engines of the Anabaptists avail nothing. For not only are they to be baptized who believe, but they who confess, and they who, according to the promise of God's Word, belong to the Church. For otherwise even the apostles would not have baptized anyone, since no apostle had absolute evidence regarding the faith of one confessing and calling himself a Christian. . . .

Eighthly—I believe that in the holy Eucharist, *i.e.,* the supper of thanksgiving, the true body of Christ is present by the contemplation of faith. . . . But that the body of Christ in essence and really, *i.e.,* the natural body itself, is either present in the supper or masticated with our mouth and teeth, as the Papists or some [the Lutherans] who look back to the fleshpots of Egypt assert, we not only deny, but constantly maintain to be an error, contrary to the Word of God. . . .

Christ Himself, the mouth and wisdom of God, saith: "The poor ye have always with you; but me ye have not always" [John 12:8]. Here the presence of the body alone is denied, for according to His divinity He is always present, because He is always everywhere, according to His other Word: "Lo, I am with you always, even unto the end of the world" [Matt. 28:20], viz., according to divinity, power and goodness. Augustine agrees with us. Neither is there any foundation for the assertion of the opponents that the humanity of Christ is wherever the divinity is, otherwise the person is divided; for this would destroy Christ's true humanity. Only the deity can be everywhere. . . .

When in departing He commended His disciples to His Father, He said: "I am no more in the world" [John 17:11]. Here we have a substantive verb ("I *am* no more in the world"), no less than in the words: "This *is* my body"; so that the opponents cannot say that there is a trope here, since they deny that substantives admit of the trope.* . . .

In view of these passages we are compelled to confess that the words: "This is my body," should not be understood naturally, but figuratively, just as the words: "This is Jehovah's passover" [Ex. 12:11]. For the lamb that was eaten every year with the celebration of the festival was not the passing over of the Lord, but it signified that such a passing over had formerly taken place. . . .

As the body cannot be nourished by a spiritual substance, so the soul cannot be nourished by a corporeal substance. But if the natural body of Christ is eaten, I ask whether it feeds the body or the soul? Not the body, hence the soul. If the soul, then the soul eats flesh, and it would not be true that spirit is only born of Spirit. . . .

The above [twelve points] I firmly believe, teach and maintain, not by my own utterances, but by those of the Word of God; and, God willing, I promise to do this as long as the mind controls these members, unless some one from the declarations of Holy Scripture,

---

*In other words, someone like Luther cannot dismiss Christ's statement, "I am no more in the world," as a metaphor, since he has so firmly insisted that "This is my body" cannot be a metaphor.

properly understood, explain and establish the reverse as clearly and plainly as we have established the above. For it is no less agreeable and delightful than fair and just for us to submit our judgment to the Holy Scriptures, and the Church, deciding in harmony with these by virtue of the Spirit.

From *Zwingli: On Providence and Other Essays,* edited and translated by William John Hinke, pages 36, 38, 40–41, 45, 49–50, 52–53, 58. Copyright © 1983 by Labyrinth Press. Used by permission of the publisher.

Martin Luther

From *That These Words of Christ, "This Is My Body," etc., Still Stand Firm Against the Fanatics*

By 1526, when Luther wrote this treatise, Zwingli and Johannes Oecolampadius, the leader of the Reformation at Basel, had challenged his understanding of the Eucharist, insisting that Christ's words, "This is my body," must be understood only in a figurative sense. Luther rejected the Catholic theory of transubstantiation, but he thought Zwingli and Oecolampadius went too far. He set out his own position in this treatise. The meeting of Luther and Zwingli at Marburg in 1529 only confirmed their differences, and the union of Lutheran and Reformed Protestants proved impossible.

Our adversary says that mere bread and wine are present, not the body and blood of the Lord. If they believe and teach wrongly here, then they blaspheme God and are giving the lie to the Holy Spirit, betray Christ, and seduce the world. . . .

Neither does it help them to assert that at all other points they have a high and noble regard for God's words and the entire gospel, except in this matter. My friend, God's Word is God's Word; this point does not require much haggling! When one blasphemously gives the lie to God in a single word, or says it is a minor matter if God is blasphemed or called a liar, one blasphemes the entire God and makes light of all blasphemy. . . .

The sum and substance of all this is that we have on our side the clear, distinct Scripture which reads, "Take, eat; this is my body," and we are not under obligation nor will we be pressed to cite Scripture beyond this text—though we could do so abundantly. On the contrary, they should produce Scripture which reads, "This represents my body," or, "This is a sign of my body." . . .

Suppose they say: The Scriptures contradict themselves, and no one reconciles them unless he believes that mere bread and wine are present in the Supper. Answer: What Scripture? Suppose they say: Oh, where the article of faith is established that Christ ascended to heaven and sits on the right hand of God in his glory. Again, eating flesh is of no avail, John 6 [:63], "The flesh is of no avail." So, if flesh and blood are in the Supper, Christ could not be sitting at the right hand of God in his glory, and he would be giving us something to eat which is of no use for salvation. Therefore name any Scripture you will, it must make of Christ's body a "sign of the body," and this must be the text of the Supper!

Who would have expected such lofty wisdom from the fanatics? Here you see the best single argument that they have. . . .

Now anyone who asks too many questions becomes unwelcome, but I must ask some more, that I may become still more clever. How do we become certain, good gentlemen, that a body may not through the power of God be at the same time in heaven and in the Supper, since the power of God has neither measure nor number, and does things which no mind can comprehend but must simply be believed? When he says, "This is my body," how shall I calm my heart and convince it that God has no means or power to do what his Word says? . . .

Here perhaps they may say: We can prove it very well. Once we climbed up to heaven secretly, just at midnight, when God was most soundly asleep. We had a lantern and a master key with us, broke into his most secret chamber, and unlocked all his chests and strong-boxes in which his power lay. We took gold scales so that we could weigh our loot accurately and be sure to hit it just right. But we found no power that can enable a body to be at the same time in heaven and in the Supper. Therefore it is certain that "body" must mean "sign of the body." May God repay you, Satan, you damnable wretch, for the shameful and cocksure way you ridicule us! But my ridicule in turn will tickle you, too, what do you bet? . . .

The Scriptures teach us, however, that the right hand of God is not a specific place in which a body must or may be, such as on a golden throne, but is the almighty power of God, which at one and the same time can be nowhere and yet must be everywhere. It cannot be at any one place, I say. For if it were at some specific place, it would have to be there in a circumscribed and determinate manner, as everything which is at one place must be at that place determinately and measurably, so that it cannot meanwhile be at any other place. But the power of God cannot be so determined and measured, for it is uncircumscribed and immeasurable, beyond and above all that is or may be.

On the other hand, it must be essentially present at all places, even in the tiniest tree leaf. The reason is this: It is God who creates, effects, and preserves all things through his almighty power and right hand, as our Creed confesses. For he dispatches no officials or angels when he creates or preserves something, but all this is the work of his divine power itself. If he is to create or preserve it, however, he must be present and must make and preserve his creation both in its innermost and outermost aspects. . . .

Listen now, you pig, dog, or fanatic, whatever kind of unreasonable ass you are: Even if Christ's body is everywhere, you do not therefore immediately eat or drink or touch him; nor do I talk with you about such things in this manner, either; go back to your pigpen and your filth. I said above that the right hand of God is everywhere, but at the same time nowhere and uncircumscribed, above and apart from all creatures. There is a difference between his being present and your touching. He is free and unbound wherever he is, and he does not have to stand there like a rogue set in a pillory, or his neck in irons.

See, the bright rays of the sun are so near you that they pierce into your eyes or your skin so that you feel it, yet you are unable to grasp them and put them into a box, even if you should try forever. Prevent them from shining in through the window—this you can do, but catch and grasp them you cannot. So too with Christ: although he is everywhere, he does not permit himself to be so caught and grasped; he can easily shell himself, so that you get the shell but not the kernel. Why? Because it is one thing if God is present, and another if he is present for you. He is there for you when he adds his Word and binds himself, saying, "Here you are to find me." Now when you have the Word, you can grasp and have him with certainty and say, "Here I have thee, according to thy Word." Just as I say of the right hand of God: although this is everywhere, as we may not deny, still because it is also nowhere, as has been said, you can actually grasp it nowhere, unless for your benefit it binds itself to you and summons you to a definite place. This God's right hand does, however, when it enters into the humanity of Christ and dwells there. There you surely find it, otherwise you will run back and forth throughout all creation, groping here and groping there yet never finding, even though it is actually there; for it is not there for you.

So too, since Christ's humanity is at the right hand of God, and also is in all and above all things according to the nature of the divine right hand, you will not eat or drink him like the cabbage and soup on your table, unless he wills it. He also now exceeds any grasp, and you will not catch him by groping about, even though he is in your bread, unless he binds himself to you and summons you to a particular table by his Word, and he himself gives meaning to the bread for you, by his Word, bidding you to eat him. This he does in the Supper, saying, "This is my body," as if to say, "At home you may eat bread also, where I am indeed sufficiently near at hand too; but this is the true *touto,* * the 'This is my body': when you eat this, you eat my body, and nowhere else. Why? Because I wish to attach myself here with my Word, in order that you may not have to buzz about, trying to seek me in all the places where I am; this would be too much for you, and you would also be too puny to apprehend me in these places without the help of my Word."

From "That These Words of Christ, 'This Is My Body,' etc., Still Stand Firm Against the Fanatics, 1527," in *Luther's Works,* Volume 37, pages 26, 33, 46–48, 57–58, 68–69. Edited and translated by Robert H. Fischer. General editor, Helmut T. Lehmann. Copyright © 1961 by Fortress Press. Used by permission of the publisher.

George Blaurock (d. 1529)

From *The Hutterite Chronicle*

Zwingli had tried to lead a gradual reformation in Zurich, one that would keep the support of a consensus of the citizens. He did not move fast enough or far enough for some. The crucial issue proved to be infant baptism: some of his young associates held that a reformation based on scripture and individual faith ought to require that adults confess their faith and then be rebaptized. After all, they argued, the New Testament never mentions baptizing infants. In this excerpt, George Blaurock recalls those beginnings of Anabaptism in Zurich.

It came to pass that Ulrich Zwingli and Conrad Grebel, one of the aristocracy, and Felix Mantz—all three much experienced and men learned in the German, Latin, Greek, and also the Hebrew, languages—came together and began to talk through matters of belief

---

*This.

among themselves and recognized that infant baptism is unnecessary and recognized further that it is in fact no baptism. Two, however, Conrad and Felix, recognized in the Lord and believed [further] that one must and should be correctly baptized according to the Christian ordinance and institution of the Lord, since Christ himself says that whoever *believes* and is baptized will be saved. Ulrich Zwingli, who shuddered before Christ's cross, shame, and persecution, did not wish this and asserted that an uprising would break out. The other two, however, Conrad and Felix, declared that God's clear commandment and institution could not for that reason be allowed to lapse. . . .

They came to one mind in these things, and in the pure fear of God they recognized that a person must learn from the divine Word and preaching a true faith which manifests itself in love, and receive the true Christian baptism on the basis of the recognized and confessed faith, in the union with God of a good conscience, [prepared] henceforth to serve God in a holy Christian life with all godliness, also to be steadfast to the end in tribulation. And it came to pass that they were together until fear began to come over them, yea, they were pressed in their hearts. Thereupon, they began to bow their knees to the Most High God in heaven and called upon him as the Knower of hearts, implored him to enable them to do his divine will and to manifest his mercy toward them. For flesh and blood and human forwardness did not drive them, since they well knew what they would have to bear and suffer on account of it. After the prayer, George Cajacob arose and asked Conrad to baptize him, for the sake of God, with the true Christian baptism upon his faith and knowledge. And when he knelt down with that request and desire, Conrad baptized him, since at that time there was no ordained deacon [*diener,* servant] to perform such work. After that was done the others similarly desired George to baptize them, which he also did upon their request. Thus they together gave themselves to the name of the Lord in the high fear of God. Each confirmed the other in the service of the gospel, and they began to teach and keep the faith. Therewith began the separation from the world and its evil works.

Translated by George Huntston Williams. From *Spiritual and Anabaptist Writers,* edited by George Huntston Williams and Angel M. Mergal (Volume XXV: The Library of Christian Classics), pages 42–44. First published MCMLVII by SCM Press Ltd., London, and The Westminster Press, Philadelphia. Used by permission of the publishers.

Thomas Müntzer (c.1489–1525)

From *Sermon Before the Princes*

*Müntzer had converted to the cause of the Reformation by the early
1520s. As preacher in the town of Zwickau, he soon pushed reform in
more radical directions: he claimed that the Holy Spirit, speaking
directly to the common people, had more authority than the scriptures
as interpreted by learned scholars, and he proclaimed that God would
soon bring the present age of the world to an end, punishing those who
oppressed the people. Müntzer preached this sermon to Duke John of
Saxony and his son and court officials in 1524, urging them to become
God's instruments in the revolution. Not surprisingly, they declined,
and in the next year Müntzer joined the peasant revolt and was killed.*

It is known that poor, ailing, disintegrating Christendom can be
neither counseled nor aided unless the diligent, untroubled servants
of God daily work through the Scriptures, singing, reading, and
preaching. But therewith the head of many a pampered priest will
continuously have to suffer great blows or [he will] miss out in his
handiwork. But how ought one otherwise to deal with him at a time
when Christendom is being so wretchedly devastated by ravenous
wolves, as it is written in Isaiah [5:1–23] and in Ps. 80 [9–14] concerning the vineyard of God? . . .

Christ the Son of God and his apostles and indeed, before him, his
holy prophets began a real pure Christianity, having sown pure
wheat in the field, that is, [they] planted the precious Word of God
in the hearts of the elect as Matthew [12:24–30], Mark [4:26–29], and
Luke [8:5–15] have written, and Ezekiel [36:29]. But the lazy, ne-
glectful ministers of this same church have not wished to accomplish
this and maintain it by dint of diligent watchfulness; but rather they
have sought their own [ends], not what was Jesus Christ's [Phil. 2:4,
21]. For this reason they have allowed the harmfulness of the godless
vigorously to take over, that is, the weeds [Ps. 80:9–14]. . . .

Thus, ye amiable princes, it is necessary that we apply utmost
diligence in these parlous days [1 Tim. 4], as all the dear fathers
have delineated in the Bible from the beginning of the world, in
order to cope with this insidious evil. For the age is dangerous and
the days are wicked [2 Tim. 3:1; Eph. 5:15–16]. Why? Simply because the noble power of God is so wretchedly disgraced and dis-
honored that the poor common people are misled by the ungodly
divines all with such rigmarole, as the prophet Micah [3:5–37] says

of it: This is now the character of almost all divines with mighty few exceptions. They teach and say that God no longer reveals his divine mysteries to his beloved friends by means of valid visions or his audible Word, etc. Thus they stick with their inexperienced way [cf. Ecclesiasticus 34:9] and make into the butt of sarcasm those persons who go around in possession of revelation, as the godless did to Jeremiah [20:7–8]. . . .

The beloved apostles had to be diligently attentive to [the meaning of] visions, as it is clearly written in their Acts. Indeed, it is a [mark of the] truly apostolic, patriarchal, and prophetic spirit to attend upon visions and to attain unto the same in painful tribulation. Therefore it is no wonder that Brother Fattened Swine and Brother Soft Life* rejects them [Job 28:12–13]. . . .

Now if you want to be true governors, you must begin government at the roots, and, as Christ commanded, drive his enemies from the elect. For you are the means to this end. Beloved, don't give us any old jokes about how the power of God should do it without your application of the sword. Otherwise may it rust away for you in its scabbard! May God grant it, whatever any divine may say to you! Christ says it sufficiently [Matt. 7:19; John 15:2, 6]: Every tree that bringeth not forth good fruit is rooted out and cast into the fire. If you do away with the mask of the world, you will soon recognize it with a righteous judgment [John 7:24]. Perform a righteous judgment at God's command! You have help enough for the purpose [Wisdom of Solomon, ch. 6], for Christ is your Master [Matt. 23:8]. Therefore let not the evildoers live longer who make us turn away from God [Deut. 13:5]. For the godless person has no right to live when he is in the way of the pious. In Ex. 22:18 God says: Thou shalt not suffer evildoers to live. Saint Paul also means this where he says of the sword of rulers that it is bestowed upon them for the retribution of the wicked as protection for the pious [Rom. 13:4]. God is your protection and will teach you to fight against his foes [Ps. 18:34]. He will make your hands skilled in fighting and will also sustain you. But you will have to suffer for that reason a great cross and temptation in order that the fear of God may be declared unto you. That cannot happen without suffering, but it costs you no more than the danger of having risked all for God's sake and the useless prattle of your adversaries. For though even pious David was drawn from his castle by Absalom, he finally came again into ascendency

---

*Martin Luther.

when Absalom got hung up and was stabbed. Therefore, you cherished fathers of Saxony, you must hazard all for the sake of the gospel. But God will chasten you out of love as his most beloved sons [cf. Deut. 1:31] when he in his momentary anger is enraged. Blessed at that time are all who trust in God. Free in the Spirit of Christ, say only [Ps. 3:6]: I will not be afraid of a hundred thousand though they have set themselves against me round about. I suppose at this point our learned divines will bring out the goodness of Christ, which they in their hypocrisy apply by force. But over against this [goodness] they ought also to take note of the sternness of Christ [John 2:15–17; Ps. 69:9], when he turned over the roots of idolatry. As Paul says in Col. 3:5–7, because of these the wrath of God cannot be done away with in the congregation. . . . That this might now take place, however, in an orderly and proper fashion, our cherished fathers, the princes, should do it, who with us confess Christ. If however, they do not do it, the sword will be taken from them [Dan. 7:26–27].

Translated by George Huntston Williams. From *Spiritual and Anabaptist Writers,* edited by George Huntston Williams and Angel M. Mergal (Volume XXV: The Library of Christian Classics), pages 49–50, 54, 61, 66–68. First published MCMLVII by SCM Press Ltd., London, and The Westminster Press, Philadelphia. Used by permission of the publishers.

From *The Schleitheim Confession of Faith*

Just as the early Anabaptists posed a radical challenge to Luther and Müntzer, so radicals within their own ranks soon challenged the moderate Anabaptists. The Swiss Anabaptists gathered in 1527 and produced this statement of faith, largely directed against extremists in their own camp. It sets out characteristic themes of Swiss and South German Anabaptism: pacifism, withdrawal from the larger world into small communities, and the use of the "ban"—the refusal to speak or interact with the offender—as a way of dealing with errant members of the community. Michael Sattler, its chief author, was killed for his faith within the year.

A very great offense has been introduced by certain false brethren among us, so that some have turned aside from the faith, in the way they intend to practice and observe the freedom of the Spirit and of Christ. But such have missed the truth and to their condemnation are given over to the lasciviousness and self-indulgence of the flesh. They think faith and love may do and permit everything, and nothing will harm them nor condemn them, since they are believers. . . .

But you are not that way. For they that are Christ's have crucified the flesh with its passions and lusts. You understand me well and [know] the brethren whom we mean. Separate yourselves from them for they are perverted. Petition the Lord that they may have the knowledge which leads to repentance, and [pray] for us that we may have constancy to persevere in the way which we have espoused, for the honor of God and of Christ, His Son, Amen.

The articles which we discussed and on which we were of one mind are these. . . .

First. Observe concerning baptism: Baptism shall be given to all those who have learned repentance and amendment of life, and who believe truly that their sins are taken away by Christ, and to all those who walk in the resurrection of Jesus Christ, and wish to be buried with Him in death, so that they may be resurrected with Him, and to all those who with this significance request it [baptism] of us and demand it for themselves. This excludes all infant baptism, the highest and chief abomination of the pope. In this you have the foundation and the testimony of the apostles: Matt. 28; Mark 16; Acts 2, 8, 16, 19. This we wish to hold simply, yet firmly and with assurance.

Second. We are agreed as follows on the ban: The ban shall be employed with all those who have given themselves to the Lord, to walk in His commandments, and with all those who are baptized into the one body of Christ and who are called brethren or sisters, and yet who slip sometimes and fall into error and sin, being inadvertently overtaken. The same shall be admonished twice in secret and the third time openly disciplined or banned according to the command of Christ: Matt. 18. But this shall be done according to the regulation of the Spirit (Matt. 5) before the breaking of bread, so that we may break and eat one bread, with one mind and in one love, and may drink of one cup. . . .

Fourth. We are agreed [as follows] on separation: A separation shall be made from the evil and from the wickedness which the devil planted in the world; in this manner, simply that we shall not have fellowship with them [the wicked] and not run with them in the multitude of their abominations. This is the way it is: Since all who do not walk in the obedience of faith, and have not united themselves with God so that they wish to do His will, are a great abomination before God, it is not possible for anything to grow or issue from them except abominable things. For truly all creatures are in but two classes, good and bad, believing and unbelieving, darkness and light, the world and those who [have come] out of the world, God's temple and idols, Christ and Belial; and none can have part with the other.

To us then the command of the Lord is clear when He calls upon us to be separate from the evil and thus He will be our God and we shall be His sons and daughters.

He further admonishes us to withdraw from Babylon and the earthly Egypt that we may not be partakers of the pain and suffering which the Lord will bring upon them. . . .

Therefore there will also unquestionably fall from us the unchristian, devilish weapons of force—such as sword, armor and the like, and all their use [either] for friends or against one's enemies—by virtue of the word of Christ, Resist not [him that is] evil. . . .

In the perfection of Christ, however, only the ban is used for a warning and for the excommunication of the one who has sinned, without putting the flesh to death—simply the warning and the command to sin no more. . . .

Keep watch on all who do not walk according to the simplicity of the divine truth which is stated in this letter from [the decisions of] our meeting, so that everyone among us will be governed by the rule of the ban and henceforth the entry of false brethren and sisters among us may be prevented.

From "The Schleitheim Confession of Faith," translated by John C. Wenger, in *The Mennonite Quarterly Review,* vol. 19, no. 4 (October 1947), pages 247–250, 252. Used by permission of *The Mennonite Quarterly Review.*

Menno Simons (1496–1561)

From *The Writings of Menno Simons*

Menno Simons was ordained a Catholic priest but joined the Anabaptist cause in 1536 and soon became the most prominent leader of the Dutch and North German Anabaptists. Menno's tireless efforts in behalf of a moderate pacifist tradition helped Anabaptists recover after their association with violence in the city of Münster. The Mennonites, descendants of the communities he helped restore, still bear his name. He begins this selection by insisting that baptism does not bring about a transformation of a Christian so much as it serves as a sign of a transformation that has already occurred. Therefore, only adults who have committed their lives to Christ should be baptized.

We are not regenerated because we have been baptized, . . . but we are baptized because we have been regenerated by faith and the Word of God [1 Peter 1:23]. Regeneration is not the result of baptism, but baptism is the result of regeneration. This can indeed not be controverted by any man, or disproved by the Scriptures.

The Scriptures know of only one remedy, which is Christ with His merits, death and blood. Hence, he who seeks the remission of his sins through baptism, rejects the blood of the Lord and makes water his idol. Therefore let every one have a care, lest he ascribe the honor and glory due to Christ to the outward ceremonies and visible elements. . . .

This [baptism] is the very least of all the commandments which He has given. It is a much greater commandment to love your enemies, to do good to those who do evil to you, to pray in spirit and in truth for those who persecute you, to subjugate the flesh under God's word, to tread under your feet all pride, covetousness, impurity, hate, envy and intemperance, to serve your neighbor with gold, silver, with house and possessions, with your hard labor, with counsel and deed, with life and death, nay to be free from all evil desire, unbecoming words and evil works, to love God and His righteousness, His will and commandments with all your heart, and to bear the cross of the Lord Jesus Christ with a joyous heart. . . .

Since, then, we do not find in all Scripture a single word by which Christ has ordained the baptism of infants, or that His apostles taught and practiced it, we say and confess rightly that infant baptism is but a human invention, an opinion of men, a perversion of the ordinance of Christ.

To baptize before that which is required for baptism, namely faith, is found is as if one would place the cart before the horse, to sow before plowing, to build before the lumber is at hand, or to seal the letter before it is written. . . .

The regenerated do not go to war nor fight. They are the children of peace who have beaten their swords into plowshares and their spears into pruning hooks and know of no war. They give to Caesar the things that are Caesar's and to God the things that are God's. Their sword is the word of the Spirit which they wield with a good conscience through the Holy Ghost.

Since we are to be conformed to the image of Christ [Rom. 8:29], how can we, then, fight our enemies with the sword? Does not the apostle Peter say: "For even hereunto were ye called, because Christ also suffered for us, leaving us an example, that ye should follow his steps; who did not sin neither was guile found in his mouth; who, when he was reviled, reviled not again; when he suffered he threatened not; but committed himself to him that judgeth righteously" [1 Peter 2:21–23; Matt. 16–24]. . . .

I am well aware that the tyrants who boast themselves Christians attempt to justify their horrible wars and shedding of blood, and would make a good work of it, by referring us to Moses, Joshua, etc. But they do not reflect that Moses and his successors, with their iron sword, have served out their time, and that Jesus Christ has now given us a new commandment and has girded our loins with another sword. They do not consider that they use the sword of war, which they wield, contrary to all evangelical Scripture, against their own brethren, namely those of like faith with them who have received the same baptism and have broken the same bread with them and are thus members of the same body.

Again, our fortress is Christ, our defence is patience, our sword is the Word of God, and our victory is the sincere, firm, unfeigned faith in Jesus Christ. Spears and swords of iron we leave to those who, alas, consider human blood and swine's blood of well nigh equal value. He that is wise, let him judge what I mean. . . .

However lamentably we may here be persecuted, oppressed, smitten, robbed, burned at the stake, drowned in the water by the hellish Pharaoh and his cruel, unmerciful servants, yet soon shall come the day of our refreshing and all the tears shall be wiped from our eyes and we shall be arrayed in the white silken robes of righteousness, follow the Lamb, and with Abraham, Isaac and Jacob sit down in the kingdom of God and possess the precious, pleasant land of eternal, imperishable joy. Praise God and lift up your heads, ye who suffer for Jesus' sake; the time is near when ye shall hear, "Come ye blessed" and ye shall rejoice with Him for evermore.

Translated by John Horsch. From *Menno Simons' Life and Writings,* by H. S. Bender, pages 78–81, 89, 91, 108–109. Copyright © 1936 by Mennonite Publishing House. Used by permission of the publisher.

From *The Formula of Concord*

In 1530 Luther gave his blessing to the Augsburg Confession as the basic statement of Lutheran faith, but in the years after Luther's death in 1546, Lutherans faced a series of theological controversies. Luther's young associate, Philipp Melanchthon (1497–1560), held that human beings can cooperate with God's grace and therefore contribute toward their salvation. Matthias Flacius Illyricus (1520–1575), another Lutheran theologian, insisted that this betrayed Luther's emphasis on grace; in sin we have no capacity for free choice. Indeed, we have ceased to be human beings; sin has become our very substance. Around 1560, Victorinus Strigel (1524–1569) responded that even a sinful human being remains a human being and a creature of God. In 1577 a group of Lutheran theologians, Martin Chemnitz (1522–1586) the most famous among them, reached a resolution on a number of issues connected to this debate. Their work, the Formula of Concord, represented the clearest statement of Lutheran orthodoxy.

In the first place, there has been dissension among a number of theologians of the Augsburg Confession about what original sin, strictly understood, is. One side contended that "man's nature and essence are wholly corrupt as a result of the fall of Adam," so that ever since the Fall the nature, substance, and essence of fallen man, at least the foremost and noblest part of his essence (namely, his rational soul in its highest degree and foremost powers), is original sin itself, which has been called "nature-sin" or "person-sin" because it is not a thought, a word or a deed but the very nature itself out of which, as the root and source, all other sins proceed. For this reason there is now after the Fall allegedly no difference whatsoever between man's nature or essence and original sin. The other party, however, took a contrary view and taught that original sin, strictly speaking, is not man's nature, substance, or essence (that is, man's body or soul), which even after the Fall are and remain God's handiwork and creation in us. They maintained that original sin is something in man's nature, in his body, soul, and all his powers, and that it is an abominable, deep, and inexpressible corruption thereof, in the sense that man lacks the righteousness in which he was originally created, that in spiritual matters he is dead to that which is good and is turned to everything evil, and that, because of this corruption and this inborn sin which inheres in his nature, all actual sins flow out of his heart. Hence, they say, we must preserve the distinction between the nature and essence of fallen man (that is, between his body and soul, which are God's handiwork and creatures in us even after the Fall) and original sin (which is a work of the devil by which man's nature has become corrupted). . . .

In the first place, it is an established truth that Christians must regard and recognize as sin not only the actual transgression of God's commandments but also, and primarily, the abominable and dreadful inherited disease which has corrupted our entire nature. In fact, we must consider this as the chief sin, the root and fountain of all actual sin. Dr. Luther calls this sin "nature-sin" or "person-sin" in order to indicate that even though a man were to think no evil, speak no evil, or do no evil—which after the Fall of our first parents is of course impossible for human nature in this life—nevertheless man's nature and person would still be sinful. This means that in the sight of God original sin, like a spiritual leprosy, has thoroughly and entirely poisoned and corrupted human nature. . . .

In the second place, it is also a clearly established truth, as Article XIX of the Augsburg Confession teaches, that God is not the creator, author, or cause of sin. . . .

Although, in Luther's words, original sin, like a spiritual poison and leprosy, has so poisoned and corrupted man's whole nature that within the corrupted nature we are not able to point out and expose the nature by itself, on the one hand, and original sin by itself, on the other, as two manifestly separate things, nevertheless our corrupted nature or the essence of corrupted man, our body and soul or man himself created by God (within which original sin, by which the nature, essence, or total man is corrupted, dwells) are not one and the same thing. Just as in a case of external leprosy the body which is leprous and the leprosy on or in the body are not one and the same thing, so, if one wishes to speak strictly, one must maintain a distinction between (a) our nature as it is created and preserved by God and in which sin dwells and (b) original sin itself which dwells in the nature. According to the Holy Scriptures we must and can consider, discuss, and believe these two as distinct from each other.

The chief articles of our Christian faith constrain and compel us to maintain such a distinction. In the first place, in the article of creation Scripture testifies not only that God created human nature before the Fall, but also that after the Fall human nature is God's creature and handiwork [Deut. 32:6; Isa. 45:11; 54:9; 64:8; Acts 17:25, 26; Rev. 4:11]. . . .

Secondly, in the article of our redemption we have the mighty testimony of Scripture that God's Son assumed our nature, though without sin, so that in every respect he was made like us, his brethren, sin alone excepted [Heb. 2:17]. Hence all the ancient orthodox teachers held that according to his assumed human nature Christ is of one and the same essence with us, his brethren, because the human nature which he assumed is in its essence and all its essential attributes—sin alone excepted—identical with ours; they also rejected the contrary doctrine as patent heresy. Now, if there were no difference between the nature or essence of corrupted man and original sin, it would have to follow that Christ either did not assume our nature inasmuch as he did not assume sin, or that Christ assumed sin inasmuch as he assumed our nature. Both statements are contrary to the Scriptures. . . .

Thirdly, in the article of sanctification we have the testimony of Scripture that God cleanses man from sin, purifies him, and sanctifies him and that Christ has saved his people from their sins. Sin thus cannot be identified with man himself, since God receives man for Christ's sake into his grace but remains the enemy of sin throughout eternity! . . .

Fourthly, concerning the doctrine of the resurrection Scripture testifies that precisely the substance of this our flesh, but without sin, shall arise, and that in eternal life we shall have and keep precisely this soul, although without sin. If there were no difference whatever between our corrupted body and soul on the one hand and original sin on the other, then it would follow, contrary to this article of our Christian faith, either that our flesh would not rise on Judgment Day and that in eternal life, instead of this essence of our body and soul, we should have another substance or another soul since we there shall be without sin, or else that sin would be raised and would be and remain in the elect in eternal life.

From this it is evident that we must reject this doctrine with all its implications and conclusions, as when it is said that original sin is the very nature of corrupted man, its substance, its essence, its body or soul, so that there is allegedly no distinction whatever between our corrupted nature or substance or being and original sin.

From "The Formula of Concord," in *The Book of Concord,* pages 508–510, 514–517. Translated and edited by Theodore G. Tappert. Copyright © 1959 by Fortress Press. Used by permission of the publisher.

CHAPTER 2

The Catholic Reformation

Historians used to describe the Catholic response to the beginnings of Protestantism as the "Counter-Reformation," but the term seems a misnomer. By 1500 any thinking Christian knew that the church needed reform; no one stood against reformation. The debates concerned what to reform, and how, and by what authority.

Those who worked for reform within the Roman Catholic Church took a number of steps. First, they sought on a practical level to end the worst of church corruption. Second, in theological work that culminated in the Council of Trent (1545–1563), they defined more clearly their church's views on issues the Protestants had brought to the center of attention—justification, the relation of faith and works, the Sacraments, the authority of scripture and tradition, and so on. Third, they developed a new spirituality, a language and practice of prayer and discipline that gave new energy to their religious tradition.

The Jesuits, founded by Ignatius of Loyola in the 1530s, provided the shock troops of the Catholic Reformation—traveling as missionaries to Asia or secretly in Protestant countries, defending the Catholic doctrine of justification, or exploring new questions about the relation of church and state. They stood for a new discipline in the church, and they made many enemies. One was a Frenchman of genius named Blaise Pascal, who not only attacked the Jesuits but approached old questions about the relation of faith and reason in new ways.

The Catholic Church, then, got its own reformation, and ended up less corrupt, less confused, more disciplined, and more energetic. But at a price—for, perhaps inevitably, it was also less tolerant and more narrow, as the age of Erasmus gave way to the age of Loyola.

From *Consilium de Emendanda Ecclesia*

Paul III, who served as Pope from 1534 to 1549, really began the substantive efforts toward Catholic reformation. In 1536 he charged a papal commission led by Cardinal Gaspero Contarini (1483–1542) to study abuses in the church and how to correct them. This document, which the commission addressed to the pope in the following year, faced a number of the issues with remarkable frankness.

That Spirit of God by whom the power of the heavens has been established, as the prophet says, has determined to rebuild through you the Church of Christ, tottering, nay, in fact collapsed. . . . We shall hope to make the surest interpretation of this divine purpose—we whom your Holiness has called to Rome and ordered to make known to you, without regard for your advantage or for anyone else's, those abuses, indeed those most serious diseases, which now for a long time afflict God's Church and especially this Roman Curia and which have now led with these diseases gradually becoming more troublesome and destructive to this great ruin which we see. . . .

Your Holiness takes care of the Church of Christ with the help of a great many servants through whom he exercises this responsibility. These moreover are all clerics to whom divine worship has been entrusted, priests especially and particularly parish priests and above all bishops. Therefore, if this government is to proceed properly, care must be taken that these servants are qualified for the office which they must discharge.

The first abuse in this respect is the ordination of clerics and especially of priests, in which no care is taken, no diligence employed, so that indiscriminately the most unskilled, men of the vilest stock and of evil morals, adolescents, are admitted to Holy Orders and to the priesthood, to the [indelible] mark, we stress, which above all denotes Christ. . . .

Another abuse of the greatest consequence is the bestowing of ecclesiastical benefices, especially parishes and above all bishoprics, in the matter of which the practice has become entrenched that provision is made for the persons on whom the benefices are bestowed, but not for the flock and Church of Christ. Therefore, in bestowing parish benefices, but above all bishoprics, care must be taken that they be given to good and learned men so that they themselves can perform those duties to which they are bound, and, in addition, that they be conferred on those who will in all likelihood reside. A benefice in Spain or in Britain then must not be conferred on an Italian, or vice versa. . . .

There is a great and dangerous abuse in the public schools, especially in Italy, where many professors of philosophy teach ungodly things. Indeed, the most ungodly disputations take place in the churches, and, if they are of a religious nature, what pertains to the divine in them is treated before the people with great irreverence. We believe, therefore, that the bishops must be instructed, where there are public schools, to admonish those who lecture that they not teach the young ungodly things, but that they show the weakness of the natural light [of reason] in questions relating to God, to the newness or the eternity of the world, and the like, and guide these youths to what is godly. . . .

The same care must also be employed in the printing of books, and all princes should be instructed by letter to be on their guard lest any books be printed indiscriminately under their authority. Responsibility in this matter should be given to the ordinaries. And because boys in elementary school are now accustomed to read the *Colloquies* of Erasmus, in which there is much to educate unformed minds to ungodly things, the reading of this book and others of this type then must be prohibited in grammar school. . . .

These are the abuses, most blessed Father, which for the present, according to the limitations of our talents, we thought should be compiled, and which seemed to us ought to be corrected. You indeed, in accord with your goodness and wisdom, will direct all these matters. . . . You have taken the name of Paul; you will imitate, we hope, the charity of Paul. He was chosen as the vessel to carry the name of Christ among the nations [Acts 9:15]. Indeed we hope that you have been chosen to restore in our hearts and in our works the name of Christ now forgotten by the nations and by us clerics, to heal the ills, to lead back the sheep of Christ into one fold, to turn away from us the wrath of God and that vengeance which we deserve, already prepared and looming over our heads.

Translated by John Higgins. From *The Catholic Reformation: Savonarola to Ignatius Loyola,* edited by John C. Olin (New York: Harper & Row, 1967), pages 186, 188–189, 194, 197. Copyright © 1969 by John C. Olin. Used by permission of the editor.

Thomas de Vio, Cardinal Cajetan (1469–1534)

From *Faith and Works—Against the Lutherans*

Cajetan was born in Italy and given the name Tommaso de Vio but is usually known by a form of the name of his hometown, Gaeta. He joined the Dominican order and served as its master general from

1508 to 1518. His commentaries on the Bible, Aristotle, and Aquinas put humanist scholarship to new uses. In 1518 he took part in finally fruitless Catholic discussions with Luther at Augsburg; this essay, written in 1532, summarizes some of the fundamental causes of disagreement. The passage quoted here begins by rejecting the Lutheran claim that we are justified while we are still sinners.

To the Supreme Pontiff, Clement VII:

Obedience to the commands of Your Holiness is always due, but now it is for me a delight since I was wanting to refute the poisonous Lutheran views on faith and works. Fearing these were infecting even the hearts of the faithful, I had shortly before receiving Your Holiness' command felt called to write this treatise. This is consequently an agreeable act of obedience which I hope proves fruitful for Christ's faithful and pleasing to Your Holiness, whose office it is also to judge this short work. . . .

4. *The third error: forgiveness of sins preceding charity.* It is intolerable that one's sins would be forgiven before charity is infused in the person forgiven, as the following will convincingly show. An enemy cannot be made a friend unless he have the attitude of friendship. A friend devoid of the quality of friendship would be incomprehensible, just as something white is incomprehensible without whiteness. But when the unrighteous man is made righteous through Christ, an enemy of God is transformed into a friend of God, as the Apostle says in Romans 5[:10], "When we were enemies we were reconciled to God by the death of his Son." Reconciliation makes the reconciled person a friend. Hence it is impossible and incomprehensible that a sinner be justified in the absence of friendship toward God. Charity is this friendship between man and God, being both man's love of friendship toward God and God's love toward man. "God is love, and he who abides in love abides in God, and God in him" [1 John 4:16]. We read in the same Epistle, "We love God, because he first loved us" [1 John 4:19].

Since friendship consists in mutual love, the forgiveness of sins takes place essentially through charity. Hence what we call the righteousness of faith is identical with charity. . . .

5. *The Lutheran teaching on works.* The Lutherans teach that our works are neither meritorious of grace and eternal life, nor do these works make satisfaction for sins. They argue that since Christ has superabundantly merited for us both the grace of forgiveness of sins and eternal life, and since he satisfied superabundantly for all, it is consequently perverse to attribute to our works the merit of grace (or

of forgiveness of sins) and of eternal life, and to say our works satisfy for our sins. Such teaching is said to insult Christ, since it is blasphemy to attribute to ourselves what is Christ's own work. If there is need of our merits and satisfaction, this detracts from the merit and satisfaction of Christ, implying they are inadequate. . . .

The Lutherans therefore teach that good works are to be done, because they are commanded by God as the fruit of justifying faith, but not because they are meritorious of eternal life and satisfactory for sins.

6. *The meaning of merit in this context.* Before determining whether our works are meritorious or not, we must first briefly examine what is meant by merit and how theologians understand it in this context concerning our works.

Merit is said of a voluntary work, whether interior or external, to which by right a payment or reward is due. . . .

Since we are discussing our merit before God, we must explain how men can merit from God a reward for their works. It appears problematical that God would by right render payment for our work, since between ourselves and God there is no right, strictly and absolutely speaking. . . . There is only a derived kind of right, which is much less than the right of a son toward his father and of a slave toward his master. . . .

All that the slave is belongs to the master. A son cannot render as much to his father as he received. Hence a right, strictly and absolutely considered, cannot exist between master and slave and between father and son. It is true to a much greater extent that all that a man is belongs to God and that man cannot render as much to God as he received. Hence man cannot merit something from God that would be due him by right, unless this be a right so weakened that it be far less than the right between master and slave and father and son. Even such a weakened right is not, absolutely speaking, found between man and God, because absolutely speaking man's every voluntary good action is due to God. In fact, the more and the better a man's interior and outward works, so much more does he owe to God, since it is God who works in us both to will and to complete our every action [Phil. 2:13]. This weakened right is found between man and God by reason of the divine ordination by which God ordained our works to be meritorious before himself.

When man merits anything before God, God never becomes man's debtor, but rather his own. If even this weakened debt were given in an absolute sense between man and God, then God would owe man the payment he earned. But it is obvious that God is in debt to no one, as Paul says in Romans 12, "He who has given the gift, shall he then reward this?" [actually Romans 11:35]. God is therefore indebted to himself alone, that he should carry out his own will by which he granted that human works would be meritorious so he would render to man the reward for his work.

This is undoubtedly true about the simple and absolute sense of merit. In other cases, an agreement is presupposed between God and man on some matter, as among men when a master makes a pact of some kind with his slave. In this case a right can arise between master and slave. Thus if God deigns to make a pact with man, a right can arise between man and God with reference to the matter of the agreement. We often read in the Old Testament that God deigned to enter covenants with men. . . .

These texts make it clear that there can be in our works an element of merit even by right, with reference to the reward concerning which an agreement has been made with God.

Keep in mind though that to whatever extent there is a pact between God and man concerning a reward, still God never falls into our debt, but is only in debt to himself. For in view of the agreement made, there is due to our works the reward on which was agreed. God does not thereby become indebted to us regarding this reward, but rather indebted to his own prior determination by which he deigned to enter a pact with us. Consequently we profess in full truth that God is indebted to no one but to himself.

Council of Trent

From *Decree Concerning Justification*

The Council of Trent was called by Pope Paul III and met at intervals from 1545 to 1563. In spite of deep disagreements within the council and disruptions on account of war, plague, and political conflict, it managed to define a clear charter for post-Reformation Catholicism. The council addressed a good many practical questions of church reform, as well as beliefs concerning original sin, the authority of scripture and tradition, and a variety of sacramental issues. But its decree on justification probably addresses most centrally the conflict with Luther.

Since there is being disseminated at this time, not without the loss of many souls and grievous detriment to the unity of the Church, a certain erroneous doctrine concerning justification, the holy, ecumenical and general Council of Trent . . . intends, for the praise and glory of Almighty God, for the tranquillity of the Church and the salvation of souls, to expound to all the faithful of Christ the true and salutary doctrine of justification. . . .

1. The holy council declares first, that for a correct and clear understanding of the doctrine of justification, it is necessary that each one recognize and confess that since all men had lost innocence in the prevarication of Adam [Rom. 5:12; 1 Cor. 15:22], having become unclean [Isa. 64:6], and, as the Apostle says, *by nature children of wrath* [Eph. 2:3], as has been set forth in the decree on original sin, they were so far *the servants of sin* [Rom. 6:17, 20] and under the power of the devil and of death, that not only the Gentiles by the force of nature, but not even the Jews by the very letter of the law of Moses, were able to be liberated or to rise therefrom, though free will, weakened as it was in its power and downward bent, was by no means extinguished in them.

2. Whence it came to pass that the heavenly Father, *the Father of mercies and the God of all comfort* [2 Cor. 1:3], *when the blessed fulness of the time was come* [Gal. 4:4], sent to men Jesus Christ, His own Son, who had both before the law and during the time of the law been announced and promised to many of the holy fathers [Gen. 49:10, 18], *that he might redeem the Jews who were under the law* [Gal. 4:5], and *that the Gentiles who followed not after justice* [Rom. 9:30] might attain to justice, and that all men might receive the adoption of sons. Him has God *proposed* as a propitiator *through faith in his blood* [Rom. 3:25] *for our sins, and not for our sins only, but also for those of the whole world* [1 John 2:2].

3. But though *He died for all* [2 Cor. 5:15], yet all do not receive the benefit of His death, but those only to whom the merit of His passion is communicated; because as truly as men would not be born unjust, if they were not born through propagation of the seed of Adam, since by that propagation they contract through him, when they are conceived, injustice as their own, so if they were not born again in Christ, they would never be justified, since in that new birth there is bestowed upon them, through the merit of His passion, the grace by which they are made just. For this benefit the Apostle exhorts us always *to give thanks to the Father, who hath made us worthy to be partakers of the lot of the saints in light, and hath delivered us from the power of darkness, and hath translated us into*

the kingdom of the Son of his love, in whom we have redemption and remission of sins [Col. 1:12–14].

4. In which words is given a brief description of the justification of the sinner, as being a translation from that state in which man is born as child of the first Adam, to the state of grace and of the adoption of the sons of God through the second Adam, Jesus Christ, our Savior. This translation however cannot, since the promulgation of the Gospel, be effected except through the laver of regeneration or its desire, as it is written: *Unless a man be born again of water and the Holy Ghost, he cannot enter into the kingdom of God* [John 3:5].

5. It is furthermore declared that in adults the beginning of that justification must proceed from the predisposing grace of God through Jesus Christ, that is, from His vocation, whereby, without any merits on their part, they are called; that they who by sin had been cut off from God, may be disposed through His quickening and helping grace to convert themselves to their own justification by freely assenting to and cooperating with that grace; so that, while God touches the heart of man through the illumination of the Holy Ghost, man himself neither does absolutely nothing while receiving that inspiration, since he can also reject it, nor yet is he able by his own free will and without the grace of God to move himself to justice in His sight. Hence, when it is said in the sacred writings: *Turn ye to me, and I will turn to you* [Zech. 1:3], we are reminded of our liberty; and when we reply: *Convert us, O Lord, to thee, and we shall be converted* [Lam. 5:21], we confess that we need the grace of God. . . .

7. This disposition or preparation is followed by justification itself, which is not only a remission of sins but also the sanctification and renewal of the inward man through the voluntary reception of the grace and gifts whereby an unjust man becomes just and from being an enemy becomes a friend, that he may be *an heir according to hope of life everlasting* [Titus 3:7]. The causes of this justification are: the final cause is the glory of God and of Christ and life everlasting; the efficient cause is the merciful God who *washes and sanctifies* [1 Cor. 6:11] gratuitously, signing and anointing *with the holy Spirit of promise, who is the pledge of our inheritance* [Eph. 1:13–14]; the meritorious cause is His most beloved only begotten, our Lord Jesus Christ, who, *when we were enemies* [Rom. 5:10], *for the exceeding charity wherewith he loved us* [Eph. 2:4], merited for us justification by His most holy passion on the wood of the cross and made satisfaction for us to God the Father; the instrumental cause is the sacrament of baptism, which is the sacrament of faith, without which no man was

ever justified; finally, the single formal cause is the justice of God, not that by which He Himself is just, but that by which He makes us just, that, namely, with which we being endowed by Him are *renewed in the spirit of our mind* [Eph. 4:23], and not only are we reputed but we are truly called and are just, receiving justice within us, each one according to his own measure, which the Holy Ghost distributes to everyone as He wills [1 Cor. 12:11] and according to each one's disposition and cooperation. For though no one can be just except he to whom the merits of the passion of our Lord Jesus Christ are communicated, yet this takes place in that justification of the sinner, when by the merit of the most holy passion, *the charity of God is poured forth by the Holy Ghost in the hearts* [Rom. 5:5] of those who are justified and inheres in them; whence man through Jesus Christ, in whom he is ingrafted, receives in that justification, together with the remission of sins, all these infused at the same time, namely, faith, hope and charity. For faith, unless hope and charity be added to it, neither unites man perfectly with Christ nor makes him a living member of His body. For which reason it is more truly said that *faith without works is dead* [James 2:17, 20] and of no profit, and *in Christ Jesus neither circumcision availeth anything nor uncircumcision, but faith that worketh by charity* [Gal. 5:6; 6:15]. . . .

14. Those who through sin have forfeited the received grace of justification, can again be justified when, moved by God, they exert themselves to obtain through the sacrament of penance the recovery, by the merits of Christ, of the grace lost. For this manner of justification is restoration for those fallen, which the holy Fathers have aptly called a second plank after the shipwreck of grace lost. For on behalf of those who fall into sins after baptism, Christ Jesus instituted the sacrament of penance when He said: *Receive ye the Holy Ghost, whose sins you shall forgive, they are forgiven them, and whose sins you shall retain, they are retained* [John 20:22f.]. Hence it must be taught that the repentance of a Christian after his fall is very different from that at his baptism, and that it includes not only a determination to avoid sins and a hatred of them, or *a contrite and humble heart* [Ps. 50:19], but also the sacramental confession of those sins, at least in desire, to be made in its season, and sacerdotal absolution, as well as satisfaction by fasts, alms, prayers and other devout exercises of the spiritual life, not indeed for the eternal punishment, which is, together with the guilt, remitted either by the sacrament or by the desire of the sacrament, but for the temporal punishment which, as the sacred writings teach, is not always wholly remitted, as is done

in baptism, to those who, ungrateful to the grace of God which they have received, have grieved the Holy Ghost [Eph. 4:30] and have not feared to *violate the temple of God* [1 Cor. 3:17]. . . .

16. Therefore, to men justified in this manner, whether they have preserved uninterruptedly the grace received or recovered it when lost, are to be pointed out the words of the Apostle: *Abound in every good work, knowing that your labor is not in vain in the Lord* [1 Cor. 15:58]. *For God is not unjust, that he should forget your work, and the love which you have shown in his name* [Heb. 6:10]; and, *Do not lose your confidence, which hath a great reward* [Heb. 10:35]. Hence, to those who work well *unto the end* [Matt. 10:22] and trust in God, eternal life is to be offered, both as a grace mercifully promised to the sons of God through Christ Jesus, and as a reward promised by God himself, to be faithfully given to their good works and merits [Rom. 6:22].

From *Canons and Decrees of the Council of Trent,* translated by H. J. Schroeder (St. Louis: B. Herder Book Co., 1941), pages 29–34, 39–41.

Ignatius Loyola (1491–1556)

From *Rules for Thinking with the Church*

Ignatius Loyola was born in Spain and began a career as a soldier. Convalescing after being wounded, he turned to the religious life. He gradually developed a book of Spiritual Exercises *with which a spiritual director could lead people through a series of meditations and prayers, and others soon sought him out for spiritual guidance. In 1540 Pope Paul III granted official recognition to Loyola and his friends as the Society of Jesus, the Jesuits, and they soon established their reputation as missionaries and scholars. These rules form one of the appendixes to the* Spiritual Exercises; *they illustrate the conjunction of theological theory and practical reform in the Catholic Reformation.*

In order to have the proper attitude of mind in the Church Militant we should observe the following rules:

1. Putting aside all private judgment, we should keep our minds prepared and ready to obey promptly and in all things the true spouse of Christ our Lord, our Holy Mother, the hierarchical Church.

2. To praise sacramental confession and the reception of the Most Holy Sacrament once a year, and much better once a month, and better still every week, with the requisite and proper dispositions.

3. To praise the frequent hearing of Mass, singing of hymns and psalms, and the recitation of long prayers, both in and out of church; also the hours arranged for fixed times for the whole Divine Office, for prayers of all kinds and for the canonical hours.

4. To praise highly religious life, virginity, and continence; and also matrimony, but not as highly as any of the foregoing. . . .

6. To praise the relics of the saints by venerating them and by praying to these saints. Also to praise the stations, pilgrimages, indulgences, jubilees, Crusade indulgences, and the lighting of candles in the churches.

7. To praise the precepts concerning fasts and abstinences, such as those of Lent, Ember Days, Vigils, Fridays, and Saturdays; likewise to praise acts of penance, both interior and exterior.

8. To praise the adornments and buildings of churches as well as sacred images, and to venerate them according to what they represent. . . .

13. If we wish to be sure that we are right in all things, we should always be ready to accept this principle: I will believe that the white that I see is black, if the hierarchical Church so defines it. For, I believe that between the Bridegroom, Christ our Lord, and the Bride, His Church, there is but one spirit, which governs and directs us for the salvation of our souls, for the same Spirit and Lord, who gave us the Ten Commandments, guides and governs our Holy Mother Church. (Implicit Church authority)

14. Although it be true that no one can be saved unless it be predestined and unless he have faith and grace, still we must be very careful of our manner of discussing and speaking of these matters.

15. We should not make predestination an habitual subject of conversation. If it is sometimes mentioned we must speak in such a way that no person will fall into error, as happens on occasion when one will say, "It has already been determined whether I will be saved or lost, and in spite of all the good or evil that I do, this will not be changed." As a result, they become apathetic and neglect the works that are conducive to their salvation and to the spiritual growth of their souls.

16. In like manner, we must be careful lest by speaking too much and with too great emphasis on faith, without any distinction or explanation, we give occasion to the people to become indolent and

lazy in the performance of good works, whether it be before or after their faith is founded in charity.

17. Also in our discourse we ought not to emphasize the doctrine that would destroy free will. We may therefore speak of faith and grace to the extent that God enables us to do so, for the greater praise of His Divine Majesty. But, in these dangerous times of ours, it must not be done in such a way that good works or free will suffer any detriment or be considered worthless.

18. Although the generous service of God for motives of pure love should be most highly esteemed, we should praise highly the fear of His Divine Majesty, for filial fear and even servile fear are pious and most holy things. When one cannot attain anything better or more useful, this fear is of great help in rising from mortal sin, and after this first step one easily advances to filial fear which is wholly acceptable and pleasing to God our Lord, since it is inseparable from Divine Love.

From *The Spiritual Exercises of St. Ignatius* by Ignatius Loyola, translated by Anthony Mottola, pages 139–142. Copyright © 1964 by Doubleday & Company, Inc. Reprinted by permission of the publisher.

Teresa of Ávila (1515–1582)

From *The Life of Teresa of Jesus*

Teresa was born in Spain and joined the Carmelite order of nuns in 1535. She overcame severe illness, lack of education, and considerable opposition from others to become an author and the reformer of her order. Her books have a vivid, personal quality and yet analyze the form and stages of mystical experience with care and detail. She finished the first draft of this autobiography in 1562.

Chapter 11. . . . A nice way of seeking the love of God is this! We expect great handfuls of it, as one might say, and yet we want to reserve our affections for ourselves! We make no effort to carry our desires into effect or to raise them far above the earth. It is hardly suitable that people who act in this way should have many spiritual consolations; the two things seem to me incompatible. So, being unable to make a full surrender of ourselves, we are never given a full supply of this treasure. May His Majesty be pleased to give it to us little by little, even though the receiving of it may cost us all the trials in the world. . . .

To say something, then, of the early experiences of those who are determined to pursue this blessing and to succeed in this enterprise . . .: it is in these early stages that their labor is hardest. . . .

The beginner must think of himself as of one setting out to make a garden in which the Lord is to take His delight, yet in soil most unfruitful and full of weeds. His Majesty uproots the weeds and will set good plants in their stead. Let us suppose that this is already done—that a soul has resolved to practise prayer and has already begun to do so. We have now, by God's help, like good gardeners, to make these plants grow, and to water them carefully, so that they may not perish, but may produce flowers which shall send forth great fragrance to give refreshment to this Lord of ours, so that He may often come into the garden to take His pleasure and have His delight among these virtues. . . .

Beginners in prayer, we may say, are those who draw up the water out of the well: this, as I have said, is a very laborious proceeding, for it will fatigue them to keep their senses recollected, which is a great labor because they have been accustomed to a life of distraction. Beginners must accustom themselves to pay no heed to what they see or hear, and they must practise doing this during hours of prayer; they must be alone and in their solitude think over their past life. . . . This is what is meant by beginning to draw up water from the well—and God grant there may be water in it! But that, at least, does not depend on us: our task is to draw it up and to do what we can to water the flowers. And God is so good that when, for reasons known to His Majesty, perhaps to our great advantage, He is pleased that the well should be dry, we, like good gardeners, do all that in us lies, and He keeps the flowers alive without water and makes the virtues grow. By water here I mean tears—or, if there be none of these, tenderness and an interior feeling of devotion.

What, then, will he do here who finds that for many days he experiences nothing but aridity, dislike, distaste and so little desire to go and draw water that he would give it up entirely if he did not remember that he is pleasing and serving the Lord of the garden; if he were not anxious that all his service should not be lost, to say nothing of the gain which he hopes for from the great labor of lowering the bucket so often into the well and drawing it up without water? . . . What, then, as I say, will the gardener do here? He will be glad and take heart and consider it the greatest of favors to work in the garden of so great an Emperor. . . .

Chapter 18. . . . In the whole of the prayer already described, and in each of its stages, the gardener is responsible for part of the labor, although in these later stages the labor is accompanied by such bliss and consolation that the soul's desire would be never to abandon it: the labor is felt to be, not labor at all, but bliss. In this state of prayer to which we have now come, there is no feeling, but only rejoicing, unaccompanied by any understanding of the thing in which the soul is rejoicing. It realizes that it is rejoicing in some good thing, in which are comprised all good things at once, but it cannot comprehend this good thing. In this rejoicing all the senses are occupied, so that none of them is free or able to act in any way, either outwardly or inwardly. Previously, as I have said, they were permitted to give some indication of the great joy that they feel; but in this state the soul's rejoicing is beyond comparison greater, and yet can be much less effectively expressed, because there is no power left in the body, neither has the soul any power, to communicate its rejoicing. . . .

The way in which this that we call union comes, and the nature of it, I do not know how to explain. It is described in mystical theology, but I am unable to use the proper terms, and I cannot understand what is meant by "mind" or how this differs from "soul" or "spirit." They all seem the same to me, though the soul sometimes issues from itself, like a fire that is burning and has become wholly flame. . . .

What I do seek to explain is the feelings of the soul when it is in this Divine union. It is quite clear what union is—two different things becoming one. . . .

While seeking God in this way, the soul becomes conscious that it is fainting almost completely away, in a kind of swoon, with an exceeding great and sweet delight. It gradually ceases to breathe and all its bodily strength begins to fail it: it cannot even move its hands without great pain; its eyes involuntarily close, or, if they remain open, they can hardly see. If a person in this state attempts to read, he is unable to spell out a single letter: it is as much as he can do to recognize one. He sees that letters are there, but, as the understanding gives him no help, he cannot read them even if he so wishes. He can hear, but he cannot understand what he hears. He can apprehend nothing with the senses, which only hinder his soul's joy. . . .

As I was about to write of this (I had just communicated and had been experiencing this very prayer of which I am writing), I was wondering what it is the soul does during that time, when the Lord said these words to me: "It dies to itself wholly, daughter, in order that it may fix itself more and more upon Me; it is no longer itself that lives, but I. As it cannot comprehend what it understands, it is an understanding which understands not." One who has experienced this will understand something of it; it cannot be more clearly expressed, since all that comes to pass in this state is so obscure. I can only say that the soul feels close to God and that there abides within it such a certainty that it cannot possibly do other than believe. All the faculties now fail and are suspended in such a way that, as I have said, it is impossible to believe they are active. If the soul has been meditating upon any subject, this vanishes from its memory as if it had never thought of it. . . . So it is that the importunate little butterfly—the memory—is now burning its wings and can no longer fly. The will must be fully occupied in loving, but it cannot understand how it loves; the understanding, if it understands, does not understand how it understands.

From Teresa of Ávila, *The Life of Teresa of Jesus,* translated by E. Allison Peers (Doubleday & Co., 1960), pages 126–129, 174, 177–180. Used with permission of Sheed & Ward, 115 East Armour Boulevard, Kansas City, MO 64141.

Francisco Suárez (1548–1617)

From *A Work on the Three Theological Virtues: Faith, Hope, and Charity*

Suárez, a Spanish Jesuit, was one of the most prolific theologians in history. He wrote on the widest range of topics, often expanding on the work of Thomas Aquinas. His most original work probably lay in political thought, where he is considered one of the founders of modern theories of international law. In this excerpt he develops the "just war" theory that has become a part of most Catholic moral teaching.

Disputation 13

Section 1. Is war intrinsically evil? . . . Our first conclusion is that war, absolutely speaking, is not intrinsically evil, nor is it forbidden to Christians. This conclusion is a matter of faith and is laid down in the Scriptures, for in the Old Testament, wars waged by most holy men are praised (Gen. 14:19–20: "Blessed be Abram"). . . . We find similar passages concerning Moses, Joshua, Samson, Gideon, David, the Maccabees, and others, whom God often ordered to wage war upon the enemies of the Hebrews. . . .

However, one may object [that] . . . war morally brings with it innumerable sins; and a given course of action is considered in itself evil and forbidden, if it is practically always accompanied by unseemly circumstances and harm to one's neighbors. [Furthermore,] one may add that war is opposed to peace, to the love of one's enemies, and to the forgiveness of injuries. . . .

Augustine replies that he deems it advisable to avoid war in so far as is possible, and to undertake it only in cases of extreme necessity, when no alternative remains; but he also holds that war is not entirely evil, since the fact that evils follow upon war is incidental, and since greater evils would result if war were never allowed.

Wherefore, in reply to the confirmation of the argument in question one may deny that war is opposed to an honorable peace; rather it is opposed to an unjust peace, for it is more truly a means of attaining peace that is real and secure. Similarly, war is not opposed to the love of one's enemies; for whoever wages war honorably hates, not individuals, but the actions which he justly punishes. . . .

I hold that defensive war not only is permitted, but sometimes is even commanded. The first part of this proposition follows . . . since all laws allow the repelling of force with force. The reason supporting it is that the right of self-defence is natural and necessary. . . .

In order that a war may be justly waged, a number of conditions must be observed, which may be grouped under three heads. First, the war must be waged by a legitimate power; secondly, the cause itself and the reason must be just; thirdly, the method of its conduct must be proper, and due proportion must be observed at its beginning, during its prosecution and after victory. All of this will be made clear in the following sections. The underlying principle of this general conclusion, indeed, is that, while a war is not in itself evil, nevertheless, on account of the many misfortunes which it brings in its train, it is one of those undertakings that are often carried on in evil fashion; and that therefore, it requires many [justifying] circumstances to make it righteous. . . .

Section 7. What is the proper mode of conducting war? . . . I hold, first that before a war is begun the [attacking] prince is bound to call to the attention of the opposing state the existence of a just cause of war, and to seek adequate reparation therefor; and if the other state offers such adequate reparation, he is bound to accept it, and desist from war; for if he does not do so, the war will be unjust. . . .

I hold, secondly, that after war has been begun, and during the whole period thereof up to the attainment of victory, it is just to visit upon the enemy all losses which may seem necessary either for obtaining satisfaction or for securing victory, provided that these losses do not involve an intrinsic injury to innocent persons, which would be in itself an evil. Of this injury we shall treat below. . . . The reason in support of this conclusion is as follows: if the end is permissible, the necessary means to that end are also permissible; and hence it follows that in the whole course, or duration, of the war hardly anything done against the enemy involves injustice, except the slaying of the innocent. For all other damages are usually held to be necessary for attaining the end to which the war is directed.

In the third place, I hold that after the winning of victory, a prince is allowed to inflict upon the conquered state such losses as are sufficient for a just punishment and satisfaction, and reimbursement for all losses suffered.

From *Selections from Three Works of Francisco Suárez, S.J.,* translated by Gwladys L. Williams, Ammi Brown, and John Waldron (Oxford: Clarendon Press, 1944), Volume 2, pages 800–803, 805, 837–838, 840. Used by permission of Oxford University Press.

Blaise Pascal (1623–1662)

From *Pensées*

Pascal was a mathematician of genius and a scientific prodigy. Initially through family connections, he became associated with the Jansenist movement centered at the French monastery of Port-Royal. Cornelis Jansen (1585–1638) had argued for greater moral rigor in the life of the church and an Augustinian doctrine of predestination. On both counts the Jansenists came into conflict with the Jesuits, who favored a rather generous attitude in hearing confessions and assigning penance and regarded predestinarianism as a substantial step toward Calvinism. In his Provincial Letters, *Pascal subjected the Jesuits to the ridicule of a master ironist. He was at work on a great defense of Christianity, but it remained uncompleted at his death. Even the fragmentary work he left behind, his* Pensées, *has become a classic; a few passages follow, including the famous wager argument.*

199. Let us imagine a number of men in chains, and all condemned to death, where some are killed each day in the sight of the others, and those who remain see their own fate in that of their fellows, and

wait their turn, looking at each other sorrowfully and without hope. It is an image of the condition of men. . . .

205. When I consider the short duration of my life, swallowed up in the eternity before and after, the little space which I fill, and even can see, engulfed in the infinite immensity of spaces of which I am ignorant, and which know me not, I am frightened, and am astonished at being here rather than there; for there is no reason why here rather than there, why now rather than then. Who has put me here? By whose order and direction have this place and time been allotted to me? *Memoria hospitis unius diei praetereuntis.* *

206. The eternal silence of these infinite spaces frightens me. . . .

210. The last act is tragic, however happy all the rest of the play is; at the last a little earth is thrown upon our head, and that is the end for ever. . . .

229. This is what I see and what troubles me. I look on all sides, and I see only darkness everywhere. Nature presents to me nothing which is not matter of doubt and concern. If I saw nothing there which revealed a Divinity, I would come to a negative conclusion; if I saw everywhere the signs of a Creator, I would remain peacefully in faith. But, seeing too much to deny and too little to be sure, I am in a state to be pitied. . . .

233. . . . Let us now speak according to natural lights.

If there is a God, He is infinitely incomprehensible, since, having neither parts nor limits, He has no affinity to us. We are then incapable of knowing either what He is or if He is. This being so, who will dare to undertake the decision of the question? Not we, who have no affinity to Him.

Who then will blame Christians for not being able to give a reason for their belief, since they profess a religion for which they cannot give a reason? They declare, in expounding it to the world, that it is a foolishness, *stultitiam;* and then you complain that they do not prove it? . . . "God is, or He is not." But to which side shall we incline? Reason can decide nothing here. There is an infinite chaos which separated us. A game is being played at the extremity of this infinite distance where heads or tails will turn up. What will you wager? According to reason, you can do neither the one thing nor the other; according to reason, you can defend neither of the propositions. . . .

---

*[The hope of a godless man is like] the memory of a guest who stayed for one day and passed on (Wisd. of Sol. 5:14, NEB).

Yes, but you must wager. It is not optional. You are embarked. . . . Let us weigh the gain and the loss in wagering that God is. Let us estimate these two chances. If you gain, you gain all; if you lose, you lose nothing. Wager, then, without hesitation that He is. . . . there is an eternity of life and happiness. And this being so, if there were an infinity of chances, of which one only would be for you, you would still be right in wagering one to win two.

. . . And so our proposition is of infinite force, when there is the finite to stake in a game where there are equal risks of gain and of loss, and the infinite to gain. . . .

"I confess it, I admit it. But, still, is there no means of seeing the faces of the cards?"—Yes, Scripture and the rest, etc. "Yes, but I have my hands tied and my mouth closed; I am forced to wager, and am not free. I am not released, and am so made that I cannot believe. What, then, would you have me do?"

True. But at least learn your inability to believe, since reason brings you to this, and yet you cannot believe. Endeavor then to convince yourself, not by increase of proofs of God, but by the abatement of your passions. You would like to attain faith, and do not know the way; you would like to cure yourself of unbelief, and ask the remedy for it. Learn of those who have been bound like you, and who now stake all their possessions. These are people who know the way which you would follow, and who are cured of an ill of which you would be cured. Follow the way by which they began; by acting as if they believed, taking the holy water, having masses said, etc. Even this will naturally make you believe, and deaden your acuteness.—"But this is what I am afraid of."—And why? What have you to lose? . . .

What harm will befall you in taking this side? You will be faithful, honest, humble, grateful, generous, a sincere friend, truthful. Certainly you will not have those poisonous pleasures, glory and luxury; but will you not have others? I will tell you that you will thereby gain in this life, and that, at each step you take on this road, you will see so great certainty of gain, so much nothingness in what you risk, that you will at last recognize that you have wagered for something certain and infinite, for which you have given nothing. . . .

347. Man is but a reed, the most feeble thing in nature; but he is a thinking reed. The entire universe need not arm itself to crush him. A vapor, a drop of water suffices to kill him. But, if the universe were to crush him, man would still be more noble than that which killed him, because he knows that he dies and the advantage which the universe has over him; the universe knows nothing of this. . . .

434. . . . What a chimera then is man! What a novelty! What a monster, what a chaos, what a contradiction, what a prodigy! Judge of all things, imbecile worm of the earth; depository of truth, a sink of uncertainty and error; the pride and refuse of the universe. . . .

It is, however, an astonishing thing that the mystery furthest removed from our knowledge, namely, that of the transmission of sin, should be a fact without which we can have no knowledge of ourselves. For it is beyond doubt that there is nothing which more shocks our reason than to say that the sin of the first man has rendered guilty those, who, being so removed from this source, seem incapable of participation in it. This transmission does not only seem to us impossible, it seems also very unjust. . . . And yet, without this mystery, the most incomprehensible of all, we are incomprehensible to ourselves. The knot of our condition takes its twists and turns in this abyss, so that man is more inconceivable without this mystery than this mystery is inconceivable to man. . . .

These foundations, solidly established on the inviolable authority of religion, make us know that there are two truths of faith equally certain: the one, that man, in the state of creation, or in that of grace, is raised above all nature, made like unto God and sharing in His divinity; the other, that in the state of corruption and sin, he is fallen from this state and made like unto the beasts.

From Blaise Pascal, *Pensées,* translated by W. F. Trotter, Everyman's Library (London: J. M. Dent & Sons Ltd., 1958), pages 60–61, 64, 66–68, 97, 121–122. Used by permission of the publisher.

CHAPTER 3

Calvin
and the English Reformation

John Calvin had no direct influence beyond the Swiss city of Geneva, and even there he battled with the city government for much of his career. Yet more than anyone else he shaped the "Reformed" tradition Zwingli and others had begun—a tradition that would form the faith of Christians from Switzerland to the Netherlands to Hungary to Scotland, England, New England, and beyond. When the Genevans invited this young Frenchman to guide the reformation of their city in 1536, they turned to a theologian of systematic vision, whose theology emphasized the sovereignty of God and the importance of manifesting one's Christian calling in daily life. That second theme led Calvin to concern about church discipline and Christian responsibility for the reform of civil society.

For Calvin, belief in the sovereignty of God meant that God gives grace to those he chooses—predestines—without regard for their merit or efforts—and leaves others to their sins. Calvinists have been debating ever since whether one could modify that doctrine. One classic debate on the issue took place in Holland just after 1600, when the followers of Jacobus Arminius urged that Christ died for all, grace was available to all, and the saved were those who chose to accept that grace. The Synod of Dort in 1619 condemned Arminianism on the grounds that it unacceptably made salvation depend on human choice, not divine grace.

A few years earlier, Scotland had been the scene of debates over the relation of Calvinist faith and civil authority. John Knox, the leader of the Scottish Reformation, had been converted to reform in the 1540s. After imprisonment as a galley slave and exile in Geneva and England, he returned to Scotland to do battle with the Catholic Mary, Queen of Scots, insisting on the independence of church and people over against their monarch.

Those issues about church and monarch also became a dominant theme in the English reformation. In the years after 1534, when King Henry VIII broke with Rome over his divorce, the English church moved from nearly

Catholic to Lutheran to Reformed and—sometimes—back again, even to a restoration of Catholicism under Queen Mary. In the eventual settlement under Queen Elizabeth a generally Reformed tradition predominated, but the Church of England sought a middle road, theologically and liturgically, between Rome and Geneva.

In the early 1600s some Englishmen thought that that middle road did not go far enough in the direction of reformation. The Puritan party sought a simpler liturgy, a more Calvinist theology, and greater moral rigor, and their religious concerns got connected to the Parliament's struggles against the king. When Oliver Cromwell and the Parliamentary forces defeated and, in 1649, beheaded King Charles I, the ascendant Puritan forces soon discovered their own deep divisions—between moderate Presbyterians, who wanted to replace bishops with regional and national presbyteries and synods, Independents who wanted local independence for each congregation, and Baptists who, like the Anabaptists in Germany a century earlier, believed that a purified church should baptize and admit only committed adult believers. On the fringes, Diggers and Quakers preached radical social change and radical religious individualism, in forms that would have horrified Calvin himself.

John Calvin (1509–1564)

From *Institutes of the Christian Religion*

Calvin was born and educated as a lawyer in France, converted to the Reformation in 1533, and reluctantly drafted to guide the Reformation in Geneva in 1536. Except for three years when the Genevans drove him out and he moved to Strassburg, he spent the rest of his life there, preaching and teaching. The brief first edition of the Institutes of the Christian Religion *appeared in 1536, but Calvin kept revising it—and adding to it—all his life; these selections come from the final edition of 1559.*

Book 1

Chapter 1. 1. Nearly all the wisdom we possess, that is to say, true and sound wisdom, consists of two parts: the knowledge of God and of ourselves. But, while joined by many bonds, which one precedes and brings forth the other is not easy to discern. In the first place, no one can look upon himself without immediately turning his thoughts to the contemplation of God, in whom he "lives and moves" [Acts 17:28]. For, quite clearly, the mighty gifts with which we are endowed are hardly from ourselves; indeed, our very being is nothing but subsistence in the one God. Then, by these benefits shed like dew from heaven upon us, we are led as by rivulets to the spring itself. Indeed, our very poverty better discloses the infinitude of benefits reposing in God. The miserable ruin, into which the rebellion of the first man cast us, especially compels us to look upward. Thus, not only will we, in fasting and hungering, seek there what we lack; but, in being aroused by fear, we shall learn humility. For, as a veritable world of miseries is to be found in mankind, and we are thereby despoiled of divine raiment, our shameful nakedness exposes a teeming horde of infamies. Each of us must, then, be so stung by the consciousness of his own unhappiness as to attain at least some knowledge of God. . . .

Chapter 6. 1. . . . Despite this, it is needful that another and better help be added to direct us aright to the very Creator of the universe. It was not in vain, then, that he added the light of his Word by which to become known unto salvation; and he regarded as worthy of this privilege those whom he pleased to gather more closely and intimately to himself. For because he saw the minds of all men tossed and agitated, after he chose the Jews as his very own flock, he fenced them about that they might not sink into oblivion as others had. With good reason he holds us by the same means in the pure knowledge of himself, since otherwise even those who seem to stand firm before all others would soon melt away. Just as old or bleary-eyed men and those with weak vision, if you thrust before them a most beautiful volume, even if they recognize it to be some sort of writing, yet can scarcely construe two words, but with the aid of spectacles will begin to read distinctly; so Scripture, gathering up the otherwise confused knowledge of God in our minds, having dispersed our dullness, clearly shows us the true God. This, therefore, is a special gift, where God, to instruct the church, not merely uses mute teachers but also opens his own most hallowed lips. Not only does he teach the elect to look upon a god, but also shows himself as the God upon whom they are to look. He has from the beginning maintained this plan for his church, so that besides these common proofs he also put forth his Word, which is a more direct and more certain mark whereby he is to be recognized. . . .

Chapter 7. 1. Before I go any farther, it is worth-while to say something about the authority of Scripture, not only to prepare our hearts to reverence it, but to banish all doubt. When that which is set forth is acknowledged to be the Word of God, there is no one so deplorably insolent—unless devoid also both of common sense and of humanity itself—as to dare impugn the credibility of Him who speaks. Now daily oracles are not sent from heaven, for it pleased the Lord to hallow his truth to everlasting remembrance in the Scriptures alone [cf. John 5:39]. Hence the Scriptures obtain full authority among believers only when men regard them as having sprung from heaven, as if there the living words of God were heard. . . .

4. . . . Yet they who strive to build up firm faith in Scripture through disputation are doing things backwards. For my part, although I do not excel either in great dexterity or eloquence, if I were struggling against the most crafty sort of despisers of God, who seek to appear shrewd and witty in disparaging Scripture, I am confident it would not be difficult for me to silence their clamorous voices. And if it were a useful labor to refute their cavils, I would with no great trouble shatter the boasts they mutter in their lurking places. But even if anyone clears God's Sacred Word from man's evil speaking, he will not at once imprint upon their hearts that certainty which piety requires. Since for unbelieving men religion seems to stand by opinion alone, they, in order not to believe anything foolishly or lightly, both wish and demand rational proof that Moses and the prophets spoke divinely. But I reply: the testimony of the Spirit is more excellent than all reason. For as God alone is a fit witness of himself in his Word, so also the Word will not find acceptance in men's hearts before it is sealed by the inward testimony of the Spirit. The same Spirit, therefore, who has spoken through the mouths of the prophets must penetrate into our hearts to persuade us that they faithfully proclaimed what had been divinely commanded. . . .

Book 2

Chapter 7. 1. The law was added about four hundred years after the death of Abraham [cf. Gal. 3:17]. From that continuing succession of witnesses which we have reviewed it may be gathered that this was not done to lead the chosen people away from Christ; but rather to hold their minds in readiness until his coming; even to kindle desire for him, and to strengthen their expectation, in order that they might not grow faint by too long delay. . . .

6. But to make the whole matter clearer, let us survey briefly the function and use of what is called the "moral law." Now, so far as I understand it, it consists of three parts.

The first part is this: while it shows God's righteousness, that is, the righteousness alone acceptable to God, it warns, informs, convicts, and lastly condemns, every man of his own unrighteousness. For man, blinded and drunk with self-love, must be compelled to know and to confess his own feebleness and impurity. . . .

10. The second function of the law is this: at least by fear of punishment to restrain certain men who are untouched by any care for what is just and right unless compelled by hearing the dire threats in the law. . . .

12. The third and principal use, which pertains more closely to the proper purpose of the law, finds its place among believers in whose hearts the Spirit of God already lives and reigns. For even though they have the law written and engraved upon their hearts by the finger of God [Jer. 31:33; Heb. 10:16], that is, have been so moved and quickened through the directing of the Spirit that they long to obey God, they still profit by the law in two ways.

Here is the best instrument for them to learn more thoroughly each day the nature of the Lord's will to which they aspire, and to confirm them in the understanding of it. It is as if some servant, already prepared with all earnestness of heart to commend himself to his master, must search out and observe his master's ways more carefully in order to conform and accommodate himself to them. And not one of us may escape from this necessity. For no man has heretofore attained to such wisdom as to be unable, from the daily instruction of the law, to make fresh progress toward a purer knowledge of the divine will.

Again, because we need not only teaching but also exhortation, the servant of God will also avail himself of this benefit of the law: by frequent meditation upon it to be aroused to obedience, be strengthened in it, and be drawn back from the slippery path of transgression. In this way the saints must press on; for, however eagerly they may in accordance with the Spirit strive toward God's righteousness, the listless flesh always so burdens them that they do not proceed with due readiness. The law is to the flesh like a whip to an idle and balky ass, to arouse it to work. . . .

Book 3

Chapter 21. 1. In actual fact, the covenant of life is not preached equally among all men, and among those to whom it is preached, it does not gain the same acceptance either constantly or in equal degree. In this diversity the wonderful depth of God's judgment is made known. For there is no doubt that this variety also serves the decision of God's eternal election. If it is plain that it comes to pass by God's bidding that salvation is freely offered to some while others are barred from access to it, at once great and difficult questions spring up, explicable only when reverent minds regard as settled what they may suitably hold concerning election and predestination. A baffling question this seems to many. For they think nothing more inconsistent than that out of the common multitude of men some should be predestined to salvation, others to destruction. But how mistakenly they entangle themselves will become clear in the following discussion. Besides, in the very darkness that frightens them not only is the usefulness of this doctrine made known but also its very sweet fruit. We shall never be clearly persuaded, as we ought to be, that our salvation flows from the wellspring of God's free mercy until we come to know his eternal election, which illumines God's grace by this contrast: that he does not indiscriminately adopt all into the hope of salvation but gives to some what he denies to others. . . .

Human curiosity renders the discussion of predestination, already somewhat difficult of itself, very confusing and even dangerous. No restraints can hold it back from wandering in forbidden bypaths and thrusting upward to the heights. If allowed, it will leave no secret to God that it will not search out and unravel. Since we see so many on all sides rushing into this audacity and impudence, among them certain men not otherwise bad, they should in due season be reminded of the measure of their duty in this regard.

First, then, let them remember that when they inquire into predestination they are penetrating the sacred precincts of divine wisdom. If anyone with carefree assurance breaks into this place, he will not succeed in satisfying his curiosity and he will enter a labyrinth from which he can find no exit. For it is not right for man unrestrainedly to search out things that the Lord has willed to be hid in himself, and to unfold from eternity itself the sublimest wisdom, which he would have us revere but not understand that through this also he should fill us with wonder. He has set forth by his Word the secrets of his will that he has decided to reveal to us. These he decided to reveal in so far as he foresaw that they would concern us and benefit us. . . .

7. . . . As Scripture, then, clearly shows, we say that God once established by his eternal and unchangeable plan those whom he long before determined once for all to receive into salvation, and those whom, on the other hand, he would devote to destruction. We assert that, with respect to the elect, this plan was founded upon his freely

given mercy, without regard to human worth; but by his just and irreprehensible but incomprehensible judgment he has barred the door of life to those whom he has given over to damnation. Now among the elect we regard the call as a testimony of election. Then we hold justification another sign of its manifestation, until they come into the glory in which the fulfillment of that election lies. But as the Lord seals his elect by call and justification, so, by shutting off the reprobate from knowledge of his name or from the sanctification of his Spirit, he, as it were, reveals by these marks what sort of judgment awaits them. . . .

Book 4

Chapter 20. 2. . . . Spiritual government, indeed, is already initiating in us upon earth certain beginnings of the Heavenly Kingdom, and in this mortal and fleeting life affords a certain forecast of an immortal and incorruptible blessedness. Yet civil government has as its appointed end, so long as we live among men, to cherish and protect the outward worship of God, to defend sound doctrine of piety and the position of the church, to adjust our life to the society of men, to form our social behavior to civil righteousness, to reconcile us with one another, and to promote general peace and tranquillity. All of this I admit to be superfluous, if God's Kingdom, such as it is now among us, wipes out the present life. But if it is God's will that we go as pilgrims upon the earth while we aspire to the true fatherland, and if the pilgrimage requires such helps, those who take these from man deprive him of his very humanity. . . .

4. . . . Accordingly, no one ought to doubt that civil authority is a calling, not only holy and lawful before God, but also the most sacred and by far the most honorable of all callings in the whole life of mortal men. . . .

6. This consideration ought continually to occupy the magistrates themselves, since it can greatly spur them to exercise their office and bring them remarkable comfort to mitigate the difficulties of their task, which are indeed many and burdensome. For what great zeal for uprightness, for prudence, gentleness, self-control, and for innocence ought to be required of themselves by those who know that they have been ordained ministers of divine justice? . . .

23. From this also something else follows: that, with hearts inclined to reverence their rulers, the subjects should prove their obedience toward them, whether by obeying their proclamations, or by paying taxes, or by undertaking public offices and burdens which

pertain to the common defense, or by executing any other commands of theirs. . . .

Let no man deceive himself here. For since the magistrate cannot be resisted without God being resisted at the same time, even though it seems that an unarmed magistrate can be despised with impunity, still God is armed to avenge mightily this contempt toward himself. . . .

29. We owe this attitude of reverence and therefore of piety toward all our rulers in the highest degree, whatever they may be like. I therefore the more often repeat this: that we should learn not to examine the men themselves, but take it as enough that they bear, by the Lord's will, a character upon which he has imprinted and engraved an inviolable majesty. . . . Therefore, if we are cruelly tormented by a savage prince, if we are greedily despoiled by one who is avaricious or wanton, if we are neglected by a slothful one, if finally we are vexed for piety's sake by one who is impious and sacrilegious, let us first be mindful of our own misdeeds, which without doubt are chastised by such whips of the Lord [cf. Dan. 9:7]. By this, humility will restrain our impatience. Let us then also call this thought to mind, that it is not for us to remedy such evils; that only this remains, to implore the Lord's help, in whose hand are the hearts of kings, and the changing of kingdoms [Prov. 21:1]. . . .

30. Here are revealed his goodness, his power, and his providence. For sometimes he raises up open avengers from among his servants, and arms them with his command to punish the wicked government and deliver his people, oppressed in unjust ways, from miserable calamity. . . .

31. But however these deeds of men are judged in themselves, still the Lord accomplished his work through them alike when he broke the bloody scepters of arrogant kings and when he overturned intolerable governments. Let the princes hear and be afraid.

But we must, in the meantime, be very careful not to despise or violate that authority of magistrates, full of venerable majesty, which God has established by the weightiest decrees, even though it may reside with the most unworthy men, who defile it as much as they can with their own wickedness. For, if the correction of unbridled despotism is the Lord's to avenge, let us not at once think that it is entrusted to us, to whom no command has been given except to obey and suffer.

I am speaking all the while of private individuals. For if there are now any magistrates of the people, appointed to restrain the willfulness of kings (as in ancient times the ephors were set against the

Spartan kings, or the tribunes of the people against the Roman consuls, or the demarchs against the senate of the Athenians; and perhaps, as things now are, such power as the three estates exercise in every realm when they hold their chief assemblies), I am so far from forbidding them to withstand, in accordance with their duty, the fierce licentiousness of kings, that, if they wink at kings who violently fall upon and assault the lowly common folk, I declare that their dissimulation involves nefarious perfidy, because they dishonestly betray the freedom of the people, of which they know that they have been appointed protectors by God's ordinance.

From *Calvin: Institutes of the Christian Religion,* edited by John T. McNeill and translated by Ford Lewis Battles (Volumes XX and XXI: The Library of Christian Classics), pages 35–36, 69–70, 74, 79, 348, 354, 358, 360–361, 920–923, 931, 1487, 1490–1491, 1510–1511, 1517–1519. Copyright © MCMLX W. L. Jenkins. Published by The Westminster Press, Philadelphia, and the SCM Press Ltd., London. Used by permission of the publishers.

The Five Arminian Articles

In 1610, after the death of Jacobus Arminius (1560–1609), his Dutch followers drew up this statement of their principles, seeking to modify the extremes of Calvinism they found unacceptable. The first article makes the point that, since salvation goes to those who persevere in the faith, it is not given arbitrarily.

Art. I. That God, by an eternal, unchangeable purpose in Jesus Christ his Son, before the foundation of the world, hath determined, out of the fallen, sinful race of men, to save in Christ, for Christ's sake, and through Christ, those who, through the grace of the Holy Ghost, shall believe on this his Son Jesus, and shall persevere in this faith and obedience of faith, through this grace, even to the end; and, on the other hand, to leave the incorrigible and unbelieving in sin and under wrath, and to condemn them as alienate from Christ, according to the word of the Gospel in John 3:36: "He that believeth on the Son hath everlasting life: and he that believeth not the Son shall not see life; but the wrath of God abideth on him," and according to other passages of Scripture also.

Art. II. That agreeably thereto, Jesus Christ, the Saviour of the world, died for all men and for every man, so that he has obtained for them all, by his death on the cross, redemption and the forgiveness of sins; yet that no one actually enjoys this forgiveness of sins except the believer, according to the word of the Gospel of John 3:16: "God so loved the world that he gave his only-begotten Son, that whosoever believeth in him should not perish, but have everlasting life." And in the First Epistle of John 2:2: "And he is the propitiation for our sins; and not for ours only, but also for the sins of the whole world."

Art. III. That man has not saving grace of himself, nor of the energy of his free will, inasmuch as he, in the state of apostasy and sin, can of and by himself neither think, will, nor do anything that is truly good (such as saving Faith eminently is); but that it is needful that he be born again of God in Christ, through his Holy Spirit, and renewed in understanding, inclination, or will, and all his powers, in order that he may rightly understand, think, will, and effect what is truly good, according to the word of Christ, John 15:5: "Without me ye can do nothing."

Art. IV. That this grace of God is the beginning, continuance, and accomplishment of all good, even to this extent, that the regenerate man himself, without prevenient or assisting, awakening, following and co-operative grace, can neither think, will, nor do good, nor withstand any temptations to evil; so that all good deeds or movements, that can be conceived, must be ascribed to the grace of God in Christ. But as respects the mode of the operation of this grace, it is not irresistible, inasmuch as it is written concerning many, that they have resisted the Holy Ghost. (Acts 7, and elsewhere in many places.)

Art. V. That those who are incorporated into Christ by a true faith, and have thereby become partakers of his life-giving Spirit, have thereby full power to strive against Satan, sin, the world, and their own flesh, and to win the victory; it being well understood that it is ever through the assisting grace of the Holy Ghost; and that Jesus Christ assists them through his Spirit in all temptations, extends to them his hand, and if only they are ready for the conflict, and desire his help, and are not inactive, keeps them from falling, so that they, by no craft or power of Satan, can be misled nor plucked out of Christ's hands, according to the Word of Christ, John 10:28: "Neither shall any man pluck them out of my hand." But whether they are capable, through negligence, or forsaking again the first beginnings of their life in Christ, of again returning to this present evil world, of turning away from the holy doctrine which was delivered them, of losing a good conscience, of becoming devoid of grace, that must be more particularly determined out of the Holy Scripture, before we ourselves can teach it with the full persuasion of our minds.

From *The Creeds of Christendom,* Volume 3, edited and translated by Philip Schaff (New York: Harper & Brothers, 1877), pages 545–549.

From *The Canons of the Synod of Dort*

In 1618 and 1619 a synod of the Dutch Reformed Church—though it also included delegates from Switzerland, Germany, and England—met to deal with the Arminian controversy, and in these canons condemned the Arminians and set a standard for high Calvinist orthodoxy.

Of divine predestination. Art. I. As all men have sinned in Adam, lie under the curse, and are obnoxious to eternal death, God would have done no injustice by leaving them all to perish, and delivering them over to condemnation on account of sin, according to the words of the Apostle [Rom. 3:19], "that every mouth may be stopped, and all the world may become guilty before God" [v. 23]; "for all have sinned, and come short of the glory of God" and [6:23], "for the wages of sin is death."

Art. II. But "in this the love of God was manifested, that he sent his only-begotten Son into the world," "that whosoever believeth on him should not perish, but have everlasting life" [1 John 4:9; John 3:16]. . . .

Art. VI. That some receive the gift of faith from God, and others do not receive it, proceeds from God's eternal decree. "For known unto God are all his works from the beginning of the world" [Acts 15:18; Eph. 1:11]. According to which decree he graciously softens the hearts of the elect, however obstinate, and inclines them to believe; while he leaves the non-elect in his just judgment to their own wickedness and obduracy. . . .

Art. IX. This election was not founded upon foreseen faith, and the obedience of faith, holiness, or any other good quality or disposition in man, as the prerequisite, cause, or condition on which it depended; but men are chosen to faith and to the obedience of faith, holiness, etc. Therefore election is the foundation of every saving good, from which proceed faith, holiness, and the other gifts of salvation. . . .

Of the corruption of man, his conversion to God, and the manner thereof. . . . Art. III. Therefore all men are conceived in sin, and are by nature children of wrath, incapable of any saving good, prone to evil, dead in sin, and in bondage thereto; and, without the regenerating grace of the Holy Spirit, they are neither able nor willing to return to God, to reform the depravity of their nature, nor to dispose themselves to reformation. . . .

Art. IX. It is not the fault of the gospel, nor of Christ offered therein, nor of God, who calls men by the gospel, and confers upon them various gifts, that those who are called by the ministry of the Word refuse to come and be converted. The fault lies in themselves; some of whom when called, regardless of their danger, reject the Word of life; others, though they receive it, suffer it not to make a lasting impression on their heart; therefore, their joy, arising only from a temporary faith, soon vanishes, and they fall away; while others choke the seed of the Word by perplexing cares and the pleasures of this world, and produce no fruit. This our Saviour teaches in the parable of the sower [Matt. 13].

Art. X. But that others who are called by the gospel obey the call and are converted, is not to be ascribed to the proper exercise of free will, whereby one distinguishes himself above others equally furnished with grace sufficient for faith and conversion (as the proud heresy of Pelagius maintains); but it must be wholly ascribed to God, who, as he hath chosen his own from eternity in Christ, so he [calls them effectually in time], confers upon them faith and repentance, rescues them from the power of darkness, and translates them into the kingdom of his own Son, that they may show forth the praises of him who hath called them out of darkness into his marvelous light; and may glory not in themselves but in the Lord, according to the testimony of the Apostles in various places.

From *Creeds of Christendom,* Volume 3, edited by Philip Schaff (New York: Harper & Brothers, 1877), pages 581–583, 587–590.

John Knox (c.1513–1572)

From *History of the Reformation of Religion Within the Realm of Scotland*

Knox embraced the Reformed cause in the mid-1540s and suffered exile and imprisonment for his faith, before returning in triumph to become the leader of the Scottish church. At his death he left uncompleted his History of the Reformation in Scotland; *this excerpt from*

*that work recounts a debate Knox had in 1561 with the Catholic
Queen Mary over the faith of her subjects.*

Whether it was by counsel of others, or of the Queen's own desire,
we know not; but the Queen spake with John Knox at Holyrood and
had long reasoning with him. . . . The Queen accused John Knox that
he had raised a part of her subjects against her mother and against
herself. . . .

To the which the said John answered, "Madam, may it please
Your Majesty patiently to hear my simple answers? First, if to teach
the Truth of God in sincerity, if to rebuke idolatry and to will a
people to worship God according to His Word, be to raise subjects
against their Princes, then can I not be excused; for it has pleased
God of His Mercy to make me one among many to disclose unto this
Realm the vanity of the Papistical Religion, and the deceit, pride and
tyranny of that Roman Antichrist. But, Madam, if the true knowledge of God and His right worshipping be the chief causes, that must
move men from their heart to obey their just Princes, as it is most
certain they are, wherein can I be reprehended?" . . .

Queen Mary: "But yet, ye have taught the people to receive another religion than their Princes can allow. How can that doctrine
be of God, seeing that God commandeth subjects to obey their
Princes?"

John Knox: "Madam, as right religion took neither original
strength nor authority from worldly princes, but from the Eternal
God alone, so are not subjects bound to frame their religion according to the appetites of their princes. Princes are oft the most ignorant
of all others in God's true religion, as we may read in the Histories,
as well before the death of Christ Jesus as after. If all the seed of
Abraham should have been of the religion of Pharaoh, to whom they
were long subjects, I pray you, Madam, what religion should there
have been in the world? Or, if all men in the days of the Apostles
should have been of the religion of the Roman Emperors, what
religion should there have been upon the face of the earth?" . . .

Queen Mary: "Yea, but none of these men raised the sword against
their princes."

John Knox: "Yet, Madam, ye cannot deny that they resisted, for
those who obey not the commandments that are given, in some sort
resist."

Queen Mary: "But yet, they resisted not by the sword?"

John Knox: "God, Madam, had not given them the power and the
means."

Queen Mary: "Think ye that subjects, having the power, may resist their princes?"

John Knox: "If their princes exceed their bounds, Madam, no doubt they may be resisted, even by power. For there is neither greater honour, nor greater obedience, to be given to kings or princes, than God hath commanded to be given unto father and mother. But the father may be stricken with a frenzy, in which he would slay his children. If the children arise, join themselves together, apprehend the father, take the sword from him, bind his hands, and keep him in prison till that his frenzy be overpast—think ye, Madam, that the children do any wrong? It is even so, Madam, with princes that would murder the children of God that are subjects unto them. Their blind zeal is nothing but a very mad frenzy, and therefore, to take the sword from them, to bind their hands, and to cast them into prison till they be brought to a more sober mind, is no disobedience against princes, but just obedience, because it agreeth with the will of God."

At these words, the Queen stood as it were amazed, more than the quarter of an hour. Her countenance altered, so that the Lord James* began to entreat her, and to demand, "What hath offended you, Madam?"

At length she said to John Knox, "Well then, I perceive that my subjects shall obey you, and not me. They shall do what they list, and not what I command; and so must I be subject to them, and not they to me."

John Knox: "God forbid that ever I take upon me to command any to obey me, or yet to set subjects at liberty to do what pleaseth them! My travail is that both princes and subjects obey God. Think not, Madam, that wrong is done you, when ye are willed to be subject to God. It is He that subjects peoples under princes, and causes obedience to be given unto them. Yea, God craves of Kings that they be foster-fathers to His Church, and commands Queens to be nurses to His people. This subjection, Madam, unto God, and unto His troubled Church, is the greatest dignity that flesh can get upon the face of the earth, for it shall carry them to everlasting glory."

From John Knox, *History of the Reformation of Religion Within the Realm of Scotland,* edited by C. J. Guthrie (London: A. & C. Black, 1899), pages 271–272, 277–279. Used by permission of A. & C. Black (Publishers) Ltd.

---

*A supporter of Knox present at this interview.

Richard Hooker (c.1554–1600)

From *The Laws of Ecclesiastical Polity*

Educated at Oxford, Hooker became the great defender of the moderate settlement which the Church of England had arrived at after Queen Elizabeth came to the throne in 1559. In this, his best-known work, he lays out a balanced account of the Anglican middle way between Roman Catholicism and more extreme forms of Protestantism. In this selection he seeks a balance between attention to scripture and the traditions of the church, and a theology of the Lord's Supper that avoids formulas from either side of earlier disputes that had led to controversy.

Book 2

Chapter 8. 7. Two opinions therefore there are concerning sufficiency of Holy Scripture, each extremely opposite unto the other, and both repugnant unto truth. The schools of Rome teach Scripture to be so unsufficient, as if, except traditions were added, it did not contain all revealed and supernatural truth, which absolutely is necessary for the children of men in this life to know that they may in the next be saved. Others justly condemning this opinion grow likewise unto a dangerous extremity, as if Scripture did not only contain all things in that kind necessary, but all things simply, and in such sort that to do any thing according to any other law were not only unnecessary but even opposite unto salvation, unlawful and sinful. Whatsoever is spoken of God or things appertaining to God otherwise than as the truth is; though it seem an honour, it is an injury. And as incredible praises given unto men do often abate and impair the credit of their deserved commendation; so we must likewise take great heed, lest in attributing unto Scripture more than it can have, the incredibility of that do cause even those things which indeed it hath most abundantly to be less reverently esteemed. I therefore leave it to themselves to consider, whether they have in this first point or not overshot themselves; which God doth know is quickly done, even when our meaning is most sincere, as I am verily persuaded theirs in this case was. . . .

Book 5

Chapter 7. 1. Neither may we in this case lightly esteem what hath been allowed as fit in the judgment of antiquity, and by the long continued practice of the whole Church; from which unnecessarily to swerve, experience hath never as yet found it safe. For wisdom's sake we reverence them no less that are young, or not much less, than if they were stricken in years. And therefore of such it is rightly said that their ripeness of understanding is "grey hair," and their virtues "old age" [Wisd. of Sol. 4:9]. But because wisdom and youth are seldom joined in one, and the ordinary course of the world is more according to Job's observation, who giveth men advice to seek "wisdom amongst the ancient, and in the length of days, understanding" [Job 12:12]; therefore if the comparison do stand between man and man, which shall hearken unto other, sith the aged for the most part are best experienced, least subject to rash and unadvised passions, it hath been ever judged reasonable that their sentence in matter of counsel should be better trusted, and more relied upon than other men's. . . .

4. We are therefore bold to make our second petition this, That in things the fitness whereof is not of itself apparent, nor easy to be made sufficiently manifest unto all, yet the judgment of antiquity concurring with that which is received may induce them to think it not unfit, who are not able to allege any known weighty inconvenience which it hath, or to take any strong exception against it. . . .

Chapter 8. 4. . . . Our dislike of them, by whom too much heretofore hath been attributed unto the Church, is grown to an error on the contrary hand; so that now from the Church of God too much is derogated. By which removal of one extremity with another, the world seeking to procure a remedy, hath purchased a mere exchange of the evil which before was felt. . . .

Surely the Church of God in this business is neither of capacity, I trust, so weak, nor so unstrengthened, I know, with authority from above, but that her laws may exact obedience at the hands of her own children, and enjoin gainsayers silence, giving them roundly to understand, that where our duty is submission, weak oppositions betoken pride.

5. We therefore crave thirdly to have it granted, that where neither the evidence of any law divine, nor the strength of any invincible argument otherwise found out by the light of reason, nor any notable public inconvenience, doth make against that which our own laws ecclesiastical have although but newly instituted for the ordering of these affairs, the very authority of the Church itself, at the least in such cases, may give so much credit to her own laws, as to make their sentence touching fitness and conveniency weightier than any bare

and naked conceit to the contrary; especially in them who can owe no less than child-like obedience to her that hath more than motherly power. . . .

Chapter 67. 12. These things considered, how should that mind which loving truth and seeking comfort out of holy mysteries hath not perhaps the leisure, perhaps not the wit nor capacity to tread out so endless mazes, as the intricate disputes of this cause have led men into, how should a virtuously disposed mind better resolve with itself than thus? "Variety of judgments and opinions argueth obscurity in those things whereabout they differ. But that which all parts receive for truth, that which every one having sifted is by no one denied or doubted of, must needs be matter of infallible certainty. Whereas therefore there are but three expositions made of 'this is my body,' the first, 'this is in itself before participation *really and truly the natural substance of my body by reason of the coexistence which my omnipotent body hath with the sanctified element of bread,*' which is the Lutherans' interpretation; the second, 'this is itself and before participation *the very true and natural substance of my body, by force of that Deity which with the words of consecration abolisheth the substance of bread and substituteth in the place thereof my Body,*' which is the popish construction; the last, '*this hallowed food, through concurrence of divine power, is in verity and truth, unto faithful receivers, instrumentally a cause of that mystical participation, whereby as I make myself wholly theirs, so I give them in hand an actual possession of all such saving grace as my sacrificed body can yield, and as their souls do presently need, this is* to them and in them *my body:*' of these three rehearsed interpretations the last hath in it nothing but what the rest do all approve and acknowledge to be most true, nothing but that which the words of Christ are on all sides confessed to enforce, nothing but that which alone is sufficient for every Christian man to believe concerning the use and force of this sacrament, finally nothing but that wherewith the writings of all antiquity are consonant and all Christian confessions agreeable. And as truth in what kind soever is by no kind of truth gainsayed, so the mind which resteth itself on this is never troubled with those perplexities which the other do both find, by means of so great contradiction between their opinions and true principles of reason grounded upon experience, nature and sense. Which albeit with boisterous courage and breath they seem oftentimes to blow away, yet whoso observeth how again they labour and sweat by subtilty of wit to make some show of agreement between their peculiar conceits and the general edicts of nature, must needs perceive they struggle with that which they cannot fully master. Besides sith of that which is proper to themselves their discourses are hungry and unpleasant, full of tedious and irksome labour, heartless and hitherto without fruit, on the other side read we them or hear we others be they of our own or of ancienter times, to what part soever they be thought to incline touching that whereof there is controversy, yet in this where they all speak but one thing their discourses are heavenly, their words sweet as the honeycomb, their tongues melodiously tuned instruments, their sentences mere consolation and joy, are we not hereby almost even with voice from heaven, admonished which we may safeliest cleave unto?"

From *The Works of Mr. Richard Hooker,* edited by John Keble (New York: D. Appleton & Co., 1844), pages 217, 302–304, 454.

Thomas Cartwright (1535–1603)

From *A Reply to an Answer Made of Master Doctor Whitgift Against the Admonition to Parliament*

Cartwright taught at Cambridge until his Puritan views forced him to flee to Geneva. He returned and continued to be a staunch defender of moderate Presbyterianism. In 1572 Archbishop Whitgift published an attack on the Puritans as radical innovators, dangerous to the public order. Cartwright published this answer on behalf of the Puritan "cause" in the same year.

The cause is charged first with newness and strangeness, then as author of confusion and of disorder, and last of all as enemy to princes, magistrates, and commonwealths. For the first, besides that it is no sufficient challenge to say it is new and strange, there is no cause why it should be counted new which is confessed of those which mislike it to have been for the most part used in the apostles' times, nor why it should be esteemed strange which is used now far and near, of this and that side the sea, and of no strangers but of those which are of the household of faith. And it shall more largely appear in this book that this is no innovation but a renovation, and the doctrine not new but renewed, no stranger but born in Sion, whereunto it, being before unjustly banished, ought now of right to be restored.

And of confusion and disorder it is yet more untruly accused. For justice may be as well accused for doing wrong as this doctrine for bringing in disorder, whose whole work is to provide that nothing be done out of place, out of time, or otherwise than the condition of every man's calling will bear; which putteth the people in subjection under their governors, the governors in degree and order one under another, as the elder underneath the pastor and the deacon underneath the elder; which teacheth that a particular church shall give place unto a provincial synod where many churches are, and the provincial to a national, and likewise that unto the general, if any be, and all unto Christ and His Word. . . .

For the third point, which is that it is an enemy to magistrates and the commonwealth: if it be enough to accuse without proof, to say and show no reason, innocency itself shall not be guiltless. . . . If the question be whether princes and magistrates be necessary in the Church, it holdeth that the use of them is more than of the sun, without the which the world cannot stand. If it be of their honor, it holdeth that with humble submission of mind, the outward also of the body, yea, the body itself and all that it hath, if need so require, are to be yielded for the defense of the prince and for that service for the which the prince will use them unto, for the glory of God and the maintenance of the commonwealth. If it be asked of the obedience due unto the prince and unto the magistrate, it answereth that all obedience in the Lord is to be rendered. And if it come to pass that any other be asked, it so refuseth that it disobeyeth not in preferring obedience to the great God before that which is to be given to mortal man. . . . And if it be showed that this is necessary for the Church, it cannot be but profitable for the commonwealth. Nay, the profit of it may easily appear for that by the censures and discipline of the Church as they are in this book described, men are kept back from committing of great disorders of stealing, adultery, murder, etc., whilst the small faults of lying and uncomely jesting, of hard and choleric speeches, which the magistrate doth not commonly punish, be corrected. And undoubtedly, seeing that the Church and commonwealth do embrace and kiss one another . . . , it cannot be but that the breaches of the commonwealth have proceeded from the hurts of the Church, and the wants of the one from the lacks of the other. Neither is it to be hoped for that the commonwealth shall flourish until the Church be reformed. And it is also certain that, as the Church shall every day more and more decay until it be made even with the ground, unless the walls be builded and the ruins repaired, so the weight of it, if it fall, will either quite pull down the commonwealth or leave it such as none which fear God will take any pleasure in it.

From Thomas Cartwright, *A Replie to an Answere Made of Doctor Whitgift Agaynst the Admonition to the Parliament* (London, 1574), pages 1–2.

Gerrard Winstanley (c.1609–c.1660)

From *The Law of Freedom in a Platform*

Of the radical Puritans who emerged under Cromwell's rule, Winstanley may have been the most radical of all. Theologically, he sometimes challenged nearly all traditional beliefs; politically, he proposed that the earth, God's creation, was common property for all to dig and plant. He and some friends actually founded a "Digger" commune in 1649; he wrote this critique of current society and account of his alternative vision in 1652.

The burden of the Clergy remains still upon us, in a three-fold nature.

First, If any man declare his Judgment in the things of God, contrary to the Clergies' report, or the mind of some high Officers, they are cashiered, imprisoned, crushed, and undone, and made sinners for a word, as they were in the Popes' and Bishops' days. . . .

Secondly, In many Parishes there are old formal ignorant Episcopal Priests established; and some Ministers, who are bitter Enemies to Commonwealth's Freedom, and Friends to Monarchy, are established Preachers, and are continually buzzing their subtle principles into the minds of the people, to undermine the Peace of our declared Commonwealth, causing a disaffection of spirit among neighbors, who otherwise would live in peace.

Thirdly, The burden of Tythes remains still upon our Estates, which was taken from us by the Kings, and given to the Clergy, to maintain them by our labors: so that though their preaching fill the minds of many with madness, contention, and unsatisfied doubting, because their imaginary and ungrounded Doctrines cannot be understood by them, yet we must pay them large Tythes for so doing; this is Oppression. . . .

It may be you will say, If Tythes be taken from the Priests and Impropriators, and Copy-hold Services from Lords of Mannors, how shall they be provided for again; for is it not unrighteous to take their estates from them?

I Answer, when Tythes were first enacted, and Lordly power drawn over the backs of the oppressed, the Kings and Conquerors made no scruple of Conscience to take it, though the people lived in sore bondage of poverty for want of it; and can there be scruple of conscience to make restitution of this which hath been so long stolen goods? It is no scruple arising from the Righteous Law, but from covetousness, who goes away sorrowful to hear he must part with all to follow Righteousness and Peace.

But though you do take away Tythes, and the Power of Lords of Mannors, yet there will be no want to them, for they have the freedom of the Common stock, they may send to the Storehouses for what they want, and live more free than now they do, for now they are in care and vexation by servants, by casualties, by being cheated in buying and selling, and many other incumbrances, but then they will be free from all, for the common Storehouses is every man's riches, not any one's.

Is not buying and selling a righteous Law? No, It is the Law of the Conqueror, but not the righteous Law of Creation: how can that be righteous which is a cheat? For is not this a common practise, when he hath a bad Horse or Cow, or any bad commodity, he will send it to the Market, to cheat some simple plain-hearted man or other, and when he comes home, will laugh at his neighbor's hurt, and much more etc.

When Mankind began to buy and sell, then did he fall from his Innocency; for then they began to oppress and cozen one another of their Creation Birth-right. . . .

But shall not one man be richer than another?

There is no need of that; for Riches make men vain-glorious, proud, and to oppress their Brethren; and are the occasion of wars.

No man can be rich, but he must be rich, either by his own labors, or by the labors of other men helping him: If a man have no help from his neighbor, he shall never gather an Estate of hundreds and thousands a year: If other men help him to work, then are those Riches his Neighbor's, as well as his; for they be the fruit of other men's labors as well as his own. . . .

And if the Earth were set free from Kingly Bondage, so that every one were sure to have a free livelihood, and if this liberty were granted, then many secrets of God, and his Works in Nature, would be made public, which men nowadays keep secret to get a living by; so that this Kingly Bondage is the cause of the spreading of ignorance in the Earth: But when Commonwealth's Freedom is established, and Pharisaical or Kingly Slavery cast out, then will *knowledge cover the Earth, as the waters cover the Seas,* and not till then.

From Gerrard Winstanley, *The Law of Freedom in a Platform,* edited by Robert W. Kenny (New York: Schocken Books, 1973), pages 52, 58–59, 111.

George Fox (1624–1691)

From *Journal*

The son of a weaver, Fox was apprenticed to a shoemaker but even in childhood had the visions he called "openings." He concluded that a building could not be the "church" but only a "steeple house," for the church lies in people's hearts. His vision of social equality, peace, and the inner light of Christ that could guide everyone inspired his contemporaries as they have inspired the readers of the Journal *he left at his death. The Society of Friends he founded in the 1650s soon became known as the "Quakers" because of their shaking in the midst of religious emotion.*

When I came to eleven years of age, I knew pureness and righteousness; for while I was a child I was taught how to walk so as to be kept pure. The Lord taught me to be faithful in all things, and to act faithfully two ways, viz. inwardly to God, and outwardly to man. . . .

At another time it was opened in me, "That God who made the world did not dwell in temples made with hands." This at the first seemed strange, because both priests and people used to call their temples or churches, dreadful places, holy ground, and the temples of God. But the Lord showed me clearly, that he did not dwell in these temples which men had commanded and set up, but in people's hearts. . . .

Then I heard of a great meeting to be at Leicester for a dispute, wherein presbyterians, independents, baptists, and common-prayer-men, were said to be all concerned. The meeting was in a steeple-house; to which I was moved by the Lord God to go, and be amongst them. I heard their discourse and reasonings, some being in pews, and the priest in the pulpit, abundance of people being gathered together. At last one woman asked a question out of Peter, What that birth was, viz., A being born again of incorruptible seed, by the Word of God, that liveth and abideth for ever? The priest said to her, I permit not a woman to speak in the church; though he had before given liberty for any to speak. Whereupon I was wrapped up as in a rapture, in the Lord's power, and I stepped up, and asked the priest, Dost thou call this place (the steeple-house) a church? or dost thou call this mixed multitude a church? . . . But, instead of answering me, he asked me, What a church was? I told him, The church was the pillar and ground of truth, made up of living stones, living members, a spiritual household, which Christ was the head of: but he was not the head of a mixed multitude, or of an old house made up of lime, stones, and wood. This set them all on a fire. . . .

When the Lord God and his Son Jesus Christ sent me forth into the world to preach his everlasting gospel and kingdom, I was glad that I was commanded to turn people to that inward light, spirit, and grace, by which all might know their salvation and their way to God; even that Divine Spirit which would lead them into all truth, and which I infallibly knew would never deceive any.

But with and by this divine power and spirit of God, and the light of Jesus, I was to bring people off from all their own ways, to Christ the new and living way; from their churches, which men had made and gathered, to the church in God, the general assembly written in heaven, which Christ is the head of. . . .

Having got a little respite from travel, I was moved to write an epistle to friends, as followeth:

"All friends of the Lord everywhere, whose minds are turned in toward the Lord, take heed to the light within you, which is the light of Christ: which, as you love it, will call your minds inward, that are abroad in the creatures: so your minds may be renewed by it, and turned to God in this which is pure, to worship the living God, the Lord of hosts over all the creatures. That which calls your minds out of the lusts of the world, will call them out of the affections and desires, and turn you to set your affections above. The same that calls the mind out of the world, will give judgment upon the world's affections and lusts, that which calls out your minds from the world's teachers and the creatures, to have your minds renewed. . . . All who hate this light, whose minds are abroad in the creatures, in the earth, and in the image of the devil, get the words of the saints (that received their wisdom from above) into the old nature and their corrupted minds. Such are murderers of the just, enemies to the cross of Christ, in whom the prince of the air lodgeth, sons of perdition, betrayers of the just. Therefore take heed to that light, which is oppressed with that nature; which light, as it arises, shall condemn all that cursed nature, shall turn it out, and shut it out of the house.

So ye will come to see the candle lighted, and the house sweeping and swept. Then the pure pearl ariseth, then the eternal God is exalted. The same light that calls in your minds out of the world . . . , the same turns them to God the father of lights. Here in the pure mind is the pure God waited upon for wisdom from above; the pure God is seen night and day, and the eternal peace, of which there is no end, enjoyed."

From George Fox, *The Journal of George Fox* (Philadelphia: Friends' Book Store, 1850), pages 55, 59–61, 67, 73–74, 274.

CHAPTER 4

Theology in the Enlightenment

In the early 1600s a generation of warfare between Protestants and Catholics tore Europe apart. Partly in reaction, many Christians began to wonder if details of doctrine really mattered so much—at least if they mattered enough to fight over them. The same period saw a great increase in the accomplishment and influence of science, and it seemed natural to contrast the advances of scientists with the continuing bickering of theologians. Perhaps, some thought, application of the scientific approach could sort out religious questions too.

That hope led to differing results. For moderates like John Locke, historical evidence established, on good empirical grounds, the occurrence of biblical miracles, and the miracles established the authenticity of Jesus' mission from God. At the more radical end of the scale, the Deists were skeptical of all claims to revelation and believed only in a God who had initially created the universe but had left it alone ever since. Both Deists and more moderate rational theologians had doubts about the Trinity and predestination. They sought a simpler theology and were convinced that we can, with free will, improve ourselves by our own efforts.

In the same period movements that were in some ways the very opposite of Deism also sought greater theological simplicity. Beginning in the 1600s the Pietist movement in Germany emphasized Bible reading by the laity. The Pietists also believed that devotion and morality were far more important for the clergy than intellectual sophistication was. In the middle 1700s John Wesley and other early Methodist preachers made great changes in English religion by simple preaching to the masses–preaching that, in Wesley's case, emphasized human free choice, conversion experiences, and practical moral improvement. Thus he shared some of the conclusions of "rational religion" while insisting that feeling as well as reason must play a role in religion.

By the end of the 1700s, questions were arising from within philosophy itself about the claims of reason. David Hume denied that miracles could

82

serve as evidence for religious claims and attacked the argument from the order of the universe to the existence of God, but he also showed the limits of reason in philosophy. Gotthold Lessing, the great German playwright, doubted the claims of miracles but still sought a place for a kind of revelation, if only the "revelation" represented by the great historical insights that shape the "education of the human race." The philosopher Immanuel Kant attacked the traditional arguments for the existence of God but argued in favor of the need to posit God as the basis of morality, as well as for a radical evil that lies in human nature, and the importance of religious communities in overcoming that evil. The sorting out of the competing claims of reason and religious tradition was proving to be a difficult business.

John Locke (1632–1704)

From *The Reasonableness of Christianity*

Trained as a physician, Locke became the most important empiricist philosopher of his time, the philosophical defender of Newtonian physics and moderate political liberalism. In The Reasonableness of Christianity, *published in 1699, he claimed to set out a reasonable Christianity based solely on the "attentive and unbiased" reading of the Bible.*

It is obvious to any one, who reads the New Testament, that the doctrine of redemption, and consequently of the Gospel, is founded upon the supposition of Adam's fall. To understand, therefore, what we are restored to by Jesus Christ, we must consider what the Scriptures show we lost by Adam. This I thought worthy of a diligent and unbiased search: since I found the two extremes that men run into on this point, either on the one hand shook the foundations of all religion, or on the other made Christianity almost nothing: for while some men would have all Adam's posterity doomed to eternal infinite punishment, for the transgression of Adam, whom millions had never heard of, and no one had authorized to transact for him, or be his representative; this seemed to others so little consistent with the justice or goodness of the great and infinite God, that they thought there was no redemption necessary, and consequently that there was none, rather than admit of it upon a supposition so derogatory to the honour and attributes of that infinite Being; and so made Jesus Christ nothing but the restorer and preacher of pure natural religion; thereby doing violence to the whole tenor of the New Testament. And, indeed, both sides will be suspected to have trespassed this way, against the written Word of God, by any one, who does but take it to be a collection of writings, designed by God, for the instruction of the illiterate bulk of mankind, in the way to salvation; and therefore, generally, and in necessary points, to be understood in the plain direct meaning of the words and phrases, such as they may be supposed to have had in the mouths of the speakers, who used them according to the language of that time and country wherein they lived; without such learned, artificial, and forced senses of them, as are sought out, and put upon them in most of the systems of divinity, according to the notions that each one has been bred up in.

To one that, thus unbiased, reads the Scriptures, what Adam fell from (is visible), was the state of perfect obedience, which is called justice in the New Testament, though the word, which in the original signifies justice, be translated righteousness: and by this fall, he lost paradise, wherein was tranquillity and the tree of life; *i.e.* he lost bliss and immortality. . . .

If any of the posterity of Adam were just, they shall not lose the reward of it, eternal life and bliss, by being his mortal issue: Christ will bring them all to life again; and then they shall be put every one upon his own trial, and receive judgment, as he is found to be righteous or not. And the righteous, as our Saviour says, Matt. 25:46, shall go into eternal life. . . .

But yet, "all having sinned," Rom. 3:23, "and come short of the glory of God", *i.e.* the kingdom of God in heaven, which is often called his glory, both Jews and Gentiles, ver. 22, so that, by the deeds of the law, no one could be justified, ver. 20, it follows, that no one could then have eternal life and bliss. . . .

This then being the case, that whoever is guilty of any sin, should certainly die and cease to be, the benefit of life, restored by Christ at the resurrection, would have been no great advantage (for as much as, here again, death must have seized upon all mankind, because all had sinned; for the wages of sin is everywhere death, as well after, as before the resurrection) if God had not found out a way to justify some, *i.e.* so many as obeyed another law, which God gave, which in the New Testament is called the "law of faith," Rom. 3:27, and is opposed to the "law of works." . . .

The difference between the law of works, and the law of faith, is only this: that the law of works makes no allowance for failing on any occasion. Those that obey are righteous; those that in any part disobey, are unrighteous, and must not expect life, the reward of righteousness. But by the law of faith, faith is allowed to supply the defect of full obedience; and so the believers are admitted to life and immortality, as if they were righteous. . . .

What we are now required to believe to obtain eternal life, is plainly set down in the Gospel. St. John tells us, John 3:36, "He that believeth on the Son, hath eternal life; and he that believeth not the Son, shall not see life." What this believing on him is, we are also told in the next chapter. "The woman saith unto him, I know that the Messiah cometh: when he is come, he will tell us all things. Jesus said unto her, I that speak unto thee am he. The woman then went into the city, and saith to the men, Come see a man that hath told me all things that ever I did. Is not this the Messiah? And many of the Samaritans believed on him; for the saying of the woman, who testified, he told me all that ever I did. So when the Samaritans were come unto him, many more believed because of his words, and said to the woman, We believe not any longer, because of thy saying; for we have heard ourselves, and we know, that this man is truly the Saviour of the world, the Messiah," John 4:25–26, 28–29, 39–42.

By which place it is plain, that believing on the Son is the believing that Jesus was the Messiah, giving credit to the miracles he did, and the profession he made of himself. For those who were said to *believe on him,* for the saying of the woman, ver. 39, tell the woman, that they now believed not any longer, because of her saying; but that having heard him themselves, they knew, *i.e. believed,* past doubt, *that he was the Messiah.* . . .

To convince men of this, he did his miracles: and their assent to, or not assenting to this, made them to be, or not to be of his church; believers, or not believers. . . .

It is not enough to believe him to be the Messiah, the Lord, without obeying him. . . .

This part of the new covenant, the apostles also, in their preaching the gospel of the Messiah, ordinarily joined with the doctrine of faith. . . .

The first place where we find Our Saviour to have mentioned the day of judgment is John 5:28, 29, in these words: "The hour is coming, in which all that are in their graves shall hear his [*i.e.* the Son of God's] voice, and shall come forth, they that have *done good,* unto the resurrection of life, and they that have *done evil,* unto the resurrection of damnation." That which puts the distinction, if we will believe Our Saviour, is the having done good or evil. . . .

It is remarkable, that every where the sentence follows, doing or not doing, without any mention of believing or not believing. Not that any to whom the Gospel hath been preached shall be saved, without believing Jesus to be the Messiah; for all being sinners, and transgressors of the law, and so unjust, are all liable to condemnation, unless they believe, and so through grace are justified by God for this faith, which shall be accounted to them for righteousness: but the rest wanting this cover, this allowance for their transgressions, must answer for all their actions; and being found transgressors of the law, shall, by the letter and sanction of that law, be condemned, for not having paid a full obedience to that law, and not for want of faith; that is not the guilt on which the punishment is laid, though it be the want of faith, which lays open their guilt uncovered; and exposes them to the sentence of the law, against all that are unrighteous.

The common objection here, is: if all sinners shall be condemned, but such as have a gracious allowance made them; and so are justified by God, for believing Jesus to be the Messiah, and so taking him for their King; whom they are resolved to obey, to the utmost of their power, "What shall become of all mankind, who lived before our Saviour's time; who never heard of his name, and consequently could not believe in him?" To this the answer is so obvious and natural, that one would wonder how any reasonable man should think it worth the urging. Nobody was, or can be, required to believe, what was never proposed to him to believe. . . . All then that was required, before his appearing in the world, was to believe what God had revealed, and to rely with a full assurance on God, for the performance of his promise; and to believe that in due time he would send them the Messiah, this anointed King, this promised Saviour and Deliverer, according to his word. . . .

There is another difficulty often to be met with, which seems to have something of more weight in it: and that is, that "though the faith of those before Christ (believing that God would send the Messiah, to be a Prince and a Saviour to his people, as he had promised), and the faith of those since his time (believing Jesus to be that Messiah, promised and sent by God), shall be accounted to them for righteousness; yet what shall become of all the rest of mankind, who, having never heard of the promise or news of a Saviour, not a word of a Messiah to be sent, or that was come, have had no thought or belief concerning him?"

To this I answer, that God will require of every man, "according to what a man hath, and not according to what he hath not." . . . Though there be many, who being strangers to the commonwealth of Israel, were also strangers to the oracles of God, committed to that people; many, to whom the promise of the Messiah never came, and so were never in a capacity to believe or reject that revelation; yet God had, by the light of reason, revealed to all mankind, who would make use of that light, that he was good and merciful. The same spark of the divine nature and knowledge in man, which, making him a man, showed him the law he was under as a man, showed him also the way of atoning the merciful, kind, compassionate Author and Father of him and his being, when he had transgressed that law. He that made use of this candle of the Lord, so far as to find what was his duty, could not miss to find also the way to reconciliation and forgiveness, when he had failed of his duty: though, if he used not his reason this way, if he put out or neglected this light, he might, perhaps, see neither.

From *The Works of John Locke,* Volume 7 (London: W. Sharpe and Son, 1823), pages 4–5, 9–11, 14, 17–18, 123, 126–129, 132–133.

Matthew Tindal (c.1657–1733)

From *Christianity as Old as the Creation*

Tindal published Christianity as Old as the Creation *in 1730. It was widely read and came to be known as "the Deist's Bible." The title suggests Tindal's basic thesis: unlike Locke, who left a place for a special revelation and saving work in Christ, Tindal held that all the important true tenets held by Christians could be known by anyone, any time, through the use of human reason. Tindal writes here in the form of a dialogue between* A *and* B.

A: By *Natural Religion,* I understand the Belief of the Existence of a God, and the Sense and Practice of those Duties which result from the Knowledge we, by our Reason, have of him and his Perfections; and of ourselves, and our own Imperfections; and of the relation we stand in to him and our Fellow-Creatures; so that the *Religion of Nature* takes in every thing that is founded on the Reason and Nature of things. . . .

I suppose you will allow, that 'tis evident by the *Light of Nature,* that there is a God; or in other words, a Being absolutely perfect, and infinitely happy in himself, who is the Source of all other Beings; and that what Perfections soever the Creatures have, they are wholly deriv'd from him.

B: This, no doubt, has been demonstrated over and over; and I must own, that I can't be more certain of my own Existence, than of the Existence of such a Being.

A: Since then it is demonstrable there is such a Being, it is equally demonstrable, that the Creatures can neither add to, or take from the Happiness of that Being; and that he could have no Motive in framing his Creatures, or in giving Laws to such of them as he made capable of knowing his Will, but their own Good.

To imagine he created them at first for his own sake, and has since required things of them for that Reason, is to suppose he was not perfectly happy in himself before the Creation; and that the Creatures, by either observing, or not observing the Rules prescrib'd them, cou'd add to, or take from his Happiness.

If then a Being infinitely happy in himself, cou'd not command his Creatures any thing for his own Good; nor an all-wise Being things to no end or purpose; nor an all-good Being any thing but for their good: It unavoidably follows, nothing can be a part of the divine Law, but what tends to promote the common Interest, and mutual Happiness of his rational Creatures; and every thing that does so, must be a part of it.

As God can require nothing of us, but what makes for our Happiness; so he, who can't envy us any Happiness our Nature is capable of, can forbid us those Things only, which tend to our Hurt; and this we are as certain of, as that there is a God infinitely happy in himself, infinitely good and wise; and as God can design nothing by his Laws but our Good, so by being infinitely powerful, he can bring every thing to pass which he designs for that End. . . .

Our Reason, which gives us a Demonstration of the divine Perfections, affords us the same concerning the Nature of those Duties God requires; not only with relation to himself, but to ourselves, and to one another: These we can't but see, if we look into ourselves, consider our own Natures, and the Circumstances God has placed us in with relation to our Fellow-Creatures, and what conduces to our mutual Happiness: Our Senses, our Reason, the Experience of others as well as our own, can't fail to give us sufficient Information.

With relation to ourselves, we can't but know how we are to act; if we consider, that God has endow'd Man with such a Nature, as makes him necessarily desire his own Good; and, therefore, he may be sure, that God, who has bestow'd this Nature on him, could not require any thing of him in prejudice of it; but, on the contrary, that he should do every thing which tends to promote the Good of it. The Health of the Body, and the Vigor of the Mind, being highly conducing to our Good, we must be sensible we offend our Maker, if we indulge our Senses to the prejudice of these. . . .

As to what God expects from Man with relation to each other; every one must know his Duty, who considers that the common Parent of Mankind has the whole Species alike under his Protection, and will equally punish him for injuring others, as he would others for injuring him; and consequently, that it is his Duty to deal with them, as he expects they should deal with him in the like Circumstances. . . .

Having thus discovered our Duty, we may be sure it will always be the same; since Inconstancy, as it argues a Defect either of Wisdom or Power, can't belong to a Being infinitely wise and powerful: What unerring Wisdom has once instituted, can have no Defects; and as God is entirely free from all Partiality, his Laws must alike extend to all Times and Places.

From these Premises, I think, we may boldly draw this Conclusion, That if Religion consists in the Practice of those Duties, that result from the Relation we stand in to God and Man, our Religion must always be the same. If God is unchangeable, our Duty to him must be so too; if Human Nature continues the same, and Men at all Times stand in the same Relation to one another, the Duties which result from thence too, must always be the same: And consequently our Duty both to God and Man must, from the Beginning of the World to the End, remain unalterable; be always alike plain and perspicuous; neither chang'd in Whole, or Part: which demonstrates that no Person, if he comes from God, can teach us any other Religion, or give us any Precepts, but what are founded on those Relations. *Heaven and Earth shall sooner pass away,* than *one Tittle of this* Eternal *Law shall either be abrogated, or alter'd.* . . .

B: In my Opinion you lay too great a Stress on fallible Reason, and too little on infallible Revelation; and therefore I must needs say, your arguing wholly from Reason would make some of less Candour than myself, take you for an errant *Free-thinker.*

A: Whatever is true by Reason, can never be false by Revelation; and if God can't be deceiv'd himself, or be willing to deceive Men, the Light he hath given to distinguish between religious Truth and Falsehood, cannot, if duly attended to, deceive them in things of so great Moment. . . .

In a word, to suppose any thing in Revelation inconsistent with Reason, and at the same time, pretend it to be the Will of God, is not only to destroy that Proof, on which we conclude it to be the Will of God, but even the Proof of the Being of a God; since if our reasoning Faculties duly attended to deceive us, we can't be sure of the Truth of any one Proposition; but every thing wou'd be alike uncertain, and we should for ever fluctuate in a State of universal Scepticism: Which shews how absurdly they act, who, on pretence of magnifying Tradition, endeavour to weaken the Force of Reason, (tho' to be sure they always except their own;) and thereby foolishly sap the Foundation, to support the Superstructure; but as long as Reason is against Men, they will be against Reason. . . .

And to suppose any thing can be true by Revelation, which is false by Reason, is not to support that thing, but to undermine Revelation; because nothing unreasonable, nay, what is not highly reasonable, can come from a God of unlimited, universal, and eternal Reason. . . .

If it be but probable, that God made any external Revelation at all, it can be but probable, tho' perhaps, not in the same Degree of Probability, that he made this, or that Revelation: And this Evidence all pretend to, since, perhaps, there never was a Time or Place, where some external Revelation was not believ'd, and its Votaries equally confident, that Theirs was a true Revelation: And indeed, the prodigious Numbers of Revelations, which from time to time have been in the World, shew how easily Mankind may in this Point be impos'd on. . . .

In a Word, when Men, in defending their own, or attacking other traditionary Religions, have recourse to the Nature or Reason of Things; does not That shew, they believe the Truth of all traditionary Religions is to be try'd by it; as being That, which must tell them what is true or false in Religion? And were there not some Truths relating to Religion or themselves so evident, as that all must agree in them, nothing relating to Religion could be prov'd, every thing would want a farther Proof; and if there are such evident Truths, must not all others be try'd by their Agreement with them? And are not these the Tests, by which we are to distinguish the only true Religion from the many false ones? And do not all Parties alike own, there are such Tests drawn from the nature of Things, each crying their Religion contains every thing worthy, and nothing unworthy of having God for its Author; thereby confessing that Reason enables them to tell what is worthy of having God for its Author. And if Reason tells them this, does it not tell them every thing that God can be suppos'd to require?

From Matthew Tindal, *Christianity as Old as the Creation,* 2nd edition (London, 1732), pages 11–15, 17, 157–158, 162–163, 165.

Philip Jacob Spener (1635–1705)

From *Pia Desideria*

A Lutheran pastor in the city of Frankfurt, Spener published Pia Desideria: or, Heartfelt Desires for a God-pleasing Improvement of the True Protestant Church *in 1675. German Protestant theology had become abstract and highly intellectual and seemed to have little impact on the lives of ordinary people. Spener and the Pietist movement he represented sought practical reforms to improve morals and religious sensitivity.*

Thought should be given to a *more extensive use of the Word of God among us.* We know that by nature we have no good in us. If there is to be any good in us, it must be brought about by God. To this end the Word of God is the powerful means, since faith must be enkindled through the gospel, and the law provides the rules for good works and many wonderful impulses to attain them. The more at home the Word of God is among us, the more we shall bring about faith and its fruits.

It may appear that the Word of God has sufficiently free course among us inasmuch as at various places (as in this city) there is daily or frequent preaching from the pulpit. When we reflect further on the matter, however, we shall find that with respect to this first proposal, more is needed. I do not at all disapprove of the preaching of sermons in which a Christian congregation is instructed by the reading and exposition of a certain text, for I myself do this. But I find that this is not enough. In the first place, we know that "all scripture is inspired by God and profitable for teaching, for reproof, for correction, and for training in righteousness" [2 Tim. 3:16]. Accordingly *all* scripture, without exception, should be known by the congregation if we are all to receive the necessary benefit. If we put together all the passages of the Bible which in the course of many years are read to a congregation in one place, they will comprise only a very small part of the Scriptures which have been given to us. The remainder is not heard by the congregation at all, or is heard only insofar as one or another verse is quoted or alluded to in sermons, without, however, offering any understanding of the entire context, which is nevertheless of the greatest importance. In the second place, the people have little opportunity to grasp the meaning of the Scriptures except on the basis of those passages which may have been expounded to them, and even less do they have opportunity to become as practiced in them as edification requires. Meanwhile, although solitary reading of the Bible at home is in itself a splendid and praiseworthy thing, it does not accomplish enough for most people.

It should therefore be considered whether the church would not be well advised to introduce the people to Scripture in still other ways than through the customary sermons on the appointed lessons.

This might be done, first of all, by diligent reading of the Holy Scriptures, especially of the New Testament. It would not be difficult for every housefather to keep a Bible, or at least a New Testament, handy and read from it every day or, if he cannot read, to have somebody else read. . . .

Then a second thing would be desirable in order to encourage people to read privately, namely, that where the practice can be introduced the books of the Bible be read one after another, at specified times in the public service, without further comment (unless one wished to add brief summaries). This would be intended for the edification of all, but especially of those who cannot read at all, or cannot read easily or well, or of those who do not own a copy of the Bible.

For a third thing it would perhaps not be inexpedient (and I set this down for further and more mature reflection) to reintroduce the ancient and apostolic kind of church meetings. In addition to our customary services with preaching, other assemblies would also be held in the manner Paul describes them in 1 Corinthians 14:26–40. One person would not rise to preach (although this practice would be continued at other times), but others who have been blessed with gifts and knowledge would also speak and present their pious opinions on the proposed subject to the judgment of the rest, doing all this in such a way as to avoid disorder and strife. . . .

The people must have impressed upon them and must accustom themselves to believing that *it is by no means enough to have knowledge of the Christian faith, for Christianity consists rather of practice.* . . .

If we can therefore awaken a fervent love among our Christians, first toward one another and then toward all men (for these two, brotherly affection and general love, must supplement each other according to 2 Peter 1:7), and put this love into practice, practically all that we desire will be accomplished. . . .

Since ministers must bear the greatest burden in all these things which pertain to a reform of the church, and since their shortcomings do correspondingly great harm, it is of the utmost importance that the office of the ministry be occupied by men who, above all, are themselves true Christians and, then, have the divine wisdom to guide others carefully on the way of the Lord. It is therefore important, indeed necessary, for the reform of the church that only such persons be called who may be suited, and that nothing at all except the glory of God be kept in view during the whole procedure of calling. This would mean that all carnal schemes involving favor, friendship, gifts, and similarly unseemly things would be set aside. Not the least among the reasons for the defect in the church are the mistakes which occur in the calling of ministers, but we shall not elaborate on this here.

However, if such suitable persons are to be called to the ministry they must be available, and hence they must be trained in *our schools and universities.* . . .

The professors could themselves accomplish a great deal here by their example (indeed, without them a real reform is hardly to be hoped for) if they would conduct themselves as men who have died unto the world, in everything would seek not their own glory, gain, or pleasure but rather the glory of their God and the salvation of those entrusted to them, and would accommodate all their studies, writing of books, lessons, lectures, disputations, and other activities to this end. Then the students would have a living example according to which they might regulate their life. . . .

Besides, students should unceasingly have it impressed upon them that holy life is not of less consequence than diligence and study, indeed that study without piety is worthless. . . .

It would be especially helpful if the professors would pay attention to the life as well as the studies of the students entrusted to them and would from time to time speak to those who need to be spoken to. The professors should act in such a way toward those students who, although they distinguish themselves in studying, also distinguish themselves in riotous living, tippling, bragging, and boasting of academic and other pre-eminence (who, in short, demonstrate that they live according to the world and not according to Christ) that they must perceive that because of their behavior they are looked down upon by their teachers, that their splendid talents and good academic record do not help by themselves, and that they are regarded as persons who will do harm in proportion to the gifts they receive. On the other hand, the professors should openly and expressly show those who lead a godly life, even if they are behind the others in their studies, how dear they are to their teachers and how very much they are to be preferred to the others. In fact, these students ought to be the first, or the only, ones to be promoted. The others ought to be excluded from all hope of promotion until they change their manner of life completely. This is the way it ought in all fairness to be. It is certain that a young man who fervently loves God, although adorned with limited gifts, will be more useful to the church of God with his meager talent and academic achievement than a vain and worldly fool with double doctor's degrees who is very clever but has not been taught by God. The work of the former is blessed, and he is aided by the Holy Spirit. The latter has only a carnal knowledge, with which he can easily do more harm than good.

From Philip Jacob Spener, *Pia Desideria,* translated and edited by Theodore G. Tappert, pages 87–89, 95–96, 103–104, 107–108. Copyright © 1964 by Fortress Press. Used by permission of the publisher.

John Wesley (1703–1791)

From *The Scripture Way of Salvation*

By one estimate, Wesley preached over 40,000 sermons and traveled 250,000 miles; his preaching changed English religion. He established groups devoted to prayer and Bible reading wherever he preached. Wesley's commitment to detailed rules of piety had early won him the name "Method-ist," though his movement broke with the Church of England only after his death. This essay, published in 1765, contains key themes of Wesley's theology: the experience of personal salvation, and the importance of sanctification, a sanctification that can even lead in this life to Christian perfection. Since the hymns of Wesley's brother Charles have become one of the great legacies of Methodism, it is fitting that Wesley here ends by quoting one of them.

"Ye are saved through faith" [Eph. 2:8]

1. . . . How easy to be understood, how plain and simple a thing, is the genuine religion of Jesus Christ, provided only that we take it in its native form, just as it is described in the oracles of God! It is exactly suited by the wise Creator and Governor of the world to the weak understanding and narrow capacity of man in his present state. How observable is this, both with regard to the end it proposes and the means to attain that end. The end is, in one word, "salvation"; the means to attain it, "faith."

2. It is easily discerned that these two little words—I mean "faith" and "salvation"—include the substance of all the Bible: the marrow, as it were, of the whole Scripture. So much the more should we take all possible care to avoid all mistake concerning them and to form a true and accurate judgment concerning both the one and the other. . . .

I. 1. And, first, let us inquire what is *salvation?* The salvation which is here spoken of is not what is frequently understood by that word: the going to heaven, eternal happiness. It is not the soul's going to paradise, termed by our Lord, "Abraham's bosom" [Luke 16:22]. It is not a blessing which lies on the other side of death or (as we usually speak) "in the other world." The very words of the text itself put this beyond all question, "Ye *are* saved." . . . So that the salvation which is here spoken of might be extended to the entire work of God, from the first dawning of grace in the soul till it is consummated in glory. . . .

3. And this consists of two general parts: justification and sanctification.

Justification is another word for pardon. It is the forgiveness of all our sins and, what is necessarily implied therein, our acceptance with God. The price whereby this hath been procured for us (commonly termed the "meritorious cause" of our justification) is the blood and righteousness of Christ; or, to express it a little more clearly, all that Christ hath done and suffered for us, till "he poured out his soul for the transgressors" [cf. Isa. 53:12]. The immediate effects of justification are *the peace of God,* a "peace that passeth all understanding" [cf. Phil. 4:7] and a "rejoicing in *hope* of the glory of God" [cf. Rom. 5:2] "with joy unspeakable and full of glory" [cf. 1 Peter 1:8].

4. And at the same time that we are justified—yea, in that very moment—*sanctification* begins. In that instant we are "born again, born from above, born of the Spirit." There is a *real* as well as a *relative* change. We are inwardly renewed by the power of God. We feel "the love of God shed abroad in our heart by the Holy Ghost which is given unto us" [cf. Rom. 5:5], producing love to all mankind, and more especially to the children of God, expelling the love of the world, the love of pleasure, of ease, of honour, of money, together with pride, anger, self-will and every other evil temper; in a word, changing the "earthly, sensual, devilish mind" into "the mind which was in Christ Jesus" [cf. Phil. 2:5]. . . .

8. From the time of our being born again, the gradual work of sanctification takes place. We are enabled "by the Spirit" to "mortify

the deeds of the body" [Rom. 8:11, 13], of our evil nature, and as we are more and more dead to sin, we are more and more alive to God. We go on from grace to grace, while we are careful to "abstain from all appearance of evil" [1 Thess. 5:22] and are "zealous of good works" [Titus 2:14] as we have opportunity, "doing good to all men" while we walk in all his ordinances blameless, therein worshipping him in spirit and in truth [cf. John 4:23] while we take up our cross [cf. Matt. 16:24] and deny ourselves every pleasure that does not lead us to God.

9. It is thus that we wait for entire sanctification, for a full salvation from all our sins—from pride, self-will, anger, unbelief—or, as the apostle expresses it, "go on unto perfection" [Heb. 6:1]. But what is perfection? The word has various senses: here it means perfect love. It is love excluding sin, love filling the heart, taking up the whole capacity of the soul. It is love "rejoicing evermore, praying without ceasing, in everything giving thanks" [cf. 1 Thess. 5:16–18]. . . .

III. 18. "But does God work this great work in the soul gradually or instantaneously?" Perhaps it may be gradually wrought in some; I mean in this sense, that they do not advert to the particular moment wherein sin ceases to be. But it is infinitely desirable, were it the will of God, that it should be done instantaneously, that the Lord should destroy sin "by the breath of his mouth" [cf. Job 15:-30] in a moment, in the twinkling of an eye. And so he generally does; a plain fact of which there is evidence enough to satisfy any unprejudiced person. Thou therefore look for it every moment! Look for it in the way above described, in all those "good works" whereunto thou art "created anew in Christ Jesus" [cf. Eph. 2:10]. . . . Stay for nothing! Why should you? Christ is ready; and he is all you want. He is waiting for you! He is at the door! Let your inmost soul cry out,

> "Come in, come in, thou heavenly Guest!
>   Nor hence again remove;
>   But sup with me and let the feast
>   Be everlasting love."
>   [Charles Wesley,
>   *Hymns on God's Everlasting Love*]

From John Wesley, *Sermons on Several Occasions* (London: Henry G. Bohn, 1845), pages 107–108, 111.

John Wesley

From *Predestination Calmly Considered*

Wesley and George Whitefield (1714–1770) were the two most influential preachers of the English revival movement, but they split on the issue of predestination. Whitefield remained a Calvinist who believed in predestination, but, as this selection, written in 1773, indicates, Wesley felt that his activity as a preacher urging conversions simply made no sense if his hearers lacked free choice.

41. Our blessed Lord does indisputably command and invite "all men every where to repent" [Acts 17:30]. He calleth all. He sends his ambassadors, in his name, "to preach the gospel to every creature" [Mark 16:15]. He himself "preached deliverance to the captives" [Luke 4:18] without any hint of restriction or limitation. But now, in what manner do you represent him while he is employed in this work? You suppose him to be standing at the prison doors, having the keys thereof in his hands, and to be continually inviting the prisoners to come forth, commanding them to accept of that invitation, urging every motive which can possibly induce them to comply with that command; adding the most precious promises, if they obey; the most dreadful threatenings, if they obey not. And all this time you suppose him to be unalterably determined in himself never to open the doors for them, even while he is crying, "Come ye, come ye, from that evil place. For why will ye die, O house of Israel?" [cf. Ezek. 18:31]. "Why" (might one of them reply), "because we cannot help it. We *cannot* help ourselves, and thou *wilt* not help us. It is not in our power to break the gates of brass [cf. Ps. 107:16], and it is not thy pleasure to open them. Why *will* we die? We *must* die, because it is not thy *will* to save us." Alas, my brethren, what kind of sincerity is this which you ascribe to God our Saviour?

42. . . . It is written, "God is love" [1 John 4:8], love in the abstract, without bounds, and "there is no end of his goodness" [cf. Ps. 52:1]. His love extends even to those who neither love nor fear him. He is good, even to the evil and the unthankful; yea, without any exception or limitation, to all the children of men. For "the Lord is loving" (or good) "unto every man, and his mercy is over all his works" [Ps. 145:9, Book of Common Prayer].

But how is God good or loving to a "reprobate," or one that is not "elected"? . . .

52. . . . Now, if man be capable of choosing good or evil, then is he a proper object of the justice of God, acquitting or condemning, rewarding or punishing. But otherwise he is not. A mere machine is not capable of being either acquitted or condemned. Justice cannot punish a stone for falling to the ground; nor (on your scheme) a man for falling into sin. For he can no more help it than the stone, if he be (in your sense) fore-ordained to this condemnation. Why does this man sin? "He cannot cease from sin." Why can't he cease from sin? "Because he has no saving grace." Why has he no saving grace? "Because God, of his own good pleasure, hath eternally decreed not to give it him." Is he then under an unavoidable necessity of sinning? "Yes, as much as a stone is of falling. He never had any more power to cease from evil than a stone has to hang in the air." And shall this man, for not doing what he never could do, and for doing what he never could avoid, be sentenced to depart into everlasting fire, prepared for the devil and his angels? [cf. Matt. 25:41]. "Yes, because it is the sovereign will of God." Then you have either found a new God, or made one! This is not the God of the Christians. Our God is just in all his ways; he reapeth not where he hath not strewed. He requireth only according to what he hath given; and where he hath given little, little is required.

From *The Works of John Wesley*, Volume 11 (London: Wesleyan Conference Office, 1872), pages 226–227, 233–234.

David Hume (1711–1776)

From *Dialogues Concerning Natural Religion*

Hume remains one of the most influential of modern philosophers. He developed a consistent empiricism that also emphasized the limits of human reason. These Dialogues, *published after Hume's death, discuss the arguments for the existence of God that had been so important to theology in the eighteenth century. Of the three characters, Philo is a skeptic; Cleanthes, a rational theologian; and Demea, a pious believer. Philo's position comes closest to Hume's own, though Hume takes all their positions seriously. This selection begins with Cleanthes' statement of an argument from the order of the universe to the existence of God and then moves to Philo's criticisms of it.*

Not to lose any time in circumlocutions, said Cleanthes, addressing himself to Demea, much less in replying to the pious declamations of Philo; I shall briefly explain how I conceive this matter. Look round the world: contemplate the whole and every part of it: you will find it to be nothing but one great machine, subdivided into an infinite number of lesser machines, which again admit of subdivisions to a degree beyond what human senses and faculties can trace and explain. All these various machines, and even their most minute parts, are adjusted to each other with an accuracy which ravishes into admiration all men who have ever contemplated them. The curious adapting of means to ends, throughout all nature, resembles exactly, though it much exceeds, the productions of human contrivance; of human designs, thought, wisdom, and intelligence. Since, therefore, the effects resemble each other, we are led to infer, by all the rules of analogy, that the causes also resemble; and that the Author of Nature is somewhat similar to the mind of man, though possessed of much larger faculties, proportioned to the grandeur of the work which he has executed. By this argument *a posteriori,* and by this argument alone, do we prove at once the existence of a Deity, and his similarity to human mind and intelligence. . . .

What I chiefly scruple in this subject, said Philo, is not so much that all religious arguments are by Cleanthes reduced to experience, as that they appear not to be even the most certain and irrefragable of that inferior kind. That a stone will fall, that fire will burn, that the earth has solidity, we have observed a thousand and a thousand times; and when any new instance of this nature is presented, we draw without hesitation the accustomed inference. The exact similarity of the cases gives us a perfect assurance of a similar event; and a stronger evidence is never desired nor sought after. But wherever you depart, in the least, from the similarity of the cases, you diminish proportionably the evidence; and may at last bring it to a very weak *analogy,* which is confessedly liable to error and uncertainty. After having experienced the circulation of the blood in human creatures, we make no doubt that it takes place in Titius and Maevius. But from its circulation in frogs and fishes, it is only a presumption, though a strong one, from analogy, that it takes place in men and other animals. The analogical reasoning is much weaker when we infer the circulation of the sap in vegetables from our experience that the blood circulates in animals; and those who hastily followed that imperfect analogy, are found, by more accurate experiments, to have been mistaken.

If we see a house, Cleanthes, we conclude, with the greatest certainty, that it had an architect or builder; because this is precisely that species of effect which we have experienced to proceed from that species of cause. But surely you will not affirm, that the universe bears such a resemblance to a house, that we can with the same uncertainty infer a similar cause, or that the analogy is here entire and perfect. The dissimilitude is so striking, that the utmost you can here pretend to is a guess, a conjecture, a presumption concerning a similar cause; and how that pretension will be received in the world, I leave you to consider. . . .

Philo raises hard questions about the evidence for belief in an omnipotent creator, but when he turns to criticize the claim that we can know that creator to be morally good and love mankind, he claims to have an even stronger case. He surveys all the tragedies and sufferings that afflict human life and then draws his conclusions.

And is it possible, Cleanthes, said Philo, that after all these reflections, and infinitely more which might be suggested, you can still persevere in your Anthropomorphism, and assert the moral attributes of the Deity, his justice, benevolence, mercy, and rectitude, to be of the same nature with these virtues in human creatures? His power we allow is infinite: whatever he wills is executed: but neither man nor any other animal is happy: therefore he does not will their happiness. His wisdom is infinite: he is never mistaken in choosing the means to any end: but the course of Nature tends not to human or animal felicity: therefore it is not established for that purpose. Through the whole compass of human knowledge, there are no inferences more certain and infallible than these. In what respect, then, do his benevolence and mercy resemble the benevolence and mercy of men?

Epicurus's old questions are yet unanswered.

Is he willing to prevent evil, but not able? then is he impotent. Is he able, but not willing? then is he malevolent. Is he both able and willing? whence then is evil? . . .

But allowing you what never will be believed, at least what you never possibly can prove, that animal, or at least human happiness, in this life, exceeds its misery, you have yet done nothing: for this is not, by any means, what we expect from infinite power, infinite wisdom, and infinite goodness. Why is there any misery at all in the world? Not by chance surely. From some cause then. Is it from the intention of the Deity? But he is perfectly benevolent. Is it contrary to his intention? But he is almighty. Nothing can shake the solidity of this reasoning, so short, so clear, so decisive; except we assert, that these subjects exceed all human capacity, and that our common measures of truth and falsehood are not applicable to them; a topic which I have all along insisted on, but which you have, from the beginning, rejected with scorn and indignation.

From *Hume's Philosophical Works,* Volume 2 (Boston: Little, Brown & Co., 1854), pages 432–434, 501, 505.

Gotthold Lessing (1729–1781)

From *On the Proof of the Spirit and of Power*

It is often difficult to identify Lessing's own religious views. Amid careers as librarian, playwright, literary critic, and diplomat he found time to write essays asking hard questions about religion, but his answers often remain unclear. This essay, written in 1777, wonders how historical claims, which can at best be only probable, could serve as the basis for the certainty that seems essential to religious faith. In the end, Lessing seems to prefer judging religions by the fruits or practical results they produce.

If I had lived at the time of Christ, then of course the prophecies fulfilled in his person would have made me pay great attention to him. If I had actually seen him do miracles; if I had no cause to doubt that these were true miracles; then in a worker of miracles who had been marked out so long before, I would have gained so much confidence that I would willingly have submitted my intellect to his, and I would have believed him in all things in which equally indisputable experiences did not tell against him.

Or: if I even now experienced that prophecies referring to Christ or the Christian religion, of whose priority in time I have long been certain, were fulfilled in a manner admitting no dispute; if even now miracles were done by believing Christians which I had to recognize as true miracles; what could prevent me from accepting this proof of the spirit and of power, as the apostle calls it? . . .

The problem is that reports of fulfilled prophecies are not fulfilled prophecies; that reports of miracles are not miracles. These, the prophecies fulfilled before my eyes, the miracles that occur before my eyes, are immediate in their effect. But those, the reports of fulfilled prophecies and miracles, have to work through a medium which takes away all their force. . . .

What is asserted is only that the reports which we have of these prophecies and miracles are as reliable as historical truths ever can be. And then it is added that historical truths cannot be demonstrated: nevertheless we must believe them as firmly as truths that have been demonstrated.

To this I answer: *First,* who will deny (not I) that the reports of these miracles and prophecies are as reliable as historical truths ever can be? But if they are only as reliable as this, why are they treated as if they were infinitely more reliable?

And in what way? In this way, that something quite different and much greater is founded upon them than it is legitimate to found upon truths historically proved.

If no historical truth can be demonstrated, then nothing can be demonstrated by means of historical truths.

That is: *accidental truths of history can never become the proof of necessary truths of reason. . . .*

That, then, is the ugly, broad ditch which I cannot get across, however often and however earnestly I have tried to make the leap. If anyone can help me over it, let him do it, I beg him, I adjure him. He will deserve a divine reward from me.

And so I repeat what I have said above in the same words. I do not for one moment deny that in Christ prophecies were fulfilled. I do not for one moment deny that Christ did miracles. But since the truth of these miracles has completely ceased to be demonstrable by miracles still happening now, since they are no more than reports of miracles (even though they be narratives which have not been, and cannot be, impugned), I deny that they can and should bind me to the very least faith in the other teachings of Christ.

What then does bind me? Nothing but these teachings themselves. Eighteen hundred years ago they were so new, so alien, so foreign to the entire mass of truths recognized in that age, nothing less than miracles and fulfilled prophecies were required if the multitude were to attend to them at all.

But to make the multitude attentive to something means to put common sense on to the right track.

And so it came about, so it now is. And what it hunted out to the left and right of this track are the fruits of those miracles and fulfilled prophecies.

These fruits I may see before me ripe and ripened, and may I not be satisfied with that? The old pious legend that the hand which scatters the seed must wash in snails' blood seven times for each throw, I do not doubt, but merely ignore it. What does it matter to me whether the legend is false or true? The fruits are excellent.

From Gotthold Lessing, *Lessing's Theological Writings,* translated by Henry Chadwick (London: A. & C. Black, Ltd., 1956), pages 51–53, 55. Used by permission of A. & C. Black (Publishers) Ltd.

Immanuel Kant (1724–1804)

From *Religion Within the Limits of Reason Alone*

Kant strongly criticized traditional arguments for the existence of God, but in the Critique of Practical Reason *he maintained that we need to posit God as a foundation of morality. The moral law calls us to do our duty without regard for consequences, but it also demands attention to human happiness. Only the existence of a God who guarantees that duty will ultimately lead to happiness rescues morality from incoherence. In* Religion Within the Limits of Reason Alone, *published in 1793, Kant scandalized his Enlightenment friends by pointing to a radical evil that lies in human nature, an evil from which we can hope to free ourselves only on the assumption of a divine assistance. He concludes that the true service of God would need to involve only an ethically good life; it need not include any particular religious activities or beliefs. And yet, Kant says, human beings seem incapable of the kind of life they ought to lead apart from specific religious traditions.*

Pure religious faith alone can found a universal church; for only [such] rational faith can be believed in and shared by everyone, whereas an historical faith, grounded solely on facts, can extend its influence no further than tidings of it can reach, subject to circumstances of time and place and dependent upon the capacity [of men] to judge the credibility of such tidings. Yet, by reason of a peculiar weakness of human nature, pure faith can never be relied on as much as it deserves, that is, a church cannot be established on it alone.

Men are conscious of their inability to know supersensible things; and although they allow all honor to be paid to faith in such things (as the faith which must be universally convincing to them), they are yet not easily convinced that steadfast diligence in morally good life-conduct is all that God requires of men, to be subjects in His kingdom and well-pleasing to Him. They cannot well think of their obligation except as an obligation to some *service* or other which they must offer to God—wherein what matters is not so much the inner moral worth of the actions as the fact that they are offered to God— to the end that, however morally indifferent men may be in themselves, they may at least please God through passive obedience. It does not enter their heads that when they fulfil their duties to men (themselves and others) they are, by these very acts, performing God's commands and are therefore in all their actions and abstentions, so far as these concern morality, *perpetually in the service of God,* and that it is absolutely impossible to serve God more directly in any other way (since they can affect and have an influence upon earthly beings alone, and not upon God). Because each great worldly lord stands in special need of being *honored* by his subjects and *glorified* through protestations of submissiveness, without which he cannot expect from them as much compliance with his behests as he requires to be able to rule them, and since, in addition, however gifted with reason a man may be, he always finds an immediate satisfaction in attestations of honor, we treat duty, so far as it is also a divine command, as the prosecution of a *transaction* with God, not with man. Thus arises the concept of a religion of *divine worship* instead of the concept of a religion purely moral.

Since all religion consists in this, that in all our duties we look upon God as the lawgiver universally to be honored, the determining of religion, so far as the conformity of our attitude with it is concerned, hinges upon knowing *how God wishes* to be honored (and obeyed). Now a divine legislative will commands either through laws in themselves *merely statutory* or through *purely moral* laws. As to the latter, each individual can know of himself, through his own reason, the will of God which lies at the basis of his religion; for the concept of the Deity really arises solely from consciousness of these laws and from the need of reason to postulate a might which can procure for these laws, as their final end, all the results conformable to them and possible in a world. The concept of a divine will, determined according to pure moral laws alone, allows us to think of only *one* religion which is purely moral, as it did of only *one* God. But if we admit statutory laws of such a will and make religion consist of our obedience to them, knowledge of such laws is possible not through our own reason alone but only through revelation. . . .

If, then, the question: How does God wish to be honored? is to be answered in a way universally valid for each man, *regarded merely as man,* there can be no doubt that the legislation of His will ought to be solely *moral;* for statutory legislation (which presupposes a revelation) can be regarded merely as contingent and as something which never has applied or can apply to every man, hence as not binding upon all men universally. Thus, "not they who say Lord! Lord! but they who do the will of God" [cf. Matt. 7:21], they who seek to become well-pleasing to Him not by praising Him (or His envoy, as a being of divine origin) according to revealed concepts which not every man can have, but by a good course of life, regarding which everyone knows His will—these are they who offer Him the true veneration which He desires.

But when we regard ourselves as obliged to behave not merely as men but also as *citizens* in a divine state on earth, and to work for the existence of such a union, under the name of a church, then the question: How does God wish to be honored in *a church* (as a congregation of God)? appears to be unanswerable by reason alone and to require statutory legislation of which we become cognizant only through revelation, *i.e.,* an historical faith which, in contradistinction to pure religious faith, we can call ecclesiastical faith....

In men's striving toward an ethical commonwealth, ecclesiastical faith thus naturally precedes* pure religious faith; *temples* (buildings consecrated to the public worship of God) were before *churches* (meeting-places for the instruction and quickening of moral dispositions), *priests* (consecrated stewards of pious rites) before *divines* (teachers of the purely moral religion); and for the most part they still are first in the rank and value ascribed to them by the great mass of people. Since, then, it remains true once for all that a statutory *ecclesiastical faith* is associated with pure religious faith as its vehicle and as the means of public union of men for its promotion, one must grant that the preservation of pure religious faith unchanged, its propagation in the same form everywhere, and even a respect for the revelation assumed therein, can hardly be provided for adequately through *tradition,* but only through *scripture;* which, again, as a revelation to contemporaries and posterity, must itself be an object of esteem, for the necessities of men require this in order that they may be sure of their duty in divine service. A holy book arouses the greatest respect even among those (indeed, most of all among those) who do not read it, or at least those who can form no coherent religious concept therefrom; and the most sophistical reasoning avails nothing in the face of the decisive assertion, which beats down every objection: *Thus it is written.* It is for this reason that the passages in it which are to lay down an article of faith are called

---

*Morally, this order ought to be reversed [Kant's footnote].

simply *texts.* The appointed expositors of such a scripture are themselves, by virtue of their occupation, like unto consecrated persons; and history proves that it has never been possible to destroy a faith grounded in scripture, even with the most devastating revolutions in the state, whereas the faith established upon tradition and ancient public observances has promptly met its downfall when the state was overthrown. How fortunate,* when such a book, fallen into men's hands, contains, along with its statutes, or laws of faith, the purest moral doctrine of religion in its completeness—a doctrine which can be brought into perfect harmony with such statutes ([which serve] as vehicles for its introduction). In this event, both because of the end thereby to be attained and because of the difficulty of rendering intelligible according to natural laws the origin of such enlightenment of the human race as proceeds from it, such a book can command an esteem like that accorded to revelation. . . .

And now a few words touching this concept of a belief in revelation.

There is only *one* (true) *religion;* but there can be *faiths* of several kinds. We can say further that even in the various churches, severed from one another by reason of the diversity of their modes of belief, one and the same true religion can yet be found. . . .

We have noted that a church dispenses with the most important mark of truth, namely, a rightful claim to universality, when it bases itself upon a revealed faith. For such a faith, being historical (even though it be far more widely disseminated and more completely secured for remotest posterity through the agency of scripture) can never be universally communicated so as to produce conviction. Yet, because of the natural need and desire of all men for something *sensibly tenable,* and for a confirmation of some sort from experience of the highest concepts and grounds of reason (a need which really must be taken into account when the universal *dissemination* of a faith is contemplated), some historical ecclesiastical faith or other, usually to be found at hand, must be utilized.

From Immanuel Kant, *Religion Within the Limits of Reason Alone,* translated by Theodore M. Greene and Hoyt H. Hudson (New York: Harper & Row, Harper Torchbooks, 1960), pages 94–98, 100. Copyright © 1934 by Open Court Publishing. Reprinted by permission of Open Court Publishing Company, La Salle, Illinois.

---

*An expression for everything wished for, or worthy of being wished for, which we can neither foresee nor bring about through our own endeavors according to the laws of experience; for which, therefore, if we wish to name its source, we can offer none other than a gracious Providence [Kant's footnote].

CHAPTER 5

Theology in the United States

In 1630, as the first settlers of the Massachusetts Bay Colony were crossing the Atlantic, their governor, John Winthrop, wrote of the common desire that their new colony might be like "a city on a hill" to inspire the world with the possibilities of a pure Christian commonwealth. That Puritan dream of offering a model to the world has helped define much of the history—and not just the theological history—of the United States, whether as an inspiring goal, a misguided ambition, or a standard that judges and condemns.

Already in the first ten years of Massachusetts Bay, debates began. John Cotton, the first minister in Boston, preached the kind of Calvinism that emphasizes the radical, unpredictable freedom with which God bestows grace. Across the river in Cambridge, his colleague Thomas Hooker insisted that those who have received grace will manifest it in lives of Christian virtue. The resulting debate over whether the saved could be identified by their outward virtue nearly tore the colony apart.

That first generation of New Englanders at least shared a common dream, but succeeding generations arrived in New England by accident of birth, not the commitment involved in a long sea voyage. How could one keep that vision of a city on a hill alive? The most dramatic answer came in the 1740s, when the Great Awakening spread religious revivals from Massachusetts to Georgia, providing the first "national" experience of the English colonies as well as the occasion for reflections by America's greatest theologian, Jonathan Edwards.

Edwards was both a revival preacher and a sophisticated intellectual, but in later generations revival religion and technical theology often went their separate ways. "Back East" in New England, theological writers such as the Unitarian William Ellery Channing, the transcendentalist Ralph Waldo Emerson, and the liberal Congregationalist Horace Bushnell regarded the emotionalism of revivalism with suspicion, while out on the frontier revival preachers like Charles Grandison Finney had little patience with intellectuals.

Of course, neither the academic nor the popular tradition of American religious thought was a unified movement. On the one side, Hooker represented an orthodox Calvinism not much touched by the Age of Reason; Edwards, a remarkable blend of Calvinism and Enlightenment philosophy; and Channing, a kind of rational religion; while Emerson and Bushnell both introduced elements of nineteenth-century Romanticism. In popular religion, Finney propagated his revivals more or less within established denominations, but other Americans founded their own churches—from moderate attempts at church unity by the Disciples of Christ to radically new religious approaches, such as those of Joseph Smith and the Mormons or Mary Baker Eddy and Christian Science.

Many of these writers shared, in very different ways, Winthrop's vision of the United States as a special place, a city on a hill set apart, but the injustices of American society, from slavery to racism to the treatment of women to economic injustice, raised questions about the authenticity of that ideal.

John Winthrop (1588–1649)

From *A Model of Christian Charity*

Winthrop, the first governor and historian of the Massachusetts Bay Colony, preached this sermon on board the ship Arbella *as the colonists crossed the Atlantic.*

Thus stands the case between God and us. We are entered into a Covenant with Him for this work. We have taken out a commission. The Lord hath given us leave to draw our own articles. . . . Now if the Lord shall please to hear us, and bring us in peace to the place we desire, then hath he ratified this Covenant and sealed our Commission, and will expect a strict performance of the articles contained in it; but if we shall neglect the observation of these articles which are the ends we have propounded, and dissembling with our God, shall fail to embrace this present world and prosecute our carnal intentions, seeking great things for ourselves and our posterity, the Lord will surely break out in wrath against us; be revenged of us a perjured people and make us know the price of the breach of such a Covenant.

Now the only way to avoid this shipwreck and to provide for our posterity is to follow the counsel of Micah, *to do justly, to love mercy, to walk humbly with our God.* For this end, we must be knit together, in this work, as one man. We must entertain each other in brotherly affection. We must be willing to abridge ourselves of our superfluities, for the supply of others' necessities. We must uphold a familiar commerce together in all meekness, gentleness, patience, and liberality. We must delight in each other; make others' conditions our own; rejoice together, mourn together, labor and suffer together, always having before our eyes our commission and community in the work, as members of the same body. So shall we *keep the unity of the spirit in the bond of peace.* The Lord will be our God, and delight to dwell among us, as his own people, and will command a blessing upon us in all our ways. So that we shall see much more of his wisdom, power, goodness and truth than formerly we have been acquainted with. We shall find that the God of Israel is among us, when ten of us shall be able to resist a thousand of our enemies; when he shall make us a praise and a glory, that men shall say of succeeding plantations: "The Lord make it like that of New England." For we must consider that we shall be as a City upon a hill. The eyes of all people are upon us. So that if we shall deal falsely with our God in this work we have undertaken, and so cause him to withdraw his present help from us, we shall be made a story and a by-word through the world. We shall open the mouths of enemies to speak evil of the ways of God and all professors* for God's sake. We shall shame the faces of many of God's worthy servants, and cause their prayers to be turned into curses upon us till we be consumed out of the good land whither we are a-going.

From *Life and Letters of John Winthrop,* edited by Robert C. Winthrop, Volume 2 (Boston: Ticknor and Fields, 1867), pages 18–19.

Thomas Hooker (1586–1647)

From *The Activity of Faith: or, Abraham's Imitators*

Hooker had already been an important figure among English and Dutch Puritans. He became the first minister in Cambridge, Massachusetts, and later one of the leaders in founding settlements in Connecticut. This sermon, published posthumously in 1651, insists that Christian faith—and thus the reception of God's grace—will manifest itself in good works.

Romans 4:12. And the Father of Circumcision to them who are not of circumcision only, but also walk in the steps of that faith of our father Abraham, which he had, being yet uncircumcised.

---

*Those who profess faith in God.

... The point is clear in the text, that if a man had circumcision, that is, if he had all those preferments that God vouchsafeth to a people in the face and bosom of his Church, this would not do him any good at all. He hath no title to the promises because of these, if he rest in them: Abraham *is not the father of those that are circumcised only.* So that I say again, all outward privileges are not able to make a man a true Saint of God. . . .

This doctrine confoundeth the carnal confidence of those professors, that living in the bosom of the Church, place all their hopes and assurance of being saved upon this bottom: because they have been baptized, and come to Church, and hear the Word, and receive the Sacrament, therefore of necessity (they presume) they must be accepted of God. . . . These are the *Fig-leaves* wherewith poor and ignorant Christians think to hide themselves at this day. Tell them of their faults, bid them walk humbly and holily before God, reprove them for their strange practices against God and his truth, in profaning his day, blaspheming his name, contemning his Word, despising his ministers, etc. and they presently cry out against us: What will you make Pagans of us? What do you think we are Heathens? Have we not received Christian Baptism? etc. This is a bottom that beareth up many: But oh poor silly creatures, this will not do it; be not deceived, you will shrink under this shelter, you will fall notwithstanding these props, when you come to trial; you may have all this, and yet perish, this will not make you saints in the sight of God. . . .

Mark what I say, a faithful man is a fruitful man: faith enableth a man to be doing. Ask the Question, By what power was it whereby *Abraham* was enabled to yield obedience to the Lord? The text answereth you, *They that walk in the footsteps* not *of Abraham,* but *in the footsteps of the faith of Abraham* . . . implying that it was the grace of faith that God bestowed on *Abraham,* that quickened and enabled him to every duty that God required of him, and called him to the performance of. So that I say, the Question becoming, whence came it that *Abraham* was so fruitful a Christian, what enabled him to do, and to suffer what he did? Surely it was faith that was the cause that produced such Effects, that helped him perform such actions. The Point then you see is evident, Faith is it that causeth fruit. . . .

When a man will say he hath faith, and in the meantime can be content to be idle and unfruitful in the work of the Lord, can be content to be a dead Christian, let him know that his case is marvellously fearful: For if faith were in him indeed, it would appear, ye cannot keep your good hearts to yourselves, wherever fire is, it will burn, and wherever faith is, it cannot be kept secret: The heart will be enlarged, the soul quickened, and there will be a change in the whole life and conversation, if ever faith take place in a man.

From Thomas Hooker, *The Saints Dignitie and Dutie* (London, 1651), pages 155–158, 160, 163, 166.

Jonathan Edwards (1703–1758)

From *Personal Narrative*

Edwards remains the greatest theological genius America has produced. As a preacher he led the revival in the 1730s in Northampton, Massachusetts, that prefigured the Great Awakening, and he later wrote the great history and defense of the Awakening itself. As a philosophical theologian, he produced a remarkable synthesis of the new philosophy of Newton and Locke and classical Calvinism. This selection, written in the early 1740s, shows Edwards' characteristic psychological care in analyzing religious experience and his central commitment to the radical sovereignty of God.

From my childhood up, my mind had been full of objections against the doctrine of God's sovereignty, in choosing whom he would to eternal life, and rejecting whom he pleased; leaving them eternally to perish, and be everlastingly tormented in hell. It used to appear like a horrible doctrine to me. But I remember the time very well, when I seemed to be convinced, and fully satisfied, as to this sovereignty of God and his justice in thus eternally disposing of men, according to his sovereign pleasure. . . . And there has been a wonderful alteration in my mind, with respect to the doctrine of God's sovereignty, from that day to this; so that I scarce ever have found so much as the rising of an objection against it, in the most absolute sense, in God's showing mercy to whom he will show mercy, and hardening whom he will. . . .

Not long after I first began to experience these things, I gave an account to my father of some things that had passed in my mind. I was pretty much affected by the discourse we had together; and when the discourse was ended, I walked abroad alone, in a solitary place in my father's pasture, for contemplation. And as I was walking there, and looking upon the sky and clouds, there came into my mind so sweet a sense of the glorious *majesty* and *grace* of God, as I know not how to express. I seemed to see them both in a sweet conjunction; majesty and meekness joined together: it was a sweet, and gentle, and holy majesty; and also a majestic meekness; an awful sweetness; a high, and great, and holy gentleness.

After this my sense of divine things gradually increased, and became more and more lively, and had more of that inward sweetness. The appearance of every thing was altered; there seemed to be, as it were, a calm, sweet cast, or appearance of divine glory, in almost every thing. God's excellency, his wisdom, his purity and love, seemed to appear in every thing; in the sun, moon and stars; in the clouds and blue sky; in the grass, flowers, trees; in the water and all nature; which used greatly to fix my mind. I often used to sit and view the moon for a long time; and in the day, spent much time in viewing the clouds and sky, to behold the sweet glory of God in these things: in the meantime, singing forth, with a low voice, my contemplations of the Creator and Redeemer. And scarce any thing, among all the works of nature, was so sweet to me as thunder and lightning; formerly nothing had been so terrible to me. Before, I used to be uncommonly terrified with thunder, and to be struck with terror when I saw a thunder storm rising; but now, on the contrary, it rejoiced me. I felt God, if I may so speak, at the first appearance of a thunder storm; and used to take the opportunity, at such times, to fix myself in order to view the clouds, and see the lightnings play, and hear the majestic and awful voice of God's thunder, which oftentimes was exceedingly entertaining, leading me to sweet contemplations of my great and glorious God. While thus engaged, it always seemed natural for me to sing, or chant forth my meditations; or, to speak my thoughts in soliloquies with a singing voice. . . .

I now sought an increase of grace and holiness, and a holy life, with much more earnestness, than ever I sought grace before I had it. I used to be continually examining myself, and studying and contriving for likely ways and means, how I should live holily, with far greater diligence and earnestness, than ever I pursued any thing in my life; but yet with too great a dependence on my own strength; which afterwards proved a great damage to me. My experience had not then taught me, as it has done since, my extreme feebleness and impotence, every manner of way; and the bottomless depths of secret corruption and deceit there was in my heart. . . .

Holiness, as I then wrote down some of my contemplations on it, appeared to me to be of a sweet, pleasant, charming, serene, calm nature; which brought an inexpressible purity, brightness, peacefulness and ravishment to the soul. In other words, that it made the soul like a field or garden of God, with all manner of pleasant flowers . . . enjoying a sweet calm, and the gently vivifying beams of the sun. The soul of a true Christian, as I then wrote my meditations, appeared like such a little white flower as we see in the spring of the year; low and humble on the ground, opening its bosom to receive the pleasant beams of the sun's glory; rejoicing, as it were, in a calm rapture; diffusing around a sweet fragrancy; standing peacefully and lovingly, in the midst of other flowers round about; all in like manner opening their bosoms, to drink in the light of the sun. There was no part of creature-holiness, that I had so great a sense of its loveliness, as humility, brokenness of heart and poverty of spirit; and there was nothing that I so earnestly longed for. My heart panted after this—to lie low before God, as in the dust; that I might be nothing, and that God, might be ALL, that I might become as a little child. . . .

I have a much greater sense of my universal, exceeding dependence on God's grace and strength, and mere good pleasure, of late, than I used formerly to have; and have experienced more of an abhorrence of my own righteousness. The very thought of any joy arising in me, on any consideration of my own amiableness, performances, or experiences, or any goodness of heart or life, is nauseous and detestable to me. And yet, I am greatly afflicted with a proud and self-righteous spirit, much more sensibly than I used to be formerly. I see that serpent rising and putting forth its head continually, every where, all around me.

Though it seems to me, that in some respects, I was a far better Christian, for two or three years after my first conversion, than I am now; and lived in a more constant delight and pleasure; yet of late years, I have had a more full and constant sense of the absolute sovereignty of God, and a delight in that sovereignty; and have had more of a sense of the glory of Christ, as a Mediator revealed in the gospel. On one Saturday night, in particular, I had such a discovery of the excellency of the gospel above all other doctrines, that I could not but say to myself, "This is my chosen light, my chosen doctrine": and of Christ, "This is my chosen Prophet." . . . I had, at the same time, a very affecting sense, how meet and suitable it was that God should govern the world, and order all things according to his own pleasure; and I rejoiced in it, that God reigned, and that his will was done.

From Jonathan Edwards, *The Works of President Edwards,* Volume 1 (Leavett & Allen, 1852), pages 16–18, 23.

David Walker (1785–1830)

From *Our Wretchedness in Consequence of the Preachers of the Religion of Jesus Christ*

Walker was born of a free black mother in North Carolina but moved to Boston, where he became active in Baptist churches and the abolition movement. He published this essay in 1829.

Religion, my brethren, is a substance of deep consideration among all nations of the earth. The Pagans have a kind, as well as the Mahometans, the Jews, and the Christians. But pure and undefiled religion, such as was preached by Jesus Christ and his apostles, is hard to be found in all the earth. God, through his instrument, Moses, handed a dispensation of his divine will to the children of Israel after they had left Egypt for the land of Canaan, or of Promise, who through hypocrisy, oppression, and unbelief, departed from the faith. He then, by his apostles handed a dispensation of his, together with the will of Jesus Christ, to the Europeans in Europe, who, in open violation of which, have made *merchandise* of us, and it does appear as though they take this very dispensation to aid them in their *infernal* depredations upon us. Indeed, the way in which religion was and is conducted by the Europeans and their descendants, one might believe it was a plan fabricated by themselves and the *devils* to oppress us. But hark! my master has taught me better than to believe it—he has taught me that his gospel as it was preached by himself and his apostles remains the same, notwithstanding Europe has tried to mingle blood and oppression with it. . . .

The Pagans, Jews and Mahometans try to make proselytes to their religions, and whatever human beings adopt their religions, they extend to them their protection. But Christian Americans not only hinder their fellow creatures, the Africans, but thousands of them will *absolutely beat a coloured person nearly to death, if they catch him on his knees, supplicating the throne of grace.* This barbarous cruelty was by all the heathen nations of antiquity, and is by the Pagans, Jews and Mahometans of the present day, left entirely to Christian Americans to inflict on the Africans and their descendants that their cup which is nearly full may be completed. I have known tyrants or usurpers of human liberty in different parts of this country to take their fellow creatures, the coloured people, and beat them until they would scarcely leave life in them; what for? Why they say,

"The black devils had the audacity to be found *making prayers and supplications to the God who made them!!!*" . . .

What the American preachers can think of us, I aver this day before my God, I have never been able to define. They have newspapers and monthly periodicals, which they receive in continual succession, but on the pages of which, you will scarcely ever find a paragraph respecting slavery, which is ten thousand times more injurious to this country than all the other evils put together; and which will be the final overthrow of its government, unless something is very speedily done; for this cup is nearly full.—Perhaps they will laugh at, or make light of this; but I tell you Americans! that unless you speedily alter your course *you* and your *Country are gone!!!!!* . . .

This language, perhaps, is too harsh for the American's delicate ears. But Oh Americans! Americans!! I warn you in the name of the Lord (whether you will hear, or forbear,) to repent and reform, or you are ruined!!! . . .

From *David Walker's Appeal to the Coloured Citizens of the World,* edited by Charles Wiltse, pages 35–37, 39–40. Copyright © 1965 by Hill & Wang, Inc. Reprinted by permission of Hill & Wang, a division of Farrar, Straus & Giroux, Inc.

William Ellery Channing (1780–1842)

From *The Essence of the Christian Religion*

Channing served as minister of the Federal Street Church in Boston from 1803 until his death and came to be recognized as the greatest leader of the Unitarians. This sermon, delivered in the winter of 1830–31, shows his moderate Unitarianism in practice—a rational simplicity in theology that still leaves room for reverence for Christ and belief in miracles.

I believe that Christianity has one great principle, which is *central,* around which all its truths gather, and which constitutes it the glorious gospel of the blessed God. I believe that no truth is so worthy of acceptation and so quickening as this. In proportion as we penetrate into it, and are penetrated by it, we comprehend our religion, and attain to a living faith. This great principle can be briefly expressed. It is the doctrine that "God purposes, in his unbounded fatherly love, to perfect the human soul; to purify it from all sin; to create it after his own image; to fill it with his own spirit; to unfold it for ever; to raise it to life and immortality in heaven:—that is, to communicate to it from himself a life of celestial power, virtue and joy." The elevation of men above the imperfections, temptations, sins, sufferings, of the present state, to a diviner being,—this is the great purpose of God, revealed and accomplished by Jesus Christ; this it is that constitutes the religion of Jesus Christ—glad tidings to all people: for it is a religion suited to fulfil the wants of every human being.

In the New Testament I learn that God regards the human soul with unutterable interest and love; that in an important sense it bears the impress of his own infinity, its powers being germs, which may expand without limit or end: that he loves it, even when fallen, and desires its restoration; that he has sent his Son to redeem and cleanse it from all iniquity; that he for ever seeks to communicate to it a divine virtue which shall spring up, by perennial bloom and fruitfulness, into everlasting life. In the New Testament I learn that what God wills is our perfection; by which I understand the freest exercise and perpetual development of our highest powers—strength and brightness of intellect, unconquerable energy of moral principle, pure and fervent desire for truth, unbounded love of goodness and greatness, benevolence free from every selfish taint, the perpetual consciousness of God and of his immediate presence, co-operation and friendship with all enlightened and disinterested spirits, and radiant glory of divine will and beneficent influence, of which we have an emblem—a faint emblem only—in the sun that illuminates and warms so many worlds. Christianity reveals to me this moral perfection of man, as the great purpose of God. . . .

This religion is not a deduction of philosophy, resting on obscure truths, and intelligible but to a few. It is a solemn annunciation from heaven of human immortality, and of a diviner life than this. And it is sealed by miracles, that is, by divine interpositions, which are equally intelligible, striking, and affecting to all. I maintain that miracles are most appropriate proofs of a religion which announces the elevation of man to spiritual perfection. For what are miracles? They are the acts and manifestations of a spiritual power in the universe, superior to the powers and laws of matter. And on the existence of such a power, the triumph of our own spiritual nature over death and material influences must depend.

The miracles of Christianity, so far from shocking me, approve themselves at once to my intellect and my heart. They seem to be among the most reasonable as well as important events in human history. I prize them, not because they satisfy the passion for the wonderful,—though this principle is one of the noble indications of our nature. But I prize them as discovering, in a way which all can comprehend, that there is some real Being mightier than Nature; that there is a mind which *can,* if it will, suspend or reverse the regular operations of the material world; that, of consequence, the power of death is not supreme, and that the mind may ascend to a perfection which Nature cannot give. Christianity, in its miracles and doctrines, is the very charter and pledge which I need of this elevation of the human soul. And on this account I recognize it as the glorious gospel of the blessed God, or as a religion making sure to its sincere disciples the most magnificent good which even Omnipotence can bestow.

From *The Works of William E. Channing, D.D.* (Boston: American Unitarian Association, 1886), pages 1001–1002.

Charles Grandison Finney (1792–1875)

From *Lectures on Revivals of Religion*

Finney grew up in upstate New York, the center of early American revivalism. He was ordained a Presbyterian minister and became the leading advocate of the "new measures" of simple, emotional preaching and the calculated planning of revivals. He published these lectures in 1835, the same year in which he joined the faculty of Oberlin College as Professor of Theology.

Religion is the work of man. It is something for man to do. It consists in obeying God with and from the heart. It is man's duty. It is true, God induces him to do it. He influences him by his Spirit, because of his great wickedness and reluctance to obey. If it were not necessary for God to influence men—if men were disposed to obey God, there would be no occasion to pray, "O Lord, revive thy work." The ground of necessity for such a prayer is, that men are wholly indisposed to obey; and unless God interpose the influence of his Spirit, not a man on earth will ever obey the commands of God.

A "Revival of Religion" presupposes a declension. Almost all the religion in the world has been produced by revivals. God has found it necessary to take advantage of the excitability there is in mankind, to produce powerful excitements among them, before he can lead them to obey. Men are so spiritually sluggish, there are so many things to lead their minds off from religion, and to oppose the influence of the Gospel, that it is necessary to raise an excitement among them, till the tide rises so high as to sweep away the opposing obstacles. They must be so excited that they will break over these counteracting influences, before they will obey God. . . .

Many good men have supposed, and still suppose, that the best way to promote religion, is to go along *uniformly,* and gather in the ungodly gradually, and without excitement. But however such reasoning may appear in the abstract, *facts* demonstrate its futility. If the church were far enough advanced in knowledge, and had stability of principle enough to *keep awake,* such a course would do; but the church is so little enlightened, and there are so many counteracting causes, that she will not go steadily to work without a special interest being awakened. . . .

A revival of religion is not a miracle. . . . It is a purely philosophical result of the right use of the constituted means—as much so as any other effect produced by the application of means. . . .

I wish this idea to be impressed on all your minds, for there has long been an idea prevalent that promoting religion has something very peculiar in it, not to be judged of by the ordinary rules of cause and effect; in short, that there is no connection of the means with the result, and no tendency in the means to produce the effect. No doctrine is more dangerous than this to the prosperity of the church, and nothing more absurd.

Suppose a man were to go and preach this doctrine among farmers, about their sowing grain. Let him tell them that God is a sovereign, and will give them a crop only when it pleases him, and that for them to plow and plant and labor as if they expected to raise a crop is very wrong, and taking the work out of the hands of God, that it interferes with his sovereignty, and is going on in their own strength; and that there is no connection between the means and the result on which they can depend. And now, suppose the farmers should believe such doctrine. Why, they would starve the world to death.

Just such results will follow from the church's being persuaded that promoting religion is somehow so mysteriously a subject of Divine sovereignty, that there is no natural connection between the means and the end. What *are* the results? Why, generation after generation has gone down to hell. No doubt more than five thousand millions have gone down to hell, while the church has been dreaming, and waiting for God to save them without the use of means. It has been the devil's most successful means of destroying souls. The connection is as clear in religion as it is when the farmer sows his grain. . . .

And yet some people are terribly alarmed at all direct efforts to promote a revival, and they cry out, "You are trying to get up a revival in your own strength. Take care, you are interfering with the sovereignty of God. Better keep along in the usual course, and let God give a revival when he thinks it is best. God is a sovereign, and it is very wrong for you to attempt to get up a revival, just because *you think* a revival is needed." This is just such preaching as the devil wants. And men cannot do the devil's work more effectually than by preaching up the sovereignty of God, as a reason why we should not put forth efforts to produce a revival.

From Charles Grandison Finney, *Lectures on Revivals of Religion* (E. J. Goodrich, 1868), pages 9–14, 20.

Sarah M. Grimké (1792–1873)

From *Letters on the Equality of the Sexes and the Condition of Woman*

Born in South Carolina of a slaveholding family, Grimké became a Quaker and a lecturer on abolitionism. She published these letters, written in 1837, partly in response to those who criticized her for, as a woman, engaging in public lecturing.

In attempting to comply with thy request to give my views on the Province of Woman, I feel that I am venturing on nearly untrodden ground, and that I shall advance arguments in opposition to a corrupt public opinion, and to the perverted interpretation of Holy Writ, which has so universally obtained. But I am in search of truth; and no obstacle shall prevent my prosecuting that search, because I believe the welfare of the world will be materially advanced by every new discovery we make of the designs of Jehovah in the creation of woman. It is impossible that we can answer the purpose of our being, unless we understand that purpose. It is impossible that we should fulfill our duties, unless we comprehend them; or live up to our privileges, unless we know what they are. . . .

We must first view woman at the period of her creation. "And God said, Let us make man in our own image, after our likeness; and let them have dominion over the fish of the sea, and over the fowl of the air, and over the cattle, and over all the earth, and over every creeping thing that creepeth upon the earth. So God created man in his own image, in the image of God created he him, male and female created he them." In all this sublime description of the creation of man, (which is a generic term including man and woman,) there is not one particle of difference intimated as existing between them. They were both made in the image of God; dominion was given to both over every other creature, but not over each other. Created in perfect equality, they were expected to exercise the viceregence intrusted to them by their Maker, in harmony and love. . . .

Here then I plant myself. God created us equal;—he created us free agents;—he is our Lawgiver, our King and our Judge, and to him alone is woman bound to be in subjection, and to him alone is she accountable for the use of those talents with which her Heavenly Father has entrusted her. . . .

Notwithstanding what has been urged, woman I am aware stands charged to the present day with having brought sin into the world. I shall not repel the charge by any counter assertions, although . . . Adam's ready acquiescence with his wife's proposal, does not savor much of that superiority *in strength of mind,* which is arrogated by man. Even admitting that Eve was the greater sinner, it seems to me man might be satisfied with the dominion he has claimed and exercised for nearly six thousand years, and that more true nobility would be manifested by endeavoring to raise the fallen and invigorate the weak, than by keeping woman in subjection. But I ask no favors for my sex. I surrender not our claim to equality. All I ask of our brethren is, that they will take their feet from off our necks and permit us to stand upright on that ground which God designed us to occupy.

From Sarah M. Grimké, *Letters on the Equality of the Sexes and the Condition of Woman* (New York: Burt Franklin, 1838), pages 3–5, 8–10.

Ralph Waldo Emerson (1803–1882)

From *The Divinity School Address*

Emerson resigned as minister of Second Church in Boston in 1832 and began a long career as America's most famous public lecturer. To the new "transcendentalism" he represented, with its optimism about human nature, its belief that individuals must find the truth within themselves and not at second hand, and its sense of the divinity of the human soul, even Boston Unitarianism seemed too theologically conservative. Emerson delivered this lecture at the Harvard Divinity School in 1838; he was never invited back.

In this refulgent summer, it has been a luxury to draw the breath of life. The grass grows, the buds burst, the meadow is spotted with fire and gold in the tint of flowers. The air is full of birds and sweet with the breath of the pine, the balm-of-Gilead, and the new hay. Night brings no gloom to the heart with its welcome shade. Through the transparent darkness the stars pour their almost spiritual rays. Man under them seems a young child, and his huge globe a toy. The cool night bathes the world as with a river, and prepares his eyes again for the crimson dawn. The mystery of nature was never displayed more happily. The corn and the wine have been freely dealt to all creatures, and the never-broken silence with which the old bounty goes forward has not yielded yet one word of explanation. One is constrained to respect the perfection of this world in which our senses converse. . . .

Speak the truth, and all things alive or brute are vouchers, and the very roots of the grass underground there do seem to stir and move to bear you witness. See again the perfection of the Law as it applies itself to the affections, and becomes the law of society. As we are, so we associate. The good, by affinity, seek the good; the vile, by affinity, the vile. Thus of their own volition, souls proceed into heaven, into hell.

These facts have always suggested to man the sublime creed that the world is not the product of manifold power, but of one will, of one mind; and that one mind is everywhere active, in each ray of the star, in each wavelet of the pool; and whatever opposes that will is everywhere balked and baffled, because things are made so, and not otherwise. Good is positive. Evil is merely privative, not absolute: it is like cold, which is the privation of heat. All evil is so much death or nonentity. Benevolence is absolute and real. . . .

Thought may work cold and intransitive in things, and find no end or unity; but the dawn of the sentiment of virtue on the heart, gives and is the assurance that Law is sovereign over all natures; and the worlds, time, space, eternity, do seem to break out into joy.

This sentiment is divine and deifying. It is the beatitude of man. It makes him illimitable. Through it, the soul first knows itself. It corrects the capital mistake of the infant man, who seeks to be great by following the great, and hopes to derive advantages *from another,*—by showing the fountain of all good to be in himself, and that he, equally with every man, is an inlet into the deeps of Reason. When he says, "I ought"; when love warms him; when he chooses, warmed from on high, the good and great deed; then, deep melodies wander through his soul from Supreme Wisdom.—Then he can worship, and be enlarged by his worship; for he can never go behind this sentiment. In the sublimest flights of the soul, rectitude is never surmounted, love is never outgrown. . . .

Jesus Christ belonged to the true race of prophets. He saw with open eye the mystery of the soul. Drawn by its severe harmony, ravished with its beauty, he lived in it, and had his being there. Alone in all history, he estimated the greatness of man. One man was true to what is in you and me. He saw that God incarnates himself in man, and evermore goes forth anew to take possession of his World. He said, in this jubilee of sublime emotion, "I am divine. Through me, God acts; through me, speaks. Would you see God, see me; or see thee, when thou also thinkest as I now think." But what a distortion did his doctrine and memory suffer in the same, in the next, and in the following ages! . . . He spoke of miracles; for he felt that man's life was a miracle, and all that man doth, and he knew that this daily miracle shines as the character ascends. But the word Miracle, as pronounced by Christian churches, gives a false impression; it is Monster. It is not one with the blowing clover and the falling rain. . . .

Men have come to speak of the revelation as somewhat long ago given and done, as if God were dead. The injury to faith throttles the preacher; and the goodliest of institutions becomes an uncertain and inarticulate voice. . . .

In how many churches, by how many prophets, tell me, is man made sensible that he is an infinite Soul; that the earth and heavens are passing into his mind; that he is drinking forever the soul of God? Where now sounds the persuasion, that by its very melody imparadises my heart, and so affirms its own origin in heaven? . . .

I once heard a preacher who sorely tempted me to say I would go to church no more. Men go, thought I, where they are wont to go, else had no soul entered the temple in the afternoon. A snow-storm was falling around us. The snow-storm was real; the preacher merely spectral, and the eye felt the sad contrast in looking at him, and then out of the window behind him, into the beautiful meteor of the snow. He had lived in vain. He had not one word intimating that he had laughed or wept, was married or in love, had been commended, or cheated, or chagrined. If he had ever lived and acted, we were none the wiser for it. The capital secret of his profession, namely to convert life into truth, he had not learned. . . .

And now, my brothers, you will ask, What in these desponding days can be done by us? The remedy is already declared in the ground of our complaint of the Church. We have contrasted the Church with the Soul. In the soul, then, let the redemption be sought. . . .

Let me admonish you, first of all, to go alone; to refuse the good models, even those which are sacred in the imagination of men, and dare to love God without mediator or veil. . . . The imitator dooms himself to hopeless mediocrity. The inventor did it, because it was natural to him, and so in him it has a charm. In the imitator, something else is natural, and he bereaves himself of his own beauty, to come short of another man's.

Yourself a newborn bard of the Holy Ghost,—cast behind you all conformity, and acquaint men at first hand with Deity. Look to it first and only, that fashion, custom, authority, pleasure, and money, are nothing to you,—are not bandages over your eyes, that you cannot see,—but live with the privilege of the immeasurable mind.

From *The Complete Works of Ralph Waldo Emerson,* Volume 1 (Boston: Houghton Mifflin Co., 1903), pages 119, 123–125, 128–129, 134, 136–138, 143–146.

Mary Baker Eddy (1821–1910)

From *Science and Health with Key to the Scriptures*

Mary Baker grew up in a Congregationalist family in New Hampshire. She suffered chronic ill health and two unhappy marriages before she found a cure for her illness in the nascent Christian healing movement. With the support of her third husband, Asa Eddy, she organized the Christian Science Association, with its many publications and local societies. This selection comes from the preface to her best-known work, Science and Health, *the first edition of which was published in 1875.*

Since the author's discovery of the might of Truth in the treatment of disease as well as of sin, her system has been fully tested and has not been found wanting; but to reach the heights of Christian Science, man must live in obedience to its divine Principle. To develop the full might of this Science, the discords of corporeal sense must yield to the harmony of spiritual sense, even as the science of music corrects false tones and gives sweet concord to sound.

Theology and physics teach that both Spirit and matter are real and good, whereas the fact is that Spirit is good and real, and matter is Spirit's opposite. The question, What is Truth, is answered by demonstration,—by healing both disease and sin; and this demonstration shows that Christian healing confers the most health and makes the best men. On this basis Christian Science will have a fair fight. Sickness has been combated for centuries by doctors using material remedies; but the question arises, Is there less sickness because of these practitioners? A vigorous "No" is the response deducible from two connate facts,—the reputed longevity of the Antediluvians,* and the rapid multiplication and increased violence of diseases since the flood. . . .

The divine Principle of healing is proved in the personal experience of any sincere seeker of Truth. Its purpose is good, and its practice is safer and more potent than that of any other sanitary method. The unbiased Christian thought is soonest touched by Truth, and convinced of it. . . .

Many imagine that the phenomena of physical healing in Christian Science present only a phase of the action of the human mind, which action in some unexplained way results in the cure of disease. On the contrary, Christian Science rationally explains that all other pathological methods are the fruits of human faith in matter,—faith in the workings, not of Spirit, but of the fleshly mind which must yield to Science.

The physical healing of Christian Science results now, as in Jesus' time, from the operation of divine Principle, before which sin and disease lose their reality in human consciousness and disappear as naturally and as necessarily as darkness gives place to light and sin to reformation. Now, as then, these mighty works are not supernatural, but supremely natural. They are the sign of Immanuel, or "God with us,"—a divine influence ever present in human consciousness and repeating itself, coming now as was promised aforetime,

> To preach deliverance to the captives [of sense],
> And recovering of sight to the blind,
> To set at liberty them that are bruised.

From Mary Baker Eddy, *Science and Health with Key to the Scriptures,* pages vii–viii, x–xi. © 1971, The Christian Science Board of Directors. Used by permission.

---

*Those who lived before Noah and the flood, reported by the Old Testament to have lived hundreds of years.

Joseph Smith (1805–1844)

From *King Follett Discourse*

Joseph Smith grew up amid the religious turmoil of upstate New York in the early nineteenth century. In the late 1820s he began to dictate a translation of a document he claimed to have discovered with angelic help, the Book of Mormon, *which described the wanderings of the lost tribes of Israel and the pre-Columbian history of America. Smith soon began to attract converts, who moved first to Ohio, then to Missouri, and then to Nauvoo, Illinois, where Smith was murdered by local opponents of the "Church of Jesus Christ of Latter-day Saints." He preached this sermon at the funeral of one of his followers, King Follett, in 1844. Many of its themes are no longer emphasized by Mormons, but it shows the theologically radical ideas Smith and others on the frontier sometimes generated.*

I will go back to the beginning before the world was, to show what kind of a being God is. What sort of a being was God in the beginning? Open your ears and hear. . . .

God himself was once as we are now, and is an exalted man, and sits enthroned in yonder heavens! That is the great secret. If the veil were rent today, and the great God who holds this world in its orbit, and who upholds all worlds and all things by his power, was to make himself visible,—I say, if you were to see him today, you would see him like a man in form—like yourselves in all the person, image and very form as a man; for Adam was created in the very fashion, image and likeness of God, and received instruction from, and walked, talked and conversed with him, as one man talks and communes with another. . . .

The scriptures inform us that Jesus said, as the Father hath power in himself, even so hath the Son power—to do what? Why, what the Father did. The answer is obvious—in a manner to lay down his body and take it up again. Jesus, what are you going to do? To lay down my life as my Father did, and take it up again. Do you believe it? If you do not believe it you do not believe the Bible. The scriptures say it, and I defy all the learning and wisdom and all the combined powers of earth and hell together to refute it. Here, then, is eternal life—to know the only wise and true God; and you have got to learn how to be gods yourselves, and to be kings and priests to God, the same as all gods have done before you, namely, by going from one small degree to another, and from a small capacity to a great one;

from grace to grace, from exaltation to exaltation, until you attain to the resurrection of the dead, and are able to dwell in everlasting burnings, and to sit in glory, as do those who sit enthroned in everlasting power. . . .

In the beginning, the head of the Gods called a council of the Gods; and they came together and concocted [prepared] a plan to create the world and people it. When we begin to learn this way, we begin to learn the only true God, and what kind of a being we have got to worship. . . .

Now, I ask all who hear me, why the learned men who are preaching salvation, say that God created the heavens and the earth out of nothing? The reason is, that they are unlearned in the things of God, and have not the gift of the Holy Ghost; they account it blasphemy in any one to contradict their idea. If you tell them that God made the world out of something, they will call you a fool. But I am learned, and know more than all the world put together. The Holy Ghost does, anyhow, and he is within me, and comprehends more than all the world; and I will associate myself with him.

You ask the learned doctors why they say the world was made out of nothing, and they will answer, "Doesn't the Bible say he created the world?" And they infer, from the word "create," that it must have been made out of nothing. Now, the word "create" came from the word "baurau," which does not mean to create out of nothing; it means to organize; the same as a man would organize materials and build a ship. Hence we infer that God had materials to organize the world out of chaos—chaotic matter, which is element, and in which dwells all the glory. Element had an existence from the time he had. The pure principles of elements are principles which can never be destroyed; they may be organized and re-organized, but not destroyed. They had no beginning and can have no end.

From *Discourses of the Prophet Joseph Smith,* compiled by Alma P. Burton, 3rd edition, pages 263–266. Copyright © 1965 by Deseret Book Company. Used by permission of the publisher.

Horace Bushnell (1802–1876)

From *Christian Nurture*

Bushnell, a Congregational minister in Hartford, Connecticut, tried to find creative theological alternatives to strict orthodoxy on the one hand and liberalism shading into Unitarianism on the other. He had original things to say about the nature of religious language and the work of Christ. Christian Nurture, *probably his most influential book, defended the growing Sunday school movement against revivalists unfriendly to the idea of gradual growth in faith from early childhood. In his criticisms of individualism and his use of organic metaphors, Bushnell shows the influence of Romantic ideas that he, like Emerson, was getting from Europe.*

What then is the true idea of Christian or divine nurture, as distinguished from that which is not Christian? What is its aim? What its method of working? . . . In ordinary cases, the better and more instructive way of handling this subject, would be to go directly into the practical methods of parental discipline, and show by what modes of government and instruction we may hope to realize the best results. But unhappily the public mind is preoccupied extensively by a view of the whole subject, which I must regard as a theoretical mistake, and one which will involve, as long as it continues, practical results systematically injurious. This mistaken view it is necessary, if possible, to remove. And accordingly what I have to say will take the form of an argument . . . it will be the aim of my argument to establish, viz: *That the child is to grow up a Christian, and never know himself as being otherwise.*

In other words, the aim, effort, and expectation should be, not, as is commonly assumed, that the child is to grow up in sin, to be converted after he comes to a mature age; but that he is to open on the world as one that is spiritually renewed, not remembering the time when he went through a technical experience, but seeming rather to have loved what is good from his earliest years. . . .

There is then, as the subject appears to us—

1. No absurdity in supposing that children are to grow up in Christ. On the other hand, if there is no absurdity, there is a very clear moral incongruity in setting up a contrary supposition, to be the aim of a system of Christian education. There could not be a worse or more baleful implication given to a child, than that he is to reject God and all holy principle, till he has come to a mature age. What authority have you from the Scriptures to tell your child, or, by any sign, to show him that you do not expect him truly to love and obey God, till after he has spent whole years in hatred and wrong? . . . Perhaps you do not give your child to expect that he is to grow up in sin; you only expect that he will yourself. That is scarcely better: for that which is your expectation, will assuredly be his; and what is more, any attempt to maintain a

discipline at war with your own secret expectations, will only make a hollow and worthless figment of that which should be an open, earnest reality. . . .

3. It is a fact that all Christian parents would like to see their children grow up in piety; and the better Christians they are, the more earnestly they desire it; and, the more lovely and constant the Christian spirit they manifest, the more likely it is, in general, that their children will early display the Christian character. This is current opinion. But why should a Christian parent, the deeper his piety and the more closely he is drawn to God, be led to desire, the more earnestly, what, in God's view, is even absurd or impossible? . . .

4. . . . The tendency of all our modern speculations is to an extreme individualism, and we carry our doctrines of free will so far as to make little or nothing of organic laws; not observing that character may be, to a great extent, only the free development of exercises previously wrought in us, or extended to us, when other wills had us within their sphere. All the Baptist theories of religion are based on this error. They assume, as a first truth, that no such thing is possible as an organic connection of character, an assumption which is plainly refuted by what we see with our eyes, and . . . by the declarations of Scripture. We have much to say also, in common with the Baptists, about the beginning of moral agency, as we seem to fancy that there is some definite moment when a child becomes a moral agent, passing out of a condition where he is a moral nullity, and where no moral agency touches his being. Whereas he is rather to be regarded, at the first, as lying within the moral agency of the parent, and passing out, by degrees, through a course of mixed agency, to a proper independency and self-possession. The supposition that he becomes, at some certain moment, a complete moral agent, which a moment before he was not, is clumsy, and has no agreement with observation. The separation is gradual. He is never, at any moment after birth, to be regarded as perfectly beyond the sphere of good and bad exercises; for the parent exercises himself in the child, playing his emotions and sentiments, and working a character in him, by virtue of an organic power.

And this is the very idea of Christian education, that it begins with nurture or cultivation. And the intention is that the Christian life and spirit of the parents, which are in and by the Spirit of God, shall flow into the mind of the child, to blend with his incipient and half-formed exercises; that they shall thus beget their own good within him— their thoughts, opinions, faith, and love, which are to become a little more, and yet a little more, his own separate exercise. . . .

All society is organic—the church, the state, the school, the family; and there is a spirit in each of these organisms, peculiar to itself, and more or less hostile, more or less favorable to religious character, and to some extent, at least, sovereign over the individual man. A very great share of the power in what is called a revival of religion, is organic power; nor is it any the less divine on that account. The child is only more within the power of organic laws than we all are. We possess only a mixed individuality all our life long. A pure, separate, individual man, living *wholly* within, and from himself, is a mere fiction. No such person ever existed, or ever can. I need not say that this view of an organic connection of character subsisting between parent and child, lays a basis for notions of Christian education, far different from those which now prevail, under the cover of a merely fictitious and mischievous individualism.

From Horace Bushnell, *Christian Nurture* (New York: Charles Scribner, 1871), pages 9–10, 15–16, 20, 29–31.

CHAPTER 6

The Nineteenth Century

All historical labels oversimplify, but there is at least some truth to the idea that in Europe at the beginning of the nineteenth century the Age of Reason gave way to an age of Romanticism. Appeals to feeling and intuition challenged the cold rigors of logical analysis. Writers, artists, and musicians took a new interest in tradition—in the particular traditions of their own nations and in the romanticized Middle Ages. All these themes appear in the work of Friedrich Schleiermacher, who dominated German theology in the early part of the century.

His colleague at the University of Berlin, G. W. F. Hegel (1770–1831), exercised a similar dominance in philosophy. Hegel believed that philosophy must grow out of the riches of history, and his philosophy owed much to the Christian tradition, but his own stance with regard to that tradition remains unclear. He certainly believed that the Trinity and the Incarnation are powerful symbols of important philosophical truths, but his interpreters have debated ever since whether he took them only as such symbols or as really embodying claims to historical or ontological truth.

In the generation after Hegel, his more important and more controversial followers took a more radical direction. As a New Testament scholar, D. F. Strauss concluded that the Gospels are unreliable as historical documents and that we can really know little about Jesus. But as a radical Hegelian, Strauss did not think it mattered, since the story of Jesus should really serve as a symbol of eternal philosophical truths. Ludwig Feuerbach went even further. In Friedrich Engels' famous phrase, he turns Hegel right side up. Where Hegel taught that God creates the world through thought, Feuerbach claimed that human beings invent God out of their own imaginations—an idea that has influenced Marx, Freud, and a host of others.

The Danish writer Søren Kierkegaard posed a different challenge to Hegel and to the general optimism of the century. Where Hegel thought we could make sense of the whole of reality by fitting it into a great system,

Kierkegaard insisted that we always live in the midst of an unfinished reality whose direction and shape cannot be proved, and we can therefore be guided only by faith. Where many of his contemporaries sought to get beyond the faith of earlier ages to a more sophisticated level of understanding, Kierkegaard found the heroic faith of earlier times more impressive than the comfortable complacency of his own world.

Some currents in Catholic theology shared that suspicion of the modern age. To be sure, some Catholic theologians, such as Johann Sebastian von Drey (1777–1853), had much in common with Schleiermacher, and at the end of the century Pope Leo XIII made progressive comments on social issues. But the First Vatican Council, in 1870, aggressively reaffirmed much that was traditional in the face of the modern world. The greatest Catholic theologian of the century, John Henry Newman, had begun as an Anglican. He and a number of his friends had founded the "Oxford Movement" in the Church of England, reemphasizing the importance of doctrine and Sacraments in the face of a liberalism that had grown theologically vague. Though Newman himself found that the logic of his position led him to the Church of Rome, the Oxford Movement's influence continues in the "high church" party of the Church of England.

The theology of Albrecht Ritschl (1822–1889) and his students dominated Germany in the later nineteenth century as that of Schleiermacher had earlier. Ritschl turned theology away from metaphysics to ethics: an ethics of love, forgiveness, and human efforts to move closer to the kingdom of God. By the end of the century, Ritschlian theology faced at least two challenges. New Testament scholarship seemed to imply that by "the kingdom of God" Jesus had meant a radical, apocalyptic end to the present age, not gradual moral improvement. And the "history of religions school" had learned both how diverse was Christianity and how morally and intellectually impressive were the non-Christian religions. The Ritschlian effort to summarize a simple essence of Christianity and show its moral superiority seemed now dubious, and the awareness of cultural diversity that had seemed such a positive force at the beginning of the century now pointed to an awkward kind of relativism.

Friedrich Schleiermacher (1768–1834)

From *On Religion: Speeches to Its Cultured Despisers*

Schleiermacher published these speeches in 1799, when he was a young hospital chaplain in Berlin. Raised in a Pietist family, he had fallen in with the avant-garde writers at the forefront of German Romanticism. He was here addressing his culturally sophisticated friends, hoping to persuade them that the concern for feeling that guided them in literature and the arts ought to lead them to greater sympathy for religion, and that the new value they put on traditions ought to lead them away from the "natural religion" of the Age of Reason and toward Christianity, the religion of their own tradition. In later works such as The Christian Faith *(1821), Schleiermacher worked more within the framework of traditional theological language. Those works probably represent his greater contribution to theology, but these speeches convey his youthful enthusiasm.*

Permit me to speak of myself. You know that what is spoken at the instigation of piety cannot be pride, for piety is always full of humility. Piety was the mother's womb, in whose sacred darkness my young life was nourished and was prepared for a world still sealed for it. In it my spirit breathed ere it had yet found its own place in knowledge and experience. It helped me as I began to sift the faith of my fathers and to cleanse thought and feeling from the rubbish of antiquity. . . .

Let us then, I pray you, examine whence exactly religion has its rise. . . . You start with the outside, with the opinions, dogmas and usages, in which every religion is presented. . . . Wherefore religion generally can be nothing but an empty pretence which, like a murky and oppressive atmosphere, has enshrouded part of the truth. . . .

If you have only given attention to these dogmas and opinions, therefore, you do not yet know religion itself, and what you despise is not it. Why have you not penetrated deeper to find the kernel of this shell? I am astonished at your voluntary ignorance, ye easy-going inquirers, and at the all too quiet satisfaction with which you linger by the first thing presented to you. Why do you not regard the religious life itself, and first those pious exaltations of the mind in which all other known activities are set aside or almost suppressed, and the whole soul is dissolved in the immediate feeling of the Infinite and Eternal? In such moments the disposition you pretend to despise reveals itself in primordial and visible form. He only who has studied and truly known man in these emotions can rediscover religion in those outward manifestations. . . .

Wherefore, you must not rest satisfied with the repeated oft-broken echo of that original sound. You must transport yourselves into the interior of a pious soul and seek to understand its inspiration. In the very act, you must understand the production of light and heat in a soul surrendered to the Universe. Otherwise you learn nothing of religion. . . .

Let me interpret in clear words what most pious persons only guess at and never know how to express. Were you to set God at the apex of your science as the foundation of all knowing as well as of all knowledge, they would accord praise and honor, but it would not be their way of having and knowing God. From their way, as they would readily grant, and as is easy enough to see, knowledge and science do not proceed.

It is true that religion is essentially contemplative. You would never call anyone pious who went about in impervious stupidity, whose sense is not open for the life of the world. But this contemplation is not turned, as your knowledge of nature is, to the existence of a finite thing, combined with and opposed to another finite thing. It has not even, like your knowledge of God—if for once I might use an old expression—to do with the nature of the first cause, in itself and in its relation to every other cause and operation. The contemplation of the pious is the immediate consciousness of the universal existence of all finite things, in and through the Infinite, and of all temporal things in and through the Eternal. Religion is to seek this and find it in all that lives and moves, in all growth and change, in all doing and suffering. It is to have life and to know life in immediate feeling, only as such an existence in the Infinite and Eternal. Where this is found religion is satisfied, where it hides itself there is for her unrest and anguish, extremity and death. Wherefore it is a life in the infinite nature of the Whole, in the One and in the All, in God, having and possessing all things in God, and God in all. Yet religion is not knowledge and science, either of the world or of God. Without being knowledge, it recognizes knowledge and science. In itself it is an affection, a revelation of the Infinite in the finite, God being seen in it and it in God. . . .

If then this, that I trust I have indicated clearly enough for you all, is really the nature of religion, I have already answered the questions, Whence do those dogmas and doctrines come that many consider the essence of religion? Where do they properly belong? And how do they stand related to what is essential in religion? They are all the result of that contemplation of feeling, of that reflection and comparison, of which we have already spoken. The conceptions that underlie these propositions are, like your conceptions from experience, nothing but general expressions for definite feelings. They are not necessary for religion itself, scarcely even for communicating religion, but reflection requires and creates them. Miracle, inspiration, revelation, supernatural intimations, much piety can be had without the need of any one of these conceptions. But when feeling is made the subject of reflection and comparison they are absolutely unavoidable. In this sense all these conceptions do certainly belong to the sphere of religion, and indeed belong without condition or the smallest limit to their application. . . .

What is a miracle? What we call miracle is everywhere else called sign, indication. Our name, which means a wonder, refers purely to the mental condition of the observer. It is only in so far appropriate that a sign, especially when it is nothing besides, must be fitted to call attention to itself and to the power in it that gives it significance. Every finite thing, however, is a sign of the Infinite, and so these various expressions declare the immediate relation of a phenomenon to the Infinite and the Whole. But does that involve that every event should not have quite as immediate relation to the finite and to nature? Miracle is simply the religious name for event. Every event, even the most natural and usual, becomes a miracle, as soon as the religious view of it can be the dominant. To me all is miracle. In your sense the inexplicable and strange alone is miracle, in mine it is no miracle. The more religious you are, the more miracle would you see everywhere. All disputing about single events, as to whether or not they are to be called miraculous, gives me a painful impression of the poverty and wretchedness of the religious sense of the combatants. One party show it by protesting everywhere against miracle, whereby they manifest their wish not to see anything of immediate relationship to the Infinite and to the Deity. The other party display the same poverty by laying stress on this and that. A phenomenon for them must be marvellous before they will regard it as a miracle, whereby they simply announce that they are bad observers.

What is revelation? Every original and new communication of the Universe to man is a revelation, as, for example, every such moment of conscious insight as I have just referred to. Every intuition and every original feeling proceeds from revelation. As revelation lies beyond consciousness, demonstration is not possible, yet we are not merely to assume it generally, but each one knows best himself what is repeated and learned elsewhere, and what is original and new. If nothing original has yet been generated in you, when it does come it will be a revelation for you also, and I counsel you to weigh it well. . . .

At present I have something else to deal with, a new opposition to vanquish. I would, as it were, conduct you to the God that has become flesh; I would show you religion when it has resigned its infinity and appeared, often in sorry form, among men; I would have you discover religion in the religions. Though they are always earthly and impure, the same form of heavenly beauty that I have tried to depict is to be sought in them. . . .

The different existing manifestations of religion you call positive religions. Under this name they have long been the object of a quite pre-eminent hate. Despite of your repugnance to religion generally, you have always borne more easily with what for distinction is called natural religion. You have almost spoken of it with esteem.

I do not hesitate to say at once that from the heart I entirely deny this superiority. For all who have religion at all and profess to love it, it would be the vilest inconsequence to admit it. They would thereby fall into the openest self-contradiction. For my own part, if I only succeeded in recommending to you this natural religion, I would consider that I had lost my pains. . . .

You will then find that the positive religions are just the definite forms in which religion must exhibit itself—a thing to which your so-called natural religions have no claim. They are only a vague, sorry, poor thought that corresponds to no reality, and you will find that in the positive religions alone a true individual cultivation of the religious capacity is possible. Nor do they, by their nature, injure the freedom of their adherents.

Why have I assumed that religion can only be given fully in a great multitude of forms of the utmost definiteness? Only on grounds that naturally follow from what has been said of the nature of religion. The whole of religion is nothing but the sum of all relations of man to God, apprehended in all the possible ways in which any man can be immediately conscious in his life. In this sense there is but one religion, for it would be but a poverty-stricken and halting life, if all these relations did not exist wherever religion ought to be. Yet all men will not by any means apprehend them in the same way, but quite differently. Now this difference alone is felt and alone can be exhibited while the reduction of all differences is only thought.

You are wrong, therefore, with your universal religion that is natural to all, for no one will have his own true and right religion, if it is the same for all. As long as we occupy a place there must be in these relations of man to the whole a nearer and a farther, which will necessarily determine each feeling differently in each life. Again, as long as we are individuals, every man has greater receptiveness for some religious experiences and feelings than for others. In this way everything is different. Manifestly then, no single relation can accord to every feeling its due. It requires the sum of them. Hence, the whole of religion can be present only, when all those different views of every relation are actually given. This is not possible, except in an endless number of different forms.

From Friedrich Schleiermacher, *On Religion: Speeches to Its Cultured Despisers,* translated by John Oman (London: Kegan Paul, Trench, Trübner & Co., 1893), pages 9, 14–16, 18, 35–36, 87–89, 211, 214, 217–218.

David Friedrich Strauss (1808–1874)

From *The Life of Jesus Critically Examined*

Strauss spent most of this massive work, published in 1835, analyzing the Gospel accounts of the life of Jesus and showing their historical unreliability. At the end of the book, he set out the theological conclusions that he believed survive this critical onslaught. Strauss uses the framework of Hegel's philosophy: Spirit can exist only by becoming concrete; the infinite must appear in the finite. But for Hegel, whether Christ is the *place where that happens or only the great symbol of how it happens everywhere remains ambiguous. Strauss resolves the ambiguity in favor of the radical interpretation. The book created great excitement, as well as enough scandal to guarantee that Strauss would never get a university teaching job.*

The results of the inquiry which we have now brought to a close have apparently annihilated the greatest and most valuable part of that which the Christian has been wont to believe concerning his Saviour Jesus, have uprooted all the animating motives which he has gathered from his faith, and withered all his consolations. The boundless store of truth and life which for eighteen centuries has been the aliment of humanity, seems irretrievably dissipated; the most sublime levelled with the dust, God divested of his grace, man of his dignity, and the tie between heaven and earth broken. Piety turns away with horror from so fearful an act of desecration, and strong in the impregnable evidence of its faith, pronounces that, let an audacious criticism attempt what it will, all which the Scriptures declare, and the Church believes of Christ, will still subsist as eternal truth, nor needs one iota of it to be renounced. Thus as the conclusion of the criticism of the history of Jesus, there presents itself this problem: to re-establish dogmatically that which has been destroyed critically. . . .

When it is said of God that he is a Spirit, and of man that he also is a

Spirit, it follows that the two are not essentially distinct. To speak more particularly, it is the essential property of a spirit, in the distribution of itself into distinct personalities, to remain identical with itself, to possess itself in another than itself. Hence the recognition of God as a spirit implies, that God does not remain as a fixed and immutable Infinite encompassing the Finite, but enters into it, produces the Finite, Nature, and the human mind, merely as a limited manifestation of himself, from which he eternally returns into unity. As man, considered as a finite spirit, limited to his finite nature, has not truth; so God considered exclusively as an infinite spirit, shut up in his infinitude, has not reality. The infinite spirit is real only when it discloses itself in finite spirits; as the finite spirit is true only when it merges itself in the infinite. The true and real existence of spirit, therefore, is neither in God by himself, nor in man by himself, but in the God-man; neither in the infinite alone, nor in the finite alone, but in the interchange of impartation and withdrawal between the two, which on the part of God is revelation, on the part of man religion.

If God and man are in themselves *one,* and if religion is the human side of this unity: then must this unity be made evident to man in religion, and become in him consciousness and reality. Certainly, so long as man knows not that he is a spirit, he cannot know that God is man: while he is under the guidance of nature only, he will deify nature; when he has learned to submit himself to law, and thus to regulate his natural tendencies by external means, he will set God before him as a lawgiver. But when, in the vicissitudes of the world's history, the natural state discloses its corruptions, the legal its misery; the former will experience the need of a God who elevates it above itself, the latter, of a God who descends to its level. Man being once mature enough to receive as his religion the truth that God is man, and man of a divine race; it necessarily follows, since religion is the form in which the truth presents itself to the popular mind, that this truth must appear, in a guise intelligible to all, as a fact obvious to the senses: in other words, there must appear a human individual who is recognized as the visible God. This God-man uniting in a single being the divine essence and the human personality, it may be said of him that he had the Divine Spirit for a father and a woman for his mother. His personality reflecting itself not in himself, but in the absolute substance, having the will to exist only for God, and not at all for itself, he is sinless and perfect. As a man of Divine essence, he is the power that subdues nature, a worker of miracles; but as God in a human manifestation, he is dependent on nature, subject to its necessities and sufferings—is in a state of abasement. Must he even pay the last tribute to nature? does not the fact that the human nature is subject to death preclude the idea that that nature is one with the divine? No: the God-man dies, and thus proves that the incarnation of God is real, that the infinite spirit does not scorn to descend into the lowest depths of the finite, because he knows how to find a way of return into himself. . . . By his entrance into the world as God-man, God showed himself reconciled to man; by his dying, in which act he cast off the limitations of mortality, he showed moreover the way in which he perpetually effects that reconciliation: namely, by remaining, throughout his manifestation of himself under the limitations of a natural existence, and his suppression of that existence, identical with himself. Inasmuch as the death of the God-man is merely the cessation of his state of alienation from the infinite, it is in fact an exaltation and return to God, and thus the death is necessarily followed by the resurrection and ascension. . . .

If reality is ascribed to the idea of the unity of the divine and human natures, is this equivalent to the admission that this unity must actually have been once manifested, as it never had been, and never more will be, in one individual? This is indeed not the mode in which Idea realizes itself; it is not wont to lavish all its fulness on one exemplar, and be niggardly toward all others—to express itself perfectly in that one individual, and imperfectly in all the rest: it rather loves to distribute its riches among a multiplicity of exemplars which reciprocally complete each other—in the alternate appearance and suppression of a series of individuals. And is this no true realization of the idea? is not the idea of the unity of the divine and human natures a real one in a far higher sense, when I regard the whole race of mankind as its realization, than when I single out one man as such a realization? is not an incarnation of God from eternity, a truer one than an incarnation limited to a particular point in time?

This is the key to the whole of Christology, that, as subject of the predicate which the church assigns to Christ, we place, instead of an individual, an idea; but an idea which has an existence in reality, not in the mind only, like that of Kant.* In an individual, a God-man, the properties and functions which the church ascribes to Christ contradict themselves; in the idea of the race, they perfectly agree. Humanity is the union of the two natures—God becomes man, the infinite manifesting itself in the finite, and the finite spirit remembering its infinitude; it is the child of the visible Mother and the invisible

---

*In *Religion Within the Limits of Reason Alone,* Kant speaks of the Son of God as "the personified idea of the good principle."

Father, Nature and Spirit; it is the worker of miracles, in so far as in the course of human history the spirit more and more completely subjugates nature, both within and around man, until it lies before him as the inert matter on which he exercises his active power; it is the sinless existence, for the course of its development is a blameless one, pollution cleaves to the individual only, and does not touch the race or its history. It is Humanity that dies, rises, and ascends to heaven, for from the negation of its phenomenal life there ever proceeds a higher spiritual life; from the suppression of its mortality, as a personal, national, and terrestial spirit, arises its union with the infinite spirit of the heavens. By faith in this Christ, especially in his death and resurrection, man is justified before God; that is, by the kindling within him of the idea of Humanity, the individual man participates in the divinely human life of the species.

From David Friedrich Strauss, *The Life of Jesus Critically Examined,* translated by George Eliot (London: Macmillan & Co., 1892), pages 757, 777–780.

Ludwig Feuerbach (1804–1872)

From *Lectures on the Essence of Religion*

Beginning in the 1830s, Feuerbach developed his radical interpretation of religion. What we really worship, he said, is our ideal of humanity, but religious people mistakenly imagine this to be a God separate from ourselves. Like Strauss, Feuerbach was too radical for academic employment, but in the revolutionary fervor of Germany in 1848 his dream of the triumph of humanity had considerable popularity, and he was invited to present his ideas in this series of public lectures.

I now come to those of my writings which embody my doctrine, religion, philosophy, or whatever you may choose to call it, and provide the subject matter of these lectures. This doctrine of mine is briefly as follows. *Theology is anthropology:* in other words, the object of religion, which in Greek we call *theos* and in our language God, expresses nothing other than the essence of man; man's God is nothing other than the deified essence of man, so that the history of religion or, what amounts to the same thing, of God—for the gods are as varied as the religions, and the religions are as varied as mankind—is nothing other than the history of man.

Let me illustrate and clarify this assertion by an example, which however is more than an example: the Greek, the Roman, or any other pagan god, as even our theologians and philosophers admit, is merely an object of pagan religion, a being who exists only in the faith and imagination of a pagan, but not in those of a Christian people or individual; consequently, he is only an expression, an image, of the pagan spirit and disposition. Similarly, the Christian God is merely an object of the Christian religion and consequently only a characteristic expression of the spirit and disposition of Christian man. The difference between the pagan god and the Christian God is solely a difference between pagan and Christian man, taken both collectively and individually. The pagan is a patriot, the Christian a cosmopolitan; consequently the pagan's god is a patriotic god, while that of the Christian is a cosmopolitan; the pagan, in other words, has a national, limited god, because the pagan did not rise above the limitations of his nationality but placed the nation above man; the Christian has a universal, world-encompassing God because he rises above the limitations of nationality and does not restrict the dignity and essence of man to any particular nation....

My primary concern is and always has been to illumine the obscure essence of religion with the torch of reason, in order that man may at least cease to be the victim, the plaything, of all those hostile powers which from time immemorial have employed and are still employing the darkness of religion for the oppression of mankind. It was my purpose to demonstrate that the powers which man worships and fears in his religious life, which he seeks to propitiate even with bloody human sacrifices, are merely creatures of his own unfree, fearful mind and of his ignorant unformed intelligence; to demonstrate that the being which man, in religion and theology, sets up as a distinct being over against himself, is his own essence. It was my purpose to demonstrate this so that man, who is always unconsciously governed and determined by his own essence alone, may in future consciously take his own, human essence as the law and determining ground, the aim and measure, of his ethical and political life. And this will inevitably come to pass. Whereas hitherto misunderstood religion, religious obscurantism, has been the supreme principle of politics and ethics, from now on, or at some future date, religion properly understood, religion seen in terms of man, will determine the destinies of mankind.

From Ludwig Feuerbach, *Lectures on the Essence of Religion,* translated by Ralph Manheim, pages 17–18, 22–23. Copyright © 1967 by Ralph Manheim. Reprinted by permission of Harper & Row, Publishers, Inc.

Søren Kierkegaard (1813–1855)

From *Attack Upon "Christendom"*

Kierkegaard's multifaceted brilliance, and his practice of writing from a variety of viewpoints under various pseudonyms, make it very difficult to offer a representative short excerpt. This selection offers only one relatively straightforward side of this amazingly complex writer. In 1854 Jakob Mynster, the leader of the Danish Lutheran church, died, and a eulogy at the funeral proclaimed him a hero of the faith and a witness to the truth. Kierkegaard had no particular dislike for Mynster, who was a friend of his family, but he wrote a series of newspaper articles challenging the implied equation of the Danish church of his contemporaries with the heroic age of the apostles.

We are what is called a "Christian" nation—but in such a sense that not a single one of us is in the character of the Christianity of the New Testament, any more than I am, who again and again have repeated, and do now repeat, that I am only a poet. The illusion of a Christian nation is due doubtless to the power which number exercises over the imagination. I have not the least doubt that every single individual in the nation will be honest enough with God and with himself to say in solitary conversation, "If I must be candid, I do not deny that I am not a Christian in the New Testament sense; if I must be honest, I do not deny that my life cannot be called an effort in the direction of what the New Testament calls Christianity, in the direction of denying myself, renouncing the world, dying from it, etc.; rather the earthly and the temporal become more and more important to me with every year I live." I have not the least doubt that everyone will, with respect to ten of his acquaintances, let us say, be able to hold fast to the view that they are not Christians in the New Testament sense, and that their lives are not even an effort in the direction of becoming such. But when there are 100,000, one becomes confused—They tell a ludicrous story about an innkeeper. . . . It is said that he sold his beer by the bottle for a cent less than he paid for it; and when a certain man said to him, "How does that balance the account? That means to spend money," he replied, "No, my friend, it's the big number that does it"—big number, that also in our time is the almighty power. When one has laughed at this story, one would do well to take to heart the lesson which warns against the power which number exercises over the imagination. For there can be no doubt that this innkeeper knew very well that one bottle of beer which he sold for 3 cents meant a loss of 1 cent when it cost him 4 cents. Also with regard to ten bottles the innkeeper will be able to hold fast that it is a loss. But 100,000 bottles! Here the big number stirs the imagination, the round number runs away with it, and the innkeeper becomes dazed—it's a profit, says he, for the big number does it. So also with the calculation which arrives at a Christian nation by adding up units which are not Christian, getting the result by means of the notion that the big number does it. . . .

Christ required "followers" and defined precisely what he meant: that they should be salt, willing to be sacrificed, and that a Christian means to be salt and to be willing to be sacrificed. But to be salt and to be sacrificed is not something to which thousands naturally lend themselves, still less millions, or (still less!) countries, kingdoms, states, and (absolutely not!) the whole world. On the other hand, if it is a question of gain and of mediocrity and of twaddle (which is the opposite of being salt), then the possibility of the thing begins already with the 100,000, increases with every million, reaching its highest point when the whole world has become Christian.

For this reason "man" is interested and employed in winning whole nations of Christians, kingdoms, lands, a whole world of Christians—for thus the thing of being a Christian becomes something different from what it is in the New Testament.

And this end has been attained, has been best attained, indeed completely, in Protestantism, especially in Denmark, in the Danish even-tempered, jovial mediocrity. When one sees what it is to be a Christian in Denmark, how could it occur to anyone that this is what Jesus Christ talks about: cross and agony and suffering, crucifying the flesh, suffering for the doctrine, being salt, being sacrificed, etc.? No, in Protestantism, especially in Denmark, Christianity marches to a different melody, to the tune of "Merrily we roll along, roll along, roll along"—Christianity is enjoyment of life, tranquillized, as neither the Jew nor the pagan was, by the assurance that the thing about eternity is settled, settled precisely in order that we might find pleasure in enjoying this life, as well as any pagan or Jew. . . .

And this in my opinion is the falsification of which official Christianity is guilty: it does not frankly and unreservedly make known the Christian requirement—perhaps because it is afraid people would shudder to see at what a distance from it we are living, without being able to claim that in the remotest way our life might be called an effort in the direction of fulfilling the requirement. . . .

In the magnificent cathedral the Honorable and Right Reverend Geheime-General-Ober-Hof-Prädikant, the elect favorite of the fashionable world, appears before an elect company and preaches *with emotion* upon the text he himself elected: "God hath elected the base things of the world, and the things that are despised"—and nobody laughs.

First Vatican Council

From *First Dogmatic Constitution on the Church of Christ*

The First Vatican Council met in Rome beginning in 1869, at the call of Pope Pius IX. Popes had claimed special authority on matters of doctrine for many centuries, and in 1854 Pius had proclaimed the immaculate conception of Mary—the belief that at conception she had been miraculously freed of the taint of original sin—as a dogma of the church without consulting any council. This document then only made explicit an infallibility the Papacy had already claimed.

The Eternal Pastor and Bishop of our souls, in order to continue for all time the life-giving work of His Redemption, determined to build up the Holy Church, wherein, as in the House of the living God, all who believe might be united in the bond of one faith and one charity. Wherefore, before He entered into His glory, He prayed unto the Father, not for the Apostles only, but for those also who through their preaching should come to believe in Him, that all might be one even as He the Son and the Father are one [John 17:21]. As then He sent the Apostles whom He had chosen to Himself from the world, as He Himself had been sent by the Father: so He willed that there should ever be pastors and teachers in His Church to the end of the world. And in order that the Episcopate also might be one and undivided, and that by means of a closely united priesthood the multitude of the faithful might be kept secure in the oneness of faith and communion, He set Blessed Peter over the rest of the Apostles, and fixed in him the abiding principle of this two-fold unity, and its visible foundation, in the strength of which the everlasting temple should arise and the Church in the firmness of that faith should lift her majestic front to Heaven. . . .

We therefore teach and declare that, according to the testimony of the Gospel, the primacy of jurisdiction over the universal Church of God was immediately and directly promised and given to Blessed Peter the Apostle by Christ the Lord. For it was to Simon alone, to whom He had already said: Thou shalt be called Cephas [John 1:42], that the Lord after the confession made by him, saying: Thou art the Christ, the Son of the living God, addressed these solemn words: Blessed art thou, Simon Bar-Jona, because flesh and blood have not revealed it to thee, but my Father who is in Heaven. And I say to thee that thou art Peter; and upon this rock I will build my Church, and the gates of hell shall not prevail against it. And I will give to thee the keys of the kingdom of Heaven. And whatsoever thou shalt bind upon earth, it shall be bound also in heaven, and whatsoever thou shalt loose on earth, it shall be loosed also in heaven [Matt. 16:16–19]. And it was upon Simon alone that Jesus after His resurrection bestowed the jurisdiction of Chief Pastor and Ruler over all His fold in the words: Feed my lambs: feed my sheep [John 21:15–17]. At open variance with this clear doctrine of Holy Scripture as it has been ever understood by the Catholic Church are the perverse opinions of those who, while they distort the form of government established by Christ the Lord in His Church, deny that Peter in his single person, preferably to all the other Apostles, whether taken separately or together, was endowed by Christ with a true and proper primacy of jurisdiction; or of those who assert that the same primacy was not bestowed immediately and directly upon Blessed Peter himself, but upon the Church, and through the Church on Peter as her Minister. . . .

But since in this very age, in which the salutary efficacy of the Apostolic office is most of all required, not a few are found who take away from its authority, we judge it altogether necessary solemnly to assert the prerogative which the only-begotten Son of God vouchsafed to join with the supreme pastoral office.

Therefore faithfully adhering to the tradition received from the beginning of the Christian faith, for the glory of God Our Saviour, the exaltation of the Catholic Religion, and the salvation of Christian people, the Sacred Council approving, We teach and define that it is a dogma divinely revealed: that the Roman Pontiff, when he speaks *ex cathedra,* that is, when in discharge of the office of Pastor and Doctor of all Christians, by virtue of his supreme Apostolic authority he defines a doctrine regarding faith or morals to be held by the Universal Church, by the divine assistance promised to him in blessed Peter, is possessed of that infallibility with which the divine

Redeemer willed that His Church should be endowed for defining doctrine regarding faith or morals: and that therefore such definitions of the Roman Pontiff are irreformable of themselves, and not from the consent of the Church.

From *Creeds of the Churches,* edited by John H. Leith (Aldine Publishing Co., 1963), pages 448–450, 456–457. Copyright © 1963 by John H. Leith. Used by permission of the editor.

John Henry Newman (1801–1890)

From *Apologia Pro Vita Sua*

Newman published this autobiographical defense of his views in 1864. Of these two excerpts, the first recalls the influence of two of his friends many years earlier when he was still at Oxford and a member of the Church of England. He begins with his older friend and mentor John Keble, author of The Christian Year. *In describing the concerns of Keble and of Richard Hurrell Froude, Newman is recalling the influences that shaped him. The second excerpt reflects on the nature of his beliefs after his conversion to Roman Catholicism in 1845.*

The Christian Year made its appearance in 1827. It is not necessary, and scarcely becoming, to praise a book which has already become one of the classics of the language. When the general tone of religious literature was so nerveless and impotent, as it was at that time, Keble struck an original note and woke up in the hearts of thousands a new music, the music of a school, long unknown in England. Nor can I pretend to analyze, in my own instance, the effect of religious teaching so deep, so pure, so beautiful. I have never till now tried to do so; yet I think I am not wrong in saying, that the two main intellectual truths which it brought home to me, were the same two, which I had learned from Butler,* though recast in the creative mind of my new master. The first of these was what may be called, in a large sense of the word, the Sacramental system; that is, the doctrine that material phenomena are both the types and the instruments of real things unseen,—a doctrine, which embraces in its fulness, not only what Anglicans, as well as Catholics, believe about Sacraments properly so called; but also the article of "the Communion of Saints"; and likewise the Mysteries of the faith. . . .

---

*Joseph Butler (1692–1752), Bishop of Durham and author of *The Analógy of Religion.*

On the second intellectual principle which I gained from Mr. Keble, I could say a great deal; if this were the place for it. It runs through very much that I have written, and has gained for me many hard names. Butler teaches us that probability is the guide of life. The danger of this doctrine, in the case of many minds, is, its tendency to destroy in them absolute certainty, leading them to consider every conclusion as doubtful, and resolving truth into an opinion, which it is safe to obey or to profess, but not possible to embrace with full internal assent. If this were to be allowed, then the celebrated saying, "O God, if there be a God, save my soul, if I have a soul!" would be the highest measure of devotion:—but who can really pray to a Being, about whose existence he is seriously in doubt?

I considered that Mr. Keble met this difficulty by ascribing the firmness of assent which we give to religious doctrine, not to the probabilities which introduced it, but to the living power of faith and love which accepted it. In matters of religion, he seemed to say, it is not merely probability which makes us intellectually certain, but probability as it is put to account by faith and love. It is faith and love which give to probability a force which it has not in itself. Faith and love are directed towards an Object; in the vision of that Object they live; it is that Object, received in faith and love, which renders it reasonable to take probability as sufficient for internal conviction. Thus the argument about Probability, in the matter of religion, became an argument from Personality, which in fact is one form of the argument from Authority. . . .

Hurrell Froude was a pupil of Keble's, formed by him, and in turn reacting upon him. I knew him first in 1826, and was in the closest and most affectionate friendship with him from about 1829 till his death in 1836. . . . His opinions arrested and influenced me, even when they did not gain my assent. He professed openly his admiration of the Church of Rome, and his hatred of the Reformers. He delighted in the notion of an hierarchical system, of sacerdotal power, and of full ecclesiastical liberty. He felt scorn of the maxim, "The Bible and the Bible only is the religion of Protestants"; and he gloried in accepting Tradition as a main instrument of religious teaching. He had a high severe idea of the intrinsic excellence of Virginity; and he considered the Blessed Virgin its great Pattern. He delighted in thinking of the Saints; he had a vivid appreciation of the idea of sanctity, its possibility and its heights; and he was more than inclined to believe a large amount of miraculous interference as occurring in the early and middle ages. He embraced the principle of penance and mortification. He had a deep devotion to the Real

Presence, in which he had a firm faith. He was powerfully drawn to the Medieval Church, but not to the Primitive. . . .

From the time that I became a Catholic, of course I have no further history of my religious opinions to narrate. In saying this, I do not mean to say that my mind has been idle, or that I have given up thinking on theological subjects; but that I have had no changes to record, and have had no anxiety of heart whatever. I have been in perfect peace and contentment; I never have had one doubt. I was not conscious . . . , on my conversion, of any change, intellectual or moral, wrought in my mind. I was not conscious of firmer faith in the fundamental truths of Revelation, or of more self-command; I had not more fervor; but it was like coming into port after a rough sea; and my happiness on that score remains to this day without interruption. . . .

People say that the doctrine of Transubstantiation* is difficult to believe; I did not believe the doctrine till I was a Catholic. I had no difficulty in believing it as soon as I believed that the Catholic Roman Church was the oracle of God, and that she had declared this doctrine to be part of the original revelation. It is difficult, impossible to imagine, I grant—but how is it difficult to believe? . . . I cannot indeed prove it, I cannot tell *how* it is, but I say, "Why should it not be? What's to hinder it? What do I know of substance or matter? just as much as the greatest philosophers, and that is nothing at all"—so much is this the case, that there is a rising school of philosophy now, which considers phenomena to constitute the whole of our knowledge in physics. The Catholic doctrine leaves phenomena alone. It does not say that the phenomena go; on the contrary, it says that they remain: nor does it say that the same phenomena are in several places at once. It deals with what no one on earth knows any thing about, the material substances themselves. And, in like manner, of that majestic Article of the Anglican as well as of the Catholic Creed,— the doctrine of the Trinity in Unity. What do I know of the Essence of the Divine Being? I know that my abstract idea of three is simply incompatible with my idea of one; but when I come to the question of concrete fact, I have no means of proving that there is not a sense in which one and three can equally be predicated of the Incommunicable God. . . .

Starting then with the being of a God, (which, as I have said, is

---

*The Catholic teaching that in the Mass the *accidents* or perceived qualities of the bread and wine remain unchanged but the *substance* becomes the body and blood of Christ.

as certain to me as the certainty of my own existence, though when I try to put the grounds of that certainty into logical shape I find a difficulty in doing so in mood and figure to my satisfaction,) I look out of myself into the world of men, and there I see a sight which fills me with unspeakable distress. The world seems simply to give the lie to that great truth, of which my whole being is so full, and the effect upon me is, in consequence, as a matter of necessity, as confusing as if it denied that I am in existence myself. . . .

What shall be said to this heart-piercing, reason-bewildering fact? I can only answer, that either there is no Creator, or this living society of men is in a true sense discarded from His presence. . . . *If* there be a God, *since* there is a God, the human race is implicated in some terrible aboriginal calamity. It is out of joint with the purposes of its Creator. This is a fact, a fact as true as the fact of its existence; and thus the doctrine of what is theologically called original sin becomes to me almost as certain as that the world exists, and as the existence of God.

And now, supposing it were the blessed and loving will of the Creator to interfere in this anarchical condition of things, what are we to suppose would be the methods which might be necessarily or naturally involved in His purpose of mercy? . . .

The necessity of some form of religion for the interests of humanity, has been generally acknowledged: but where was the concrete representative of things invisible, which would have the force and the toughness necessary to be a breakwater against the deluge? Three centuries ago the establishment of religion, material, legal, and social, was generally adopted as the best expedient for the purpose, in those countries which separated from the Catholic Church; and for a long time it was successful; but now the crevices of those establishments are admitting the enemy. Thirty years ago, education was relied upon: ten years ago there was a hope that wars would cease for ever, under the influence of commercial enterprise and the reign of the useful and fine arts; but will any one venture to say that there is any thing any where on this earth, which will afford a fulcrum for us, whereby to keep the earth from moving onwards?

The judgment, which experience passes whether on establishments or on education, as a means of maintaining religious truth in this anarchical world, must be extended even to Scripture, though Scripture be divine. Experience proves surely that the Bible does not answer a purpose for which it was never intended. It may be accidentally the means of the conversion of individuals; but a book, after all, cannot make a stand against the wild living intellect of man, and in this day it begins to testify, as regards its own structure and contents, to the power of that universal solvent, which is so successfully acting upon religious establishments.

Supposing then it to be the Will of the Creator to interfere in human affairs, and to make provisions for retaining in the world a knowledge of Himself, so definite and distinct as to be proof against the energy of human scepticism, in such a case,—I am far from saying that there was no other way,—but there is nothing to surprise the mind, if He should think fit to introduce a power into the world, invested with the prerogative of infallibility in religious matters. Such a provision would be a direct, immediate, active, and prompt means of withstanding the difficulty; it would be an instrument suited to the need; and, when I find that this is the very claim of the Catholic Church, not only do I feel no difficulty in admitting the idea, but there is a fitness in it, which recommends it to my mind. And thus I am brought to speak of the Church's infallibility, as a provision, adapted by the mercy of the Creator, to preserve religion in the world, and to restrain that freedom of thought, which of course in itself is one of the greatest of our natural gifts, and to rescue it from its own suicidal excesses.

From John Henry Newman, *Apologia Pro Vita Sua* (New York: Longmans, Green & Co., 1890), pages 18–19, 23–24, 238–245.

Adolf Harnack (1851–1930)

From *What Is Christianity?*

Harnack, the greatest historian of dogma of his time, was the most famous of Albrecht Ritschl's students. This book, which appeared in 1900, summarized many of the themes of liberal Ritschlian theology.

If, however, we take a general view of Jesus' teaching, we shall see that it may be grouped under three heads. They are each of such a nature as to contain the whole, and hence it can be exhibited in its entirety under any one of them.

Firstly, the kingdom of God and its coming.

Secondly, God the Father and the infinite value of the human soul.

Thirdly, the higher righteousness and the commandment of love.

That Jesus' message is so great and so powerful lies in the fact that it is so simple and on the other hand so rich; so simple as to be exhausted in each of the leading thoughts which he uttered; so rich that every one of these thoughts seems to be inexhaustible and the full meaning of the sayings and parables beyond our reach. But more than that—he himself stands behind everything that he said. His words speak to us across the centuries with the freshness of the present. It is here that that profound saying is truly verified: "Speak, that I may see thee." . . .

I. The kingdom of God and its coming. Jesus' message of the kingdom of God runs through all the forms and statements of the prophecy which, taking its color from the Old Testament, announces the day of judgment and the visible government of God in the future, up to the idea of an inward coming of the kingdom, starting with Jesus' message and then beginning. . . .

The kingdom has a triple meaning. Firstly, it is something supernatural, a gift from above, not a product of ordinary life. Secondly, it is a purely religious blessing, the inner link with the living God; thirdly, it is the most important experience that a man can have, that on which everything else depends; it permeates and dominates his whole existence, because sin is forgiven and misery banished. . . .

II. God the Father and the infinite value of the human soul. To our modern way of thinking and feeling, Christ's message appears in the clearest and most direct light when grasped in connection with the idea of God the Father and the infinite value of the human soul. Here the elements which I would describe as the restful and restgiving in Jesus' message, and which are comprehended in the idea of our being children of God, find expression. I call them *restful* in contrast with the impulsive and stirring elements; although it is just they that are informed with a special strength. But the fact that the whole of Jesus' message may be reduced to these two heads—God as the Father, and the human soul so ennobled that it can and does unite with him—shows us that the Gospel is in nowise a positive religion like the rest; that it contains no statutory or particularistic elements; *that it is, therefore, religion itself.* . . .

III. The higher righteousness and the commandment of love. This is the third head, and the whole of the Gospel is embraced under it. To represent the Gospel as an ethical message is no depreciation of its value. . . .

Firstly: Jesus severed the connection existing in his day between ethics and the external forms of religious worship and technical observance. He would have absolutely nothing to do with the purposeful and self-seeking pursuit of "good works" in combination with the ritual of worship. He exhibited an indignant contempt for those who allow their neighbors, nay, even their parents, to starve, and on the other hand send gifts to the temple. He will have no compromise in the matter. Love and mercy are ends in themselves; they lose all value and are put to shame by having to be anything else than the service of one's neighbor.

Secondly: in all questions of morality he goes straight to the root, that is, to the disposition and the intention. It is only thus that what he calls the "higher righteousness" can be understood. The "higher righteousness" is the righteousness that will stand when the depths of the heart are probed. Here, again, we have something that is seemingly very simple and self-evident. Yet the truth, as he uttered it, took the severe form: "It was said of old . . . but I say unto you." After all, then, the truth was something new; he was aware that it had never yet been expressed in such a consistent form and with such claims to supremacy. . . .

Thirdly: what he freed from its connection with self-seeking and ritual elements, and recognized as the moral principle, he reduces to *one* root and to *one* motive—love. He knows of no other, and love itself, whether it takes the form of love of one's neighbor or of one's enemy, or the love of the Samaritan, is of one kind only. It must completely fill the soul; it is what remains when the soul dies to itself. In this sense love is the new life already begun. But it is always the love which *serves,* and only in this function does it exist and live.

From Adolf Harnack, *What Is Christianity?,* translated by Thomas Bailey Saunders (New York: G. P. Putnam's Sons, 1901), pages 51–52, 61–63, 70–72.

Albert Schweitzer (1875–1965)

From *The Quest of the Historical Jesus*

In this book, which appeared in 1906, Schweitzer looked back over the many nineteenth-century efforts to recover the truth about the historical Jesus. He found that all the authors had painted Jesus in their own images—liberals found a liberal Jesus, conservative churchmen a conservative churchman, and so on. Schweitzer himself concluded that the expectation of an imminent end of the world had stood at the center of Jesus' teaching. Thus, since Jesus' crucial expectation was simply wrong—here we still are, two thousand years later—there is no way to appropriate Jesus' teaching directly for our time. If this eschatological interpretation of Jesus is wrong, Schweitzer believed, then it is impossible to know what Jesus taught at all—we are reduced to skepticism. In that sense, as he says at the beginning of this reading, the results of the "quest of the historical Jesus" have been negative— the Jesus imagined by nineteenth-century theologians never existed. Yet Schweitzer found in Jesus, even in a heroically mistaken Jesus, the inspiration for his own long career as a medical missionary in Africa.

Those who are fond of talking about negative theology can find their account here. There is nothing more negative than the result of the critical study of the Life of Jesus.

The Jesus of Nazareth who came forward publicly as the Messiah, who preached the ethic of the Kingdom of God, who founded the Kingdom of Heaven upon earth, and died to give His work its final consecration, never had any existence. He is a figure designed by rationalism, endowed with life by liberalism, and clothed by modern theology in an historical garb.

This image has not been destroyed from without, it has fallen to pieces, cleft and disintegrated by the concrete historical problems which came to the surface one after another, and in spite of all the artifice, art, artificiality, and violence which was applied to them, refused to be planed down to fit the design on which the Jesus of the theology of the last hundred and thirty years had been constructed. . . .

Whatever the ultimate solution may be, the historical Jesus of whom the criticism of the future, taking as its starting point the problems which have been recognized and admitted, will draw the portrait, can never render modern theology the services which it claimed from its own half-historical, half-modern, Jesus. He will be a Jesus, who was Messiah, and lived as such, either on the ground of a literary fiction of the earliest Evangelist, or on the ground of a purely eschatological Messianic conception.

In either case, He will not be a Jesus Christ to whom the religion of the present can ascribe, according to its long-cherished custom, its own thoughts and ideas, as it did with the Jesus of its own making. Nor will He be a figure which can be made by a popular historical treatment so sympathetic and universally intelligible to the multitude. The historical Jesus will be to our time a stranger and an enigma. . . .

Jesus means something to our world because a mighty spiritual force streams forth from Him and flows through our time also. This fact can neither be shaken nor confirmed by any historical discovery. It is the solid foundation of Christianity. . . .

It is a good thing that the true historical Jesus should overthrow the modern Jesus, should rise up against the modern spirit and send upon earth, not peace, but a sword. He was not teacher, not a casuist; He was an imperious ruler. It was because He was so in His inmost being that He could think of Himself as the Son of Man. That was only the temporally conditioned expression of the fact that He was an authoritative ruler. The names in which men expressed their recognition of Him as such, Messiah, Son of Man, Son of God, have become for us historical parables. We can find no designation which expresses what He is for us.

He comes to us as One unknown, without a name, as of old, by the lake-side, He came to those men who knew Him not. He speaks to us the same word: "Follow thou me!" and sets us to the tasks which He has to fulfil for our time. He commands. And to those who obey Him, whether they be wise or simple, He will reveal Himself in the toils, the conflicts, the sufferings which they shall pass through in His fellowship, and, as an ineffable mystery, they shall learn in their own experience Who He is.

From Albert Schweitzer, *The Quest of the Historical Jesus,* translated by W. Montgomery (London: Adam & Charles Black, 1910), pages 398–399, 403.

Ernst Troeltsch (1865–1923)

From *The Place of Christianity Among the World Religions*

Troeltsch was the leading theologian of the "history of religions" school. In earlier works he had sought to reconcile his historical study of religions with claims for an essential core shared by all forms of Christianity and for the absolute validity of Christianity. In this lecture, intended for delivery at Oxford in 1923, he criticized his own earlier approach. Troeltsch died before the lecture could be delivered.

The further investigations, especially into the history of Christianity, of which I have given the results in my *Social Teachings (Die Soziallehren der christlichen Kirchen und Gruppen,* 1912), have shown me how thoroughly individual is historical Christianity after all, and how invariably its various phases and denominations have been due to varying circumstances and conditions of life. Whether you regard it as a whole or in its several forms, it is a purely historical, individual, relative phenomenon, which could, as we actually find it, only have arisen in the territory of the classical culture, and among the Latin and Germanic races. The Christianity of the Oriental peoples—the Jacobites, Nestorians, Armenians, Abyssinians—is of quite a different type, indeed even that of the Russians is a world of its own. The inference from all that is, however, that a religion, in the several forms assumed by it, always depends upon the intellectual, social, and national conditions among which it exists. On the other hand, a study of the non-Christian religions convinced me more and more that their naïve claims to absolute validity are also genuinely such. I found Buddhism and Brahminism especially to be really humane and spiritual religions, capable of appealing in precisely the same way to the inner certitude and devotion of their followers as Christianity, though the particular character of each has been determined by the historical, geographical, and social conditions of the countries in which it has taken shape. . . .

Indeed, even the validity of science and logic seemed to exhibit, under different skies and upon different soil, strong individual differences present even in their deepest and innermost rudiments. What was really common to mankind, and universally valid for it, seemed, in spite of a general kinship and capacity for mutual understanding, to be at bottom exceedingly little, and to belong more to the province of material goods than to the ideal values of civilization.

The effect of these discoveries upon the conclusions reached in my earlier book was as follows:

The individual character of European civilization, and of the Christian religion which is intimately connected with it, receives now much greater emphasis, whilst the somewhat rationalistic concept of validity, and specifically of *supreme validity,* falls considerably into the background. It is impossible to deny facts or to resist the decrees of fate. And it is historical facts that have welded Christianity into the closest connection with the civilizations of Greece, Rome and Northern Europe. All our thoughts and feelings are impregnated with Christian motives and Christian presuppositions; and, conversely, our whole Christianity is indissolubly bound up with elements of the ancient and modern civilizations of Europe. From being a Jewish sect Christianity has become the religion of all Europe. It stands or falls with European civilization; whilst, on its own part, it has entirely lost its Oriental character and has become hellenized and westernized. Our European conceptions of personality and its eternal, divine right, and of progress towards a kingdom of the spirit and

of God, our enormous capacity for expansion and for the intercon-
nection of spiritual and temporal, our whole social order, our science, our art—all these rest, whether we know it or not, whether we
like it or not, upon the basis of this deorientalized Christianity.

Its primary claim to validity is thus the fact that only through it
have we become what we are, and that only in it can we preserve
the religious forces that we need. Apart from it we lapse either into
a self-destructive titanic attitude, or into effeminate trifling, or into
crude brutality. And at the same time our life is a consistent compromise as little unsatisfactory as we can manage between its lofty
spirituality and our practical everyday needs—a compromise that
has to be renewed at every fresh ascent and every bend of the road.
This tension is characteristic of our form of human life and rouses
us to many a heroic endeavor, though it may also lead us into the
most terrible mendacity and crime. Thus we are, and thus we shall
remain, as long as we survive. We cannot live without a religion,
yet the only religion that we can endure is Christianity, for Christianity has grown up with us and has become a part of our very
being. . . .

But this does not preclude the possibility that other racial groups,
living under entirely different cultural conditions, may experience
their contact with the Divine Life in quite a different way, and may
themselves also possess a religion which has grown up with them,
and from which they cannot sever themselves so long as they remain
what they are. And they may quite sincerely regard this as absolutely
valid for them, and give expression to this absolute validity according
to the demands of their own religious feeling. . . . If we wish to
determine their relative value, it is not the religions alone that we
must compare, but always only the civilizations of which the religion
in each case constitutes a part incapable of severance from the rest.
But who will presume to make a really final pronouncement here?
Only God Himself, who has determined these differences, can do
that.

From Ernest Troeltsch, *Christian Thought: Its History and Application* (London:
Hodder & Stoughton, 1923), pages 22–27.

CHAPTER 7

The Twentieth Century

Distance provides a measure of perspective. It seems easier to sort out the trends and trivialities of the history of theology when dealing with the distant past than when one turns to our own century. But some themes emerge clearly enough. In the nineteenth century—or the thirteenth—Christians could write plausibly about a progressing Western culture inspired by a kind of Christian vision. Somewhere in the trenches of World War I or the death camps of Auschwitz that kind of optimism about Christianity and Western culture lost its plausibility.

The Swiss theologian Karl Barth attacked it most forcefully. In the aftermath of World War I he shouted a resounding "No!" to all efforts to connect the revelation of God in Jesus Christ to the best of Western culture or human religiousness. In Germany in the 1930s the Nazis tried to organize the Protestant churches as a department of the propaganda ministry, and Barth's rejection of connections with any kind of natural theology that might emerge from one's culture became, in his words, "a summons, a challenge, a battle-cry, a confession." Barth provided much of the theological foundation for the Confessing Church, which opposed the Nazi efforts, but not all Christians opposed to Nazism agreed with his approach. For example, Dietrich Bonhoeffer, a German theologian a generation younger than Barth, participated in a plot to kill Hitler and was himself killed by the Nazis just before the end of the war. He shared Barth's suspicion of "religion," but he felt Barth's uncompromising appeal to the authority of scripture was too simple an answer for the modern age.

Theologians such as Reinhold Niebuhr introduced ideas like Barth's to the United States. Niebuhr particularly emphasized that the fact of human sin means that no human cause or party can ever be unambiguously identified with the work of God. Particularly in the United States, opposition to such "neo-orthodox" theology came not only from liberals in the tradition of Schleiermacher but also from a more conservative tradition that placed a central emphasis on the inspiration and authority of the Bible.

In his critique of cultural Christianity, Barth regarded all theological connections with philosophy with suspicion, but in this century even theologians who have made such connections have turned most often to existentialism, a philosophical school without much optimism about the progress of culture. The great scholar Rudolf Bultmann reinterpreted the gospel in existentialist terms, and writers like Paul Tillich used such categories to make connections between Christianity and culture.

Some trends in recent Roman Catholic theology have also taken a more open attitude toward contemporary culture. In 1870 the First Vatican Council had in many ways urged Catholics to barricade themselves off from the modern world. In the 1960s the Second Vatican Council opened the church in all kinds of ways and emphasized the common concerns of church and world. Catholic theologians like Karl Rahner attended the council as experts and then used the freedom it had created to explore new theological possibilities.

One theme that emerges increasingly from the theology of this century is the suffering of God. Whether in the metaphysical analyses of Alfred North Whitehead and the "process theologians" influenced by him, or in the Christology of such theologians as Jürgen Moltmann, or in the practical concerns of Christians fighting for social causes, Christians have found it hard to believe in a God characterized above all by power and impassibility. But a God of compassion, Christ suffering on the cross, still speaks to a century full of tragedy.

Karl Barth (1886–1968)

From *Church Dogmatics*

Barth first made his reputation as a young Swiss pastor with a commentary on Paul's letter to the Romans, first published in 1918 and completely revised in 1921. In the early 1930s he began his Church Dogmatics, *left incomplete at his death thirteen volumes later. The richness of the world Barth creates makes him unusually hard to excerpt, but this early section from the* Church Dogmatics *captures the passion of his radical attack on "religion."*

We begin by stating that religion is unbelief. It is a concern, indeed, we must say that it is the one great concern, of godless man. . . .

In the light of what we have already said, this proposition is not in any sense a negative value judgment. It is not a judgment of religious science or philosophy based upon some prior negative judgment concerned with the nature of religion. It does not affect only other men with their religion. Above all it affects ourselves also as adherents of the Christian religion. It formulates the judgment of divine revelation upon all religion. It can be explained and expounded, but it cannot be derived from any higher principle than revelation, nor can it be proved by any phenomenology or history of religion. Since it aims only to repeat the judgment of God, it does not involve any human renunciation of human values, any contesting of the true and the good and the beautiful which a closer inspection will reveal in almost all religions, and which we naturally expect to find in abundant measure in our own religion, if we hold to it with any conviction. What happens is simply that man is taken by God and judged and condemned by God. That means, of course, that we are struck to the very roots, to the heart. Our whole existence is called in question. But where that is the case there can be no place for sad and pitiful laments at the non-recognition of relative human greatness. . . .

To realize that religion is really unbelief, we have to consider it from the standpoint of the revelation attested in Holy Scripture. There are two elements in that revelation which make it unmistakably clear.

1. Revelation is God's self-offering and self-manifestation. Revelation encounters man on the presupposition and in confirmation of the fact that man's attempts to know God from his own standpoint are wholly and entirely futile; not because of any necessity in principle, but because of a practical necessity of fact. In revelation God tells man that He is God, and that as such He is his Lord. In telling him this, revelation tells him something utterly new, something which apart from revelation he does not know and cannot tell either himself or others. . . .

If man tries to grasp at truth of himself, he tries to grasp at it *a priori.* But in that case he does not do what he has to do when the truth comes to him. He does not believe. If he did, he would listen; but in religion he talks. If he did, he would accept a gift; but in religion he takes something for himself. If he did, he would let God Himself intercede for God: but in religion he ventures to grasp at God. Because it is a grasping, religion is the contradiction of revelation, the concentrated expression of human unbelief, i.e., an attitude and activity which is directly opposed to faith. . . .

2. As the self-offering and self-manifestation of God, revelation is the act by which in grace He reconciles man to Himself by grace. As a radical teaching about God, it is also the radical assistance of God which comes to us as those who are unrighteous and unholy, and as

such damned and lost. In this respect, too, the affirmation which revelation makes and presupposes of man is that he is unable to help himself either in whole or even in part. . . . The revelation of God in Jesus Christ maintains that our justification and sanctification, our conversion and salvation, have been brought about and achieved once and for all in Jesus Christ.

From Karl Barth, *Church Dogmatics,* Volume 1, Part 2, translated by G. T. Thomson and Harold Knight (Edinburgh: T. & T. Clark, 1956), pages 299–303, 307–308. Used by permission of the publisher.

In the 1920s Barth had moved to become a theological professor in Germany and so found himself in the midst of the church conflict when the Nazis came to power. The so-called "German Christians" cooperated with the Nazis; the "Confessing Church" opposed them and stated the basis of its opposition in the Barmen Declaration of 1934. Barth was the principal author of Barmen and soon had to flee to Switzerland. In this section from the Church Dogmatics, *published in 1948, he looks back on the significance of Barmen in the context of his own interpretation of the history of modern theology.*

The *Theological Declaration* of the Synod of Barmen . . . is important and apposite because it represents the first confessional document in which the Evangelical Church has tackled the problem of natural theology. . . . The question became a burning one at the moment when the Evangelical Church in Germany was unambiguously and consistently confronted by a definite and new form of natural theology, namely, by the demand to recognize in the political events of the year 1933, and especially in the form of the God-sent Adolf Hitler, a source of specific new revelation of God, which, demanding obedience and trust, took its place beside the revelation attested in Holy Scripture, claiming that it should be acknowledged by Christian proclamation and theology as equally binding and obligatory. When this demand was made, and a certain audience was given to it, there began, as is well known, the so-called German Church conflict. It has since become clear that behind this first demand stood quite another. According to the dynamic of the political movement, what was already intended, although only obscurely outlined, in 1933 was the proclamation of this new revelation as the only revelation, and therefore the transformation of the Christian Church into the temple of the German nature- and history-myth.

The same had already been the case in the developments of the preceding centuries. There can be no doubt that not merely a part but the whole had been intended and claimed when it had been demanded that side by side with its attestation in Jesus Christ and therefore in Holy Scripture the Church should also recognize and proclaim God's revelation in reason, in conscience, in the emotions, in history, in nature, and in culture and its achievements and developments. The history of the proclamation and theology of these centuries is simply a history of the wearisome conflict of the Church with the fact that the "also" demanded and to some extent acknowledged by it really meant an "only." . . . The logic of the matter demands that, even if we only lend our little finger to natural theology, there necessarily follows the denial of the revelation of God in Jesus Christ. A natural theology which does not strive to be the only master is not a natural theology. . . . But the naivete reigned at every point. . . . Happy little hyphens were used between, say, the words "modern" and "positive," or "religious" and "social," or "German" and "Evangelical," as if the meaning then became self-evident. The fact was overlooked that all this pointed to the presence of a trojan horse within which the superior enemy was already drawn into the city. . . .

This was how matters stood when the Church was confronted with the myth of the new totalitarian state of 1933—a myth at first lightly masked, but unmasked soon enough. . . . Once again, as so often for two hundred years—or so it seemed—the representative of a new trend and movement of the human spirit knocked at the door of the Church. Its petition was very understandable in the light of every precedent. It asked simply that its ideas and ideals should be allowed into the Church like those of all earlier times and phases. . . . Exactly the same thing had happened at the beginning of the 18th century with the reviving humanism of the Stoa; or a century later with Idealism; or, in its train, with Romanticism; and then with the positivism of the bourgeois society and scholarship of the 19th century; and the nationalism of the same period; and a little later socialism: they had all wanted to have their say in the Church. And in the face of these clear precedents there could be no basic reason for silencing this new nationalism of race. . . . If it was admissible and right and perhaps even orthodox to combine the knowability of God in Jesus Christ with His knowability in nature, reason and history, the proclamation of the Gospel with all kinds of other proclamations—and this had been the case, not only in Germany but in the Church in all lands for a long time—it is hard to see why the German Church should not be allowed to make its own particular use of the procedure. And the fact that it did so with customary German thoroughness is not really a ground of reproach. . . .

It was, therefore, an astonishing fact—and this is the significance of the first article of the Barmen *Declaration*—that within Germany there arose an opposition to the new combination which was aimed not only at this particular combination, but basically at the long-accustomed process of combination, at the "and" which had become orthodox in Germany and in the whole world, at the little hyphen as such and therefore at no more and no less than the condominion of natural theology in the Church. For when in Barmen Jesus Christ as attested to us in Holy Scripture was designated as the one Word of God whom we have to trust and to obey in life and in death; when the doctrine of a course of Church proclamation different from this one Word of God was repudiated as false doctrine; and when, in the concluding article of the whole *Declaration,* the acknowledgment of this truth and the repudiation of this error were declared to be the indispensable theological foundation of the German Evangelical Church—an assertion was made (far above the heads of the poor "German Christians" and far beyond the whole momentary position of the Church in Germany) which, if it was taken seriously, contained in itself a purifying of the Church not only from the concretely new point at issue, but from all natural theology.

From Karl Barth, *Church Dogmatics,* Volume 2, Part 1, translated by T. H. L. Parker, W. B. Johnston, Harold Knight, and J. L. M. Haire (Edinburgh: T. & T. Clark, 1957), pages 172–175. Used by permission of the publisher.

From *The Barmen Declaration*

This declaration came from a joint synod of the Reformed and Lutheran churches of Germany, gathered the year after the Nazis took power. Barth did most of the writing.

1. "I am the way and the truth and the life: no man cometh unto the Father, but by me" [John 14:6].

"Verily, verily, I say unto you. He that entereth not by the door into the sheepfold, but climbeth up some other way, the same is a thief and a robber. . . . I am the door: by me if any man enter in, he shall be saved" [John 10:1, 9].

Jesus Christ, as he is testified to us in the Holy Scripture, is the one Word of God, whom we are to hear, whom we are to trust and obey in life and in death.

We repudiate the false teaching that the church can and must recognize yet other happenings and powers, images and truths as divine revelation alongside this one Word of God, as a source of her preaching.

2. "But of him are ye in Christ Jesus, who of God is made unto us wisdom, and righteousness, and sanctification, and redemption" [1 Cor. 1:30].

Just as Jesus Christ is the pledge of the forgiveness of all our sins, just so—and with the same earnestness—is he also God's mighty claim on our whole life; in him we encounter a joyous liberation from the godless claims of this world to free and thankful service to his creatures.

We repudiate the false teaching that there are areas of our life in which we belong not to Jesus Christ but another lord, areas in which we do not need justification and sanctification through him.

3. "But speaking the truth in love, may grow up into him in all things, which is the head, even Christ: from whom the whole body [is] fitly joined together and compacted . . ." [Eph. 4:15–16].

The Christian church is the community of brethren, in which Jesus Christ presently works in the word and sacraments through the Holy Spirit. With her faith as well as her obedience, with her message as well as her ordinances, she has to witness in the midst of the world of sin as the church of forgiven sinners that she is his alone, that she lives and wishes to live only by his comfort and his counsel in expectation of his appearance.

We repudiate the false teaching that the church can turn over the form of her message and ordinances at will or according to some dominant ideological and political convictions.

From *The Barmen Declaration,* translated by Franklin Hamlin Littell, in *The German Phoenix* (Garden City, N.Y.: Doubleday & Co., 1960), pages 186–187. Copyright © 1960 by Franklin Hamlin Littell. Used by permission of the translator.

Dietrich Bonhoeffer (1906–1945)

From *Letters and Papers from Prison*

Bonhoeffer, the son of a Berlin psychiatrist, became a leader of the Confessing Church and was arrested for his part in a plot to kill Hitler. He had written a number of important earlier works, but in his letters from prison to his friend Eberhard Bethge he was searching for a new theological position. Fragmentary and cryptic, the letters have never-

theless been deeply influential. His jailers killed Bonhoeffer just before the end of the war.

30 April 1944

... What is bothering me incessantly is the question what Christianity really is, or indeed who Christ really is, for us today. The time when people could be told everything by means of words, whether theological or pious, is over, and so is the time of inwardness and conscience—and that means the time of religion in general. We are moving towards a completely religionless time; people as they are now simply cannot be religious any more. Even those who honestly describe themselves as "religious" do not in the least act up to it, and so they presumably mean something quite different by "religious."

Our whole nineteen-hundred-year-old Christian preaching and theology rest on the "religious *a priori*" of mankind. "Christianity" has always been a form—perhaps the true form—of "religion." But if one day it becomes clear that this *a priori* does not exist at all, but was a historically conditioned and transient form of human self-expression, and if therefore man becomes radically religionless—and I think that that is already more or less the case (how else is it, for example, that this war, in contrast to all previous ones, is not calling forth any "religious" reaction?)—what does that mean for "Christianity"? ...

How can Christ become the Lord of the religionless as well? Are there religionless Christians? If religion is only a garment of Christianity—and even this garment has looked very different at different times—then what is a religionless Christianity?

Barth, who is the only one to have started along this line of thought, did not carry it to completion, but arrived at a positivism of revelation, which in the last analysis is essentially a restoration. For the religionless working man (or any other man) nothing decisive is gained here. The questions to be answered would surely be: What do a church, a community, a sermon, a liturgy, a Christian life mean in a religionless world? How do we speak of God—without religion, i.e., without the temporally conditioned presuppositions of metaphysics, inwardness, and so on? How do we speak (or perhaps we cannot now even "speak" as we used to) in a "secular" way about "God"? ...

Religious people speak of God when human knowledge (perhaps simply because they are too lazy to think) has come to an end, or when human resources fail. . . . I've come to be doubtful of talking about any human boundaries (is even death, which people now hardly fear, and is sin, which they now hardly understand, still a genuine boundary today?). It always seems to me that we are trying anxiously in this way to reserve some space for God; I should like to speak of God not only on the boundaries but at the center, not in weaknesses but in strength; and therefore not in death and guilt but in man's life and goodness. As to the boundaries, it seems to me better to be silent and leave the insoluble unsolved. Belief in the resurrection is *not* the "solution" of the problem of death. God's "beyond" is not the beyond of our cognitive faculties. The transcendence of epistemological theory has nothing to do with the transcendence of God. God is beyond in the midst of our life. The church stands, not at the boundaries where human powers give out, but in the middle of the village. That is how it is in the Old Testament, and in this sense we still read the New Testament far too little in the light of the Old. How this religionless Christianity looks, what form it takes, is something that I am thinking about a great deal. . . .

May 1944

. . . Our church, which has been fighting in these years only for its self-preservation, as though that were an end in itself, is incapable of taking the word of reconciliation and redemption to mankind and the world. Our earlier words are therefore bound to lose their force and cease, and our being Christians today will be limited to two things: prayer and righteous action among men. All Christian thinking, speaking, and organizing must be born anew out of this prayer and action. . . . It is not for us to prophesy the day (though the day will come) when men will once more be called so to utter the word of God that the world will be changed and renewed by it. It will be a new language, perhaps quite non-religious, but liberating and redeeming—as was Jesus' language; it will shock people and yet overcome them by its power; it will be the language of a new righteousness and truth. . . . Till then the Christian cause will be a silent and hidden affair, but there will be those who pray and do right and wait for God's own time.

Translated by Reginald Fuller and others. From Dietrich Bonhoeffer, *Letters and Papers from Prison,* edited by Eberhard Bethge (London: SCM Press/New York: The Macmillan Company, 1971), pages 279–282, 300. Copyright © 1967, 1971 by SCM Press. Reprinted with permission of Macmillan Publishing Company and SCM Press.

Charles Hodge (1797–1878)

From *Systematic Theology*

Hodge may seem out of place here. He does not fit chronologically— or, his critics would argue, in other ways—in the twentieth century. He seems to live in a radically different world from that of Bonhoeffer. But in the United States biblical conservatism remains an important theological force, and its principles have never again been articulated as well as Hodge presented them. In his long career as a teacher at Princeton Theological Seminary he influenced generations of students and helped make the "Princeton School" the center of intellectually sophisticated conservative theology.

The infallibility and divine authority of the Scriptures are due to the fact that they are the word of God; and they are the word of God because they were given by the inspiration of the Holy Ghost. . . .

On this subject the common doctrine of the Church is, and ever has been, that inspiration was an influence of the Holy Spirit on the minds of certain select men, which rendered them the organs of God for the infallible communication of his mind and will. They were in such a sense the organs of God, that what they said God said. . . .

It is to be remembered, however, that when God uses any of his creatures as his instruments, He uses them according to their nature. He uses angels as angels, men as men, the elements as elements. Men are intelligent voluntary agents; and as such were made the organs of God. The sacred writers were not made unconscious or irrational. The spirits of the prophets were subject to the prophets [1 Cor. 14:32]. They were not like calculating machines which grind out logarithms with infallible correctness. The ancients, indeed, were accustomed to say, as some theologians have also said, that the sacred writers were as pens in the hand of the Spirit; or as harps, from which He drew what sounds He pleased. These representations were, however, intended simply to illustrate one point, namely, that the words uttered or recorded by inspired men were the words of God. The Church has never held what has been stigmatized as the mechanical theory of inspiration. . . . It was men, not machines; not unconscious instruments, but living, thinking, willing minds, whom the Spirit used as his organs. Moreover, as inspiration did not involve the suspension or suppression of the human faculties, so neither did it interfere with the free exercise of the distinctive mental characteristics of the individual. If a Hebrew was inspired, he spake Hebrew; if a Greek, he spake Greek; if an educated man, he spoke as a man of culture; if uneducated, he spoke as such a man is wont to speak. If his mind was logical, he reasoned, as Paul did; if emotional and contemplative, he wrote as John wrote. All this is involved in the fact that God uses his instruments according to their nature. The sacred writers impressed their peculiarities on their several productions as plainly as though they were the subjects of no extraordinary influence. This is one of the phenomena of the Bible patent to the most cursory reader. . . . Nevertheless, and none the less, they spoke as they were moved by the Holy Ghost, and their words were his words. . . .

The view presented above is known as the doctrine of plenary inspiration. Plenary is opposed to partial. The Church doctrine denies that inspiration is confined to parts of the Bible; and affirms that it applies to all the books of the sacred canon. It denies that the sacred writers were merely partially inspired; it asserts that they were fully inspired as to all that they teach, whether of doctrine or fact. This of course does not imply that the sacred writers were infallible except for the special purpose for which they were employed. They were not imbued with plenary knowledge. As to all matters of science, philosophy, and history, they stood on the same level with their contemporaries. They were infallible only as teachers, and when acting as the spokesmen of God. Their inspiration no more made them astronomers than it made them agriculturists. Isaiah was infallible in his predictions, although he shared with his countrymen the views then prevalent as to the mechanism of the universe. Paul could not err in anything he taught, although he could not recollect how many persons he had baptized in Corinth. . . .

The second great objection to the plenary inspiration of the Scripture is that it teaches what is inconsistent with historical and scientific truth.

Here again it is to be remarked, (1) That we must distinguish between what the sacred writers themselves thought or believed, and what they teach. They may have believed that the sun moves round the earth, but they do not so teach. (2) The language of the Bible is the language of common life; and the language of common life is founded on apparent, and not upon scientific truth. It would be ridiculous to refuse to speak of the sun rising and setting, because we know that it is not a satellite of our planet. (3) There is a great distinction between theories and facts. Theories are of men. Facts are of God. The Bible often contradicts the former, never the latter. (4) There is also a distinction to be made between the Bible and our interpretation. The latter may come into competition with settled facts; and then it must yield. Science has in many things taught the Church how to understand the Scriptures. The Bible was for ages understood and explained according to the Ptolemaic system of the universe; it is now explained without doing the least violence to its language, according to the Copernican system. Christians have commonly believed that the earth has existed only a few thousands of years. If geologists finally prove that it has existed for myriads of ages, it will be found that the first chapter of Genesis is in full accord with the facts, and that the last results of science are embodied on the first page of the Bible. It may cost the Church a severe struggle to give up one interpretation and adopt another, as it did in the seventeenth century, but no real evil need be apprehended. The Bible has stood, and still stands in the presence of the whole scientific world with its claims unshaken.

From Charles Hodge, *Systematic Theology,* Volume 1 (New York: Charles Scribner's Sons, 1901), pages 153–154, 156–157, 165, 170–171.

Reinhold Niebuhr (1892–1971)

From *Christianity and Power Politics*

Born in Missouri, Niebuhr began his career as a pastor in a poor Detroit neighborhood, involved with socialism and labor organizing, and then went on to many years of teaching at Union Seminary in New York. In the 1940s and 1950s his was an important voice on behalf of progressive politics that were yet strongly critical of Marxism, and his "realistic" attitude to the world of power politics deeply influenced political thinkers as well as theologians. He wrote this essay in 1940, as the United States was about to enter World War II.

There may be an advantage in stating the thesis, with which we enter this debate, immediately. The thesis is, that the failure of the Church to espouse pacifism is not apostasy, but is derived from an understanding of the Christian gospel which refuses simply to equate the gospel with the "law of love." Christianity is not simply a new law, namely, the law of love. The finality of Christianity cannot be proved by analyses which seek to reveal that the law of love is stated more unambiguously and perfectly in the life and teachings of Christ than anywhere else. Christianity is a religion which measures the total dimension of human existence not only in terms of the final norm of human conduct, which is expressed in the law of love, but also in terms of the fact of sin. It recognizes that the same man who can become his true self only by striving infinitely for self-realization beyond himself is also inevitably involved in the sin of infinitely making his partial and narrow self the true end of existence. It believes, in other words, that though Christ is the true norm (the "second Adam") for every man, every man is also in some sense a crucifier of Christ.

The good news of the gospel is not the law that we ought to love one another. The good news of the gospel is that there is a resource of divine mercy which is able to overcome a contradiction within our own souls, which we cannot ourselves overcome. This contradiction is that, though we know we ought to love our neighbor as ourself, there is a "law in our members which wars against the law that is in our mind," so that, in fact, we love ourselves more than our neighbor. . . .

In this doctrine of forgiveness and justification, Christianity measures the full seriousness of sin as a permanent factor in human history. Naturally the doctrine has no meaning for modern secular civilization, nor for the secularized and moralistic versions of Christianity. They cannot understand the doctrine precisely because they believe there is some fairly simple way out of the sinfulness of human history. . . .

In one of its aspects modern Christian pacifism is simply a version of Christian perfectionism. It expresses a genuine impulse in the heart of Christianity, the impulse to take the law of Christ seriously and not to allow the political strategies, which the sinful character of man makes necessary, to become final norms. . . .

In medieval ascetic perfectionism and in Protestant sectarian perfectionism (of the type of Menno Simons,* for instance) the effort to achieve a standard of perfect love in individual life was not presented as a political alternative. On the contrary, the political problem and task were specifically disavowed. This perfectionism did not give itself to the illusion that it had discovered a method for eliminating the element of conflict from political strategies. On the contrary, it regarded the mystery of evil as beyond its power of solution. It was content to set up the most perfect and unselfish individual life as a

---

*The late-sixteenth-century pacifist leader of the Anabaptists, after whom the Mennonites are named (see Chapter 1).

symbol of the Kingdom of God. It knew that this could only be done by disavowing the political task and by freeing the individual of all responsibility for social justice.

It is this kind of pacifism which is not a heresy. It is rather a valuable asset for the Christian faith. It is a reminder to the Christian community that the relative norms of social justice, which justify both coercion and resistance to coercion, are not final norms, and that Christians are in constant peril of forgetting their relative and tentative character and of making them too completely normative.

There is thus a Christian pacifism which is not a heresy. Yet most modern forms of Christian pacifism are heretical. Presumably inspired by the Christian gospel, they have really absorbed the Renaissance faith in the goodness of man, have rejected the Christian doctrine of original sin as an outmoded bit of pessimism, have reinterpreted the Cross so that it is made to stand for the absurd idea that perfect love is guaranteed a simple victory over the world, and have rejected all other profound elements of the Christian gospel as "Pauline" accretions which must be stripped from the "simple gospel of Jesus." This form of pacifism is not only heretical when judged by the standards of the total gospel. It is equally heretical when judged by the facts of human existence. There are no historical realities which remotely conform to it. . . .

Such a belief has no more justification in the facts of experience than the communist belief that the sole cause of man's sin is the class organization of society and the corollary faith that a "classless" society will be essentially free of human sinfulness. All of these beliefs are pathetic alternatives to the Christian faith. They all come finally to the same thing. They do not believe that man remains a tragic creature who needs the divine mercy as much at the end as at the beginning of his moral endeavors. They believe rather that there is some fairly easy way out of the human situation of "self-alienation."

From Reinhold Niebuhr, *Christianity and Power Politics,* copyright, 1940, by Charles Scribner's Sons, pages 1–7. Used by permission of Ursula Niebuhr. (This material has recently been reprinted in *The Essential Reinhold Niebuhr,* edited by Robert McAfee Brown and published by Yale University Press.)

Rudolf Bultmann (1884–1976)

From *New Testament and Mythology*

Bultmann, a German Lutheran, was not only a theologian but the greatest New Testament scholar of his generation. The philosopher

Martin Heidegger deeply influenced his theology. Heidegger contrasted "inauthentic existence," in which we accept the roles and rules other people set for us, with "authentic existence," in which we accept responsibility for the shape of our own lives. Bultmann concluded that only faith in God's love disclosed in Christ makes authentic existence possible. This essay, written in 1941, played a central role in shaping German theology after World War II.

The cosmology of the New Testament is essentially mythical in character. The world is viewed as a three-storied structure, with the earth in the center, the heaven above, and the underworld beneath. Heaven is the abode of God and of celestial beings—the angels. The underworld is hell, the place of torment. Even the earth is more than the scene of natural, everyday events, of the trivial round and the common task. It is the scene of the supernatural activity of God and his angels on the one hand, and of Satan and his daemons on the other. These supernatural forces intervene in the course of nature and in all that men think and will and do. Miracles are by no means rare. Man is not in control of his own life. Evil spirits may take possession of him. Satan may inspire him with evil thoughts. Alternatively, God may inspire his thought and guide his purposes. . . .

All this is the language of mythology, and the origin of the various themes can be easily traced in the contemporary mythology of Jewish Apocalyptic and in the redemption myths of Gnosticism. To this extent *the kerygma* is incredible to modern man, for he is convinced that the mythical view of the world is obsolete.* We are therefore bound to ask whether, when we preach the Gospel today, we expect our converts to accept not only the Gospel message, but also the mythical view of the world in which it is set. If not, does the New Testament embody a truth which is quite independent of its mythical setting? If it does, theology must undertake the task of stripping the Kerygma from its mythical framework, of "demythologizing" it.

Can Christian preaching expect modern man *to accept the mythical view of the world as true?* To do so would be both senseless and impossible. It would be senseless, because there is nothing specifically Christian in the mythical view of the world as such. It is simply the cosmology of a pre-scientific age. Again, it would be impossible, because no man can adopt a view of the world by his own volition—it is already determined for him by his place in history. . . .

---

*Preaching; the central message of the gospel.

Man's knowledge and mastery of the world have advanced to such an extent through science and technology that it is no longer possible for anyone seriously to hold the New Testament view of the world—in fact, there is no one who does. What meaning, for instance, can we attach to such phrases in the creed as "descended into hell" or "ascended into heaven"? . . . It is impossible to use electric light and the wireless and to avail ourselves of modern medical and surgical discoveries, and at the same time to believe in the New Testament world of spirits and miracles. We may think we can manage it in our own lives, but to expect others to do so is to make the Christian faith unintelligible and unacceptable to the modern world. . . .

If the truth of the New Testament proclamation is to be preserved, the only way is to demythologize it. But our motive in so doing must not be to make the New Testament relevant to the modern world at all costs. The question is simply whether the New Testament message consists exclusively of mythology, or whether it actually demands the elimination of myth if it is to be understood as it is meant to be. . . .

The real purpose of myth is not to present an objective picture of the world as it is, but to express man's understanding of himself in the world in which he lives. Myth should be interpreted not cosmologically, but anthropologically, or better still, existentially. Myth speaks of the power or the powers which man supposes he experiences as the ground and limit of his world and of his own activity and suffering. . . .

Myth is an expression of man's conviction that the origin and purpose of the world in which he lives are to be sought not within it but beyond it—that is, beyond the realm of known and tangible reality—and that this realm is perpetually dominated and menaced by those mysterious powers which are its source and limit. Myth is also an expression of man's awareness that he is not lord of his own being. It expresses his sense of dependence not only within the visible world, but more especially on those forces which hold sway beyond the confines of the known. Finally, myth expresses man's belief that in this state of dependence he can be delivered from the forces within the visible world.

Thus myth contains elements which demand its own criticism—namely, its imagery with its apparent claim to objective validity. The real purpose of myth is to speak of a transcendent power which controls the world and man, but that purpose is impeded and obscured by the terms in which it is expressed.

Hence the importance of the New Testament mythology lies not in its imagery but in the understanding of existence which it enshrines. The real question is whether this understanding of existence is true. Faith claims that it is, and faith ought not to be tied down to the imagery of New Testament mythology. . . .

St. Paul sees that the life of man is weighed down by anxiety [*merimnan,* 1 Cor. 7:32ff.]. Every man focuses his anxiety upon some particular object. This natural man focuses it upon security, and in proportion to his opportunities and his success in the visible sphere he places his "confidence" in the "flesh" [Phil. 3:3f.], and the consciousness of security finds its expression in "glorying" [*kauchasthai*].

Such a pursuit is, however, incongruous with man's real situation, for the fact is that he is not secure at all. Indeed, this is the way in which he loses his true life and becomes the slave of that very sphere which he had hoped to master, and which he hoped would give him security. . . . Since the visible and tangible sphere is essentially transitory, the man who bases his life on it becomes the prisoner and slave of corruption. An illustration of this may be seen in the way our attempts to secure visible security for ourselves bring us into collision with others; we can seek security for ourselves only at their expense. . . . Everybody tries to hold fast to his own life and property, because he has a secret feeling that it is all slipping away from him.

The authentic life, on the other hand, would be a life based on unseen, intangible realities. Such a life means the abandonment of all self-contrived security. This is what the New Testament means by "life after the Spirit" or "life in faith."

For this life we must have faith in *the grace of God.* It means faith that the unseen, intangible reality actually confronts us as love, opening up our future and signifying not death but life.

The grace of God means *the forgiveness of sin,* and brings deliverance from the bondage of the past. The old quest for visible security, the hankering after tangible realities, and the clinging to transitory objects, is sin, for by it we shut out invisible reality from our lives and refuse God's future which comes to us as a gift. But once we open our hearts to the grace of God, our sins are forgiven; we are released from the past. This is what is meant by "faith": to open ourselves freely to the future. But at the same time faith involves obedience, for faith means turning our backs on self and abandoning all security. It means giving up every attempt to carve out a niche in life for ourselves, surrendering all our self-confidence, and resolving to trust in God alone. . . .

We have now suggested an existentialist unmythological interpretation of the Christian understanding of Being. But is this interpretation true to the New Testament? We seem to have overlooked one important point, which is that in the New Testament faith is always *faith in Christ.* Faith, in the strict sense of the word, was only there at a certain moment in history. It had to be *revealed;* it *came* [Gal. 3:23, 25]. This might of course be taken as part of the story of man's spiritual evolution. But the New Testament means more than that. It claims that faith only became possible at a definite point in history in consequence of an *event*—viz., the event of Christ. Faith in the sense of obedient self-commitment and inward detachment from the world is only possible when it is faith in Jesus Christ. . . .

Philosophers are convinced that all we need is to be told about the "nature" of man in order to realize it. . . . Is this self-confidence of the philosophers justified? Whatever the answer may be, it is at least clear that this is the point where they part company with the New Testament. For the latter affirms the total incapacity of man to release himself from his fallen state. That deliverance can come only by an act of God. . . . So in practice authentic life becomes possible only when man is delivered from himself. It is the claim of the New Testament that this is exactly what has happened. This is precisely the meaning of that which was wrought in Christ. At the very point where man can do nothing, God steps in and acts—indeed he has acted already—on man's behalf. . . .

But what of the resurrection? Is it not a mythical event pure and simple? . . . An historical fact which involves a resurrection from the dead is utterly inconceivable!

Yes indeed: the resurrection of Jesus cannot be a miraculous proof by which the sceptic might be compelled to believe in Christ. The difficulty is not simply the incredibility of a mythical event like the resuscitation of a dead person. . . . Nor is it merely the impossibility of establishing the objective historicity of the resurrection no matter how many witnesses are cited, as though once it was established it might be believed beyond all question and faith might have its unimpeachable guarantee. No; the real difficulty is that the resurrection is itself an article of faith, and you cannot establish one article of faith by invoking another. . . . Indeed, *faith in the resurrection is really the same thing as faith in the saving efficacy of the cross,* faith in the cross as the cross of Christ. Hence you cannot first believe in Christ and then in the strength of that faith believe in the cross. . . .

The real Easter faith is faith in the word of preaching which brings illumination. If the event of Easter Day is in any sense an historical event additional to the event of the cross, it is nothing else than the rise of faith in the risen Lord, since it was this faith which led to the apostolic preaching. The resurrection itself is not an event of past history. All that historical criticism can establish is the fact that the first disciples came to believe in the resurrection. The historian can perhaps to some extent account for that faith from the personal intimacy which the disciples had enjoyed with Jesus during his earthly life, and so reduce the resurrection appearances to a series of subjective visions. But the historical problem is not of interest to Christian belief in the resurrection. For the historical event of the rise of the Easter faith means for us what it meant for the first disciples— namely, the self-attestation of the risen Lord, the act of God in which the redemptive event of the cross is completed.

From Rudolf Bultmann, "New Testament and Mythology," in *Kerygma and Myth: A Theological Debate* edited by Hans Werner Bartsch, translated by Reginald Fuller (London: SPCK, 1953), pages 1, 3–5, 10–11, 18–19, 22, 27, 38–42. Reprinted with permission of The Society for the Promotion of Christian Knowledge.

Paul Tillich (1886–1965)

From *Systematic Theology*

When the Nazis came to power, Tillich fled his native Germany and held teaching positions at a number of major American universities. Influenced by existentialist philosophy, he played a particularly important role in connecting Christian theology with the concerns of contemporary psychology, literature, and the arts.

Ultimate concern is the abstract translation of the great commandment: "The Lord, our God, the Lord is one; and you shall love the Lord your God with all your heart, and with all your soul, and with all your mind, and with all your strength" [Mark 12:29]. The religious concern is ultimate; it excludes all other concerns from ultimate significance; it makes them preliminary. The ultimate concern is unconditional, independent of any conditions of character, desire, or circumstance. The unconditional concern is total: no part of ourselves or of our world is excluded from it; there is no "place" to flee from it [Ps. 139]. The total concern is infinite: no moment of relaxation and rest is possible in the face of a religious concern which is ultimate, unconditional, total, and infinite.

The word "concern" points to the "existential" character of religious experience. We cannot speak adequately of the "object of religion" without simultaneously removing its character as an object. That which is ultimate gives itself only to the attitude of ultimate concern. It is the correlate of an unconditional concern but not a "highest thing" called "the absolute" or "the unconditioned," about which we could argue in detached objectivity. It is the object of total surrender, demanding also the surrender of our subjectivity while we look at it. It is a matter of infinite passion and interest (Kierkegaard), making us its object whenever we try to make it our object. . . . This, then, is the first formal criterion of theology: *The object of theology is what concerns us ultimately. Only those propositions are theological which deal with their object in so far as it can become a matter of ultimate concern for us. . . .*

Idolatry is the elevation of a preliminary concern to ultimacy. Something essentially conditioned is taken as unconditional, something essentially partial is boosted into universality, and something essentially finite is given infinite significance (the best example is the contemporary idolatry of religious nationalism). The conflict between the finite basis of such a concern and its infinite claim leads to a conflict of ultimates; it radically contradicts the biblical commandments and the first theological criterion. . . .

The question now arises: What is the content of our ultimate concern? What *does* concern us unconditionally? The answer, obviously, cannot be a special object, not even God, for the first criterion of theology must remain formal and general. If more is to be said about the nature of our ultimate concern, it must be derived from an analysis of the concept "ultimate concern." *Our ultimate concern is that which determines our being or not-being. Only those statements are theological which deal with their object in so far as it can become a matter of being or not-being for us.* This is the second formal criterion of theology.

Nothing can be of ultimate concern for us which does not have the power of threatening and saving our being. The term "being" in this context does not designate existence in time and space. Existence is continuously threatened and saved by things and events which have no ultimate concern for us. But the term "being" means the whole of human reality, the structure, the meaning, and the aim of existence. All this is threatened; it can be lost or saved. Man is ultimately concerned about his being and meaning. "To be or not to be" in *this* sense is a matter of ultimate, unconditioned, total, and infinite concern. . . .

It is not an exaggeration to say that today man experiences his present situation in terms of disruption, conflict, self-destruction, meaninglessness, and despair in all realms of life. This experience is expressed in the arts and in literature, conceptualized in existential philosophy, actualized in political cleavages of all kinds, and analyzed in the psychology of the unconscious. It has given theology a new understanding of the demonic-tragic structures of individual and social life. The question arising out of this experience is not, as in the Reformation, the question of a merciful God and the forgiveness of sins; nor is it, as in the early Greek church, the question of finitude, of death and error; nor is it the question of the personal religious life or of the Christianization of culture and society. It is the question of a reality in which the self-estrangement of our existence is overcome, a reality of reconciliation and reunion, of creativity, meaning and hope. We shall call such a reality the "New Being." . . .

But this answer is not sufficient. It leads immediately to the further question, "Where is this New Being manifest?" Systematic theology answers this question by saying: "In Jesus the Christ." This answer also has presuppositions and implications which it is the main purpose of the whole system to develop. Only this must be said here—that this formula accepts the ancient Christian baptismal confession of Jesus as the Christ. He who is the Christ is he who brings the new eon, the new reality. And it is the man Jesus who in a paradoxical assertion is called the Christ. Without this paradox the New Being would be an ideal, not a reality, and consequently not an answer to the question implied in our human situation.

From Paul Tillich, *Systematic Theology,* Volume 1 (University of Chicago Press, 1951), pages 11–14, 49–50. © 1951 by The University of Chicago. Used by permission of the publisher.

Second Vatican Council

From *Pastoral Constitution on the Church in the Modern World*

In 1959 Pope John XXIII announced a new council of the bishops of the Roman Catholic Church. The council met from 1962 to 1965 and made dramatic changes in the liturgy of the church—moving the Mass from Latin to the local language of each country, for instance— and showed a new openness both to Protestants and to non-Christians. This document illustrates the council's general themes and some of its social concerns.

1. The joys and the hopes, the griefs and the anxieties of the men of this age, especially those who are poor or in any way afflicted, these too are the joys and hopes, the griefs and anxieties of the followers of Christ. Indeed, nothing genuinely human fails to raise an echo in their hearts. For theirs is a community composed of men. United in Christ, they are led by the Holy Spirit in their journey to the kingdom of their Father and they have welcomed the news of salvation which is meant for every man. That is why this community realizes that it is truly and intimately linked with mankind and its history. . . .

7. . . . Unlike former days, the denial of God or of religion, or the abandonment of them, are no longer unusual and individual occurrences. . . .

20. Modern atheism often takes on a systematic expression, which, in addition to other arguments against God, stretches the desire for human independence to such a point that it finds difficulties with any kind of dependence on God. . . .

21. In her loyal devotion to God and men, the Church has already repudiated and cannot cease repudiating, sorrowfully but as firmly as possible, those poisonous doctrines and actions which contradict reason and the common experience of humanity, and dethrone man from his native excellence. . . .

The remedy which must be applied to atheism, however, is to be sought in a proper presentation of the Church's teaching as well as in the integral life of the Church and her members. . . . What does the most to reveal God's presence, however, is the brotherly charity of the faithful who are united in spirit as they work together for the faith of the gospel and who prove themselves a sign of unity.

While rejecting atheism, root and branch, the Church sincerely professes that all men, believers and unbelievers alike, ought to work for the rightful betterment of this world in which all alike live. Such an ideal cannot be realized, however, apart from sincere and prudent dialogue. Hence the Church protests against the distinction which some state authorities unjustly make between believers and unbelievers, thereby ignoring fundamental rights of the human person. . . .

27. Coming down to practical and particularly urgent consequences, this Council lays stress on reverence for man; everyone must consider his every neighbor without exception as another self, taking into account first of all his life and the means necessary to living it with dignity, so as not to imitate the rich man who had no concern for the poor man Lazarus.

In our times a special obligation binds us to make ourselves the neighbor of absolutely every person, and of actively helping him when he comes across our path, whether he be an old person abandoned by all, a foreign laborer unjustly looked down upon, a refugee, a child born of an unlawful union and wrongly suffering for a sin he did not commit, or a hungry person who disturbs our conscience by recalling the voice of the Lord: "As long as you did it for one of these, the least of my brethren, you did it for me" [Matt. 25:40].

Furthermore, whatever is opposed to life itself, such as any type of murder, genocide, abortion, euthanasia, or willful self-destruction, whatever violates the integrity of the human person, such as mutilation, torments inflicted on body or mind, attempts to coerce the will itself; whatever insults human dignity, such as subhuman living conditions, arbitrary imprisonment, deportation, slavery, prostitution, the selling of women and children; as well as disgraceful working conditions, where men are treated as mere tools for profit, rather than as free and responsible persons; all these things and others of their like are infamies indeed. They poison human society, but they do more harm to those who practice them than those who suffer from the injury. Moreover, they are a supreme dishonor to the Creator. . . .

40. Everything we have said about the dignity of the human person, and about the human community and the profound meaning of human activity, lays the foundation for the relationship between the Church and the world, and provides the basis for dialogue between them. . . . The Church, at once a visible assembly and a spiritual community, goes forward together with humanity and experiences the same earthly lot which the world does. She serves as a leaven and as a kind of soul for human society as it is to be renewed in Christ and transformed into God's family.

That the earthly and the heavenly city penetrate each other is a fact accessible to faith alone. It remains a mystery of human history, which sin will keep in great disarray until the splendor of God's sons is fully revealed. Pursuing the saving purpose which is proper to her, the Church not only communicates divine life to men, but in some way casts the reflected light of that life over the entire earth.

Translated by Joseph Gallagher. Reprinted from *The Documents of Vatican II*, Walter J. Abbott, S.J., general editor, pages 199–200, 205, 217–220, 226–227, 238–239. © 1966. By permission of New Century Publishers, Inc., Piscataway, NJ 08854.

Karl Rahner (1904–1984)

From *In Search of a Short Formula of the Christian Faith*

Rahner, a Jesuit born in Germany who spent a long career teaching at universities in Germany and Austria, served as one of the theological advisers at Vatican II; his voluminous works established him as probably the greatest Catholic theologian of his generation. This essay, published in 1967, illustrates some characteristic themes of his thought: the implicit faith in God that lies behind much human activity, and the way in which non-Christians can be what Rahner elsewhere calls "anonymous Christians" and mentions here as "advent Christians."

If the Church wants her mission to be effective in the situation of modern unbelief, she must be able to express the Christian message in such a way that it becomes really intelligible for modern man. This truism, however, demands something very difficult and very often dealt with in an unsatisfactory manner. For the message must be expressed in such a way that the essential stands out clearly from everything secondary and can in fact be "realized." Otherwise a modern "pagan" cannot distinguish this essence of Christianity from the often not very inviting and even repellent outward "image" of the Church (in preaching, religious practice, social relationships, etc.), and he will then extend to Christianity itself his partly justified objection to Christians. . . . In what follows I have attempted to draft such a "modern" confession of faith. . . .

In his spiritual existence, man will always fall back on a sacred mystery as the very ground of his being, whether he admits this explicitly or not, whether he lets this truth come through or tries to suppress it. This mystery, which permanently contains and sustains the small circle of our knowing and doing in our daily experience, our perception of reality and our free activity, as an ineffable and therefore not articulated circumference, lies at the very root of our being; it is self-evident but, by the same token, most hidden and unheeded; it speaks in its silence and is present in its absence while it shows us our limitations. We call this God. We may overlook him, but even when in our action we show ourselves uninterested in him, he is still affirmed as the ground on which this action rests, in the way in which a logical argument is still operative in an action that denies its validity; or in the way in which a statement about the absolute meaninglessness of all is considered more meaningful than the acceptance of a meaning to existence: such an explicit statement affirms once again "meaning" as the ground of reality. As the ground of the individual's existence, involved in perception and action, the sacred mystery that we call God is most deeply within us and at the same time so far beyond us that it does not need us. Reverence and worship befit him. Where these are present, where man accepts his existence in full responsibility, where man seeks and expects his ultimate meaning trustingly, there he has already found God by whatever name he may call him, since his ultimate name can forever be spoken only in a love that is speechless before his incomprehensibility.

However hard and uncertain it may be for us to interpret this deepest and totally primordial experience in the ground of our being, man nevertheless experiences in his most inward development that this silent, infinitely distant, sacred mystery, always pointing to the limitations of his finite being and revealing his guilt, allows him nevertheless to approach it; it enfolds him in an ultimate and radical love that meets him as salvation and as the real meaning of his existence as long as he allows the possibilities of this love to be wider than his own limitation and guilt.

This love, experienced in the ground of our being, is nothing else than God's absolute self-communication in which God gives himself (and not merely something finite) and in which the infinitely distant becomes the circumference of our existence; and it is this we call deifying grace. . . .

Insofar as history allows God's pledge of himself, accepted in faith, hope and love, and in his radical self-communication to man, to break through with increasing clarity, we speak of history of salvation and revelation. . . .

This history of man's self-discovery in the ground of his deified being (a deification which is at least present as an "offer"), the history of this tangible self-discovery of God in time and space (always in virtue of that divine promise we call grace), reaches its historical climax and the final goal which in a hidden way carries this whole historical process, in him whom we simply call the God-Man in this deified humanity. All seek him, not explicitly, yet really, whenever they desire that the ultimate experience of the radical meaning of their being, of their being subject to death and of God's ultimate acceptance become manifest in their history, and thus wholly present and finally confirmed. To this degree, insofar as we are concerned, every man who is faithful to his conscience is an "advent" Christian, a Christian who looks forward to the *one* man in whom the real issue (which we actually *are* and do not simply think up arbitrarily) and God's pledge have become one in one person and so have become manifest as ultimately valid. As Christians we have the courage to believe that what is here sought, has been found. It is Jesus of Nazareth. . . .

Insofar as God remains forever the sacred incomprehensible mystery in his self-communication, sharing his divinity without losing it, we call him Father. Insofar as God communicates himself to us as our most intimate and eternally valid life through his deifying grace in the ground of our being, we call him Holy Spirit. Insofar as he appears historically in the God-Man as the real truth of our existence, we call him the Word of God and the Son of God. Insofar as both these ways of God's self-communication, which mutually support and condition each other, really communicate God himself, and not a merely creaturely and finite representation of God, we confess that God, while in himself and in his own being he remains one, is distinguishably Father, Word and Spirit, so that we call him triune, Father, Son and Spirit, one God.

From Karl Rahner, "In Search of a Short Formula of the Christian Faith," translated by Theodore L. Westow, in *The Pastoral Approach to Atheism,* edited by Karl Rahner, pages 70, 75–80. Copyright © 1967 by Paulist Fathers, Inc., and Stichting Concilium. Used by permission of the publishers.

Alfred North Whitehead (1861–1947)

From *Process and Reality*

Whitehead began his career in England as a mathematician and logician but turned his interest to metaphysics about the time he came to teach at Harvard in 1924. In his "process philosophy," the world is not made up of isolated objects but of interconnected processes. God is one such process. The "primordial nature of God" sets the range of possibilities for the universe; the "consequent nature of God" synthesizes the actual events of the universe. Whitehead's idea that God is perfect because he is related to and influenced by all things, as opposed to the Aristotelian picture of a God who is perfect because he is unchanging and unaffected, has shaped a tradition known as "process theology."

The notion of God as the "unmoved mover" is derived from Aristotle, at least so far as Western thought is concerned. The notion of God as "eminently real" is a favorite doctrine of Christian theology. The combination of the two into the doctrine of an aboriginal, eminently real, transcendent creator, at whose fiat the world came into being, and whose imposed will it obeys, is the fallacy which has infused tragedy into the histories of Christianity and Mahometanism.

When the Western world accepted Christianity, Caesar conquered; and the received text of Western theology was edited by his lawyers. The code of Justinian and the theology of Justinian are two volumes expressing one movement of the human spirit. . . . The Church gave unto God the attributes which belonged exclusively to Caesar. . . .

There is, however, in the Galilean origin of Christianity yet another suggestion which does not . . . emphasize the ruling Caesar, or the ruthless moralist, or the unmoved mover. It dwells upon the tender elements in the world, which slowly and in quietness operate by love, and it finds purpose in the present immediacy of a kingdom not of this world. Love neither rules, nor is it unmoved; also it is a little oblivious as to morals. It does not look to the future; for it finds its own reward in the immediate present. . . .

In the first place, God is not to be treated as an exception to all metaphysical principles, invoked to save their collapse. He is their chief exemplification.

Viewed as primordial, he is the unlimited conceptual realization of the absolute wealth of potentiality. In this aspect, he is not *before* all creation, but *with* all creation. But, as primordial, so far is he from "eminent reality," that in this abstraction he is "deficiently actual"— and this in two ways. His feelings are only conceptual and so lack the fullness of actuality. Secondly, conceptual feelings, apart from complex integration with physical feelings, are devoid of consciousness in their subjective forms.

Thus, when we make a distinction of reason, and consider God in the abstraction of a primordial actuality, we must ascribe to him neither fullness of feeling, nor consciousness. He is the unconditioned actuality of conceptual feeling at the base of things; so that, by reason of this primordial actuality, there is an order in the relevance of eternal objects to the process of creation. . . .

But God, as well as being primordial, is also consequent. He is the beginning and the end. He is not the beginning in the sense of being in the past of all members. He is the presupposed actuality of conceptual operation, in unison of becoming with every other creative act. Thus by reason of the relativity of all things, there is a reaction of the world on God. The completion of God's nature into a fullness of physical feeling is derived from the objectification of the world in God. He shares with every new creation its actual world; and the concrescent creature is objectified in God as a novel element in God's objectification of that actual world. . . .

Thus, analogously to all actual entities, the nature of God is dipolar. He has a primordial nature and a consequent nature. The consequent nature of God is conscious; and it is the realization of the actual world in the unity of his nature, and through the transformation of his wisdom. The primordial nature is conceptual, the consequent nature is the weaving of God's physical feelings upon his primordial concepts. . . .

But the principle of universal relativity is not to be stopped at the consequent nature of God. This nature itself passes into the temporal world according to its gradation of relevance to the various concrescent occasions. There are thus four creative phases in which the universe accomplishes its actuality. There is first the phase of conceptual origination, deficient in actuality, but infinite in its adjustment of valuation. Secondly, there is the temporal phase of physical origination, with its multiplicity of actualities. In this phase full actuality is attained; but there is deficiency in the solidarity of individuals with each other. This phase derives its determinate conditions from the first phase. Thirdly, there is the phase of perfected actuality, in which the many are one everlastingly, without the qualification of any loss either of individual identity or of completeness of unity. In everlastingness, immediacy is reconciled with objective immortality. This phase derives the conditions of its being from the two antecedent phases. In the fourth phase, the creative action completes itself. For the perfected actuality passes back into the temporal world, and qualifies this world so that each temporal actuality includes it as an immediate fact of relevant experience. For the kingdom of heaven is with us today. The action of the fourth phase is the love of God for the world. It is the particular providence for particular occasions. What is done in the world is transformed into a reality in heaven, and the reality in heaven passes back into the world. By reason of this reciprocal relation, the love in the world passes into the love in heaven, and floods back again into the world. In this sense, God is the great companion—the fellow-sufferer who understands.

Reprinted with permission of Macmillan Publishing Company from *Process and Reality* by Alfred North Whitehead, pages 403–407, 413. Copyright, 1929, The Macmillan Company, renewed 1957 by Evelyn Whitehead.

Jürgen Moltmann (b. 1926)

From *The Crucified God*

Moltmann, a German Reformed theologian, first came to prominence with Theology of Hope, *published in 1965.* The Crucified God, *published in 1973, illustrates his increasing interest in the cross and the Trinity. As much as any other Protestant, he has made connections between German academic theology and the various "liberation theologies."*

In their struggle against each other, theism and atheism begin from the presupposition that God and man are fundamentally one being. Therefore what is ascribed to God must be taken from man and what is ascribed to man must have been taken from God. Theism thinks of God at man's expense as an all-powerful, perfect and infinite being. Consequently man appears here as a helpless, imperfect and finite being. There are good historical grounds for arguing that while the Christian church gained the ancient world with its proclamation of God, from Justinian at the latest the Caesars conquered in the church. . . .

A God who is conceived of in his omnipotence, perfection and infinity at man's expense cannot be the God who is love in the cross of Jesus, who makes a human encounter in order to restore their lost humanity to unhappy and proud divinities, who "became poor to make many rich." . . . It is indispensable for the liberated believer to dispense with the inhuman God, a God without Jesus, for the sake of the cross. Here "Christian atheism" is in the right.

But atheism in rebellion against this kind of political, moral and philosophical theism has long been nothing more than a reversed form of theism, especially in modern times. It has not been able to break free from its opponent. It thinks of man at God's expense as a powerful, perfect, infinite and creative being. It makes "man the supreme being for man" (Marx) and applies all the old theistic divine predicates to man for the purpose of man's incarnation. It is not God who created man in his image but man who creates God in his. Man is the ground and creator of himself *(causa sui)*. Humanity is perfect and infinite in its totality. . . .

This antitheistic atheism leads unavoidably to anthropotheism, to the divinization of man, of humanity and those parties who claim to be a cadre representing non-alienated, divine humanity in the realm of alienation. If for this atheism "man is finally man's God," this may be morally fine as an ideal in face of the situation where man is man's wolf. But a century's experience with such anthropotheism has shown that even these human deities can become man's wolf. If the consequence of Feuerbach's dethroning of God is that "the state is unlimited, infinite, true, perfect divine man," and politics becomes religion, then the history of atheism against theism returns to its beginning, and the old theism would have to be called relatively human, in so far as it ascribes to God the properties and functions which it is better for men not to exercise against other men. If God is other than man, then a man can at least not play god over other men. . . .

With a trinitarian theology of the cross faith escapes the dispute between the alternative of theism and atheism: God is not only other-worldly but also this-worldly; he is not only God, but also man; he is not only rule, authority and law but the event of suffering, liberating love. Conversely, the death of the Son is not the "death of God," but the beginning of that God event in which the life-giving spirit of love emerges from the death of the Son and the grief of the Father. . . .

The faith which springs from the God event on the cross does not give a theistic answer to the question of suffering, why it must be as it is, nor is it ossified into a mere gesture of protest, but leads sorely tried, despairing love back to its origin. "Whoever abides in love abides in God and God in him" [1 John 4:17]. Where we suffer because we love, God suffers in us. Where he has suffered the death of Jesus and in so doing has shown the force of his love, men also find the power to continue to love, to sustain that which annihilates them and to "endure what is dead" (Hegel).

From *The Crucified God,* by Jürgen Moltmann, translated by R. A. Wilson and John Bowden (New York: Harper & Row, 1974), pages 249–253. Copyright © 1974 by SCM Press Ltd. Reprinted by permission of SCM Press and Harper & Row, Publishers, Inc.

Martin Luther King, Jr. (1929–1968)

From *Letter from Birmingham Jail*

King, a black Baptist minister who had completed his graduate theological education at Boston University, led many of the civil disobedience campaigns of the civil rights struggle in the South. He was arrested after one demonstration in Birmingham, Alabama, and wrote this letter from his jail cell on April 16, 1963, to some local white ministers who had written a public letter sympathizing with his goals but criticizing his impatience and his violation of the law.

For years now I have heard the word "Wait!" It rings in the ear of every Negro with piercing familiarity. This "Wait" has almost always meant "Never." We must come to see, with one of our distinguished jurists, that "justice too long delayed is justice denied."

We have waited for more than 340 years for our constitutional and God-given rights. The nations of Asia and Africa are moving with jetlike speed toward gaining political independence, but we still creep at horse-and-buggy pace toward gaining a cup of coffee at a lunch counter. Perhaps it is easy for those who have never felt the stinging darts of segregation to say, "Wait." But when you have seen vicious mobs lynch your mothers and fathers at will and drown your sisters and brothers at whim; when you have seen hate-filled policemen curse, kick and even kill your black brothers and sisters; when you see the vast majority of your twenty million Negro brothers smothering in an airtight cage of poverty in the midst of an affluent society; when you suddenly find your tongue twisted and your speech stammering as you seek to explain to your six-year-old daughter why she can't go to the public amusement park that has just been advertised on television, and see tears welling up in her eyes when she is told that Funtown is closed to colored children, and see ominous clouds of inferiority beginning to form in her little mental sky, and see her beginning to distort her personality by developing an unconscious bitterness toward white people; when you have to concoct an answer for a five-year-old son who is asking: "Daddy, why do white people treat colored people so mean?"; when you take a cross-country drive and find it necessary to sleep night after night in the uncomfortable corners of your automobile because no motel will accept you; when you are humiliated day in and day out by nagging signs reading "white" and "colored"; when your first name becomes "nigger," your middle name becomes "boy" (however old you are) and your last name becomes "John," and your wife and mother are never given the respected title "Mrs."; when you are harried by day and haunted by night by the fact that you are a Negro, living constantly at tiptoe stance, never quite knowing what to expect next, and are plagued with inner fears and outer resentments; when you are forever fighting a degenerating sense of "nobodiness"—then you will understand why we find it difficult to wait. There comes a time when the cup of endurance runs over, and men are no longer willing to be plunged into the abyss of despair. I hope, sirs, you can understand our legitimate and unavoidable impatience.

You express a great deal of anxiety over our willingness to break laws. This is certainly a legitimate concern. Since we so diligently urge people to obey the Supreme Court's decision of 1954 outlawing segregation in the public schools, at first glance it may seem rather paradoxical for us consciously to break laws. One may well ask: "How can you advocate breaking some laws and obeying others?" The answer lies in the fact that there are two types of laws: just and unjust. I would be the first to advocate obeying just laws. One has not only a legal but a moral responsibility to obey just laws. Conversely, one has a moral responsibility to disobey unjust laws. I would agree with St. Augustine that "an unjust law is no law at all."

Now, what is the difference between the two? How does one determine whether a law is just or unjust? A just law is a man-made code that squares with the moral law or the law of God. An unjust law is a code that is out of harmony with the moral law. To put it in the terms of St. Thomas Aquinas: An unjust law is a human law that is not rooted in eternal law and natural law. Any law that uplifts human personality is just. Any law that degrades human personality is unjust. All segregation statutes are unjust because segregation distorts the soul and damages the personality. It gives the segregator a false sense of superiority and the segregated a false sense of inferiority. Segregation, to use the terminology of the Jewish philosopher Martin Buber, substitutes an "I-it" relationship for an "I-thou" relationship and ends up relegating persons to the status of things. Hence segregation is not only politically, economically and sociologically unsound, it is morally wrong and sinful. Paul Tillich has said that sin is separation. Is not segregation an existential expression of man's tragic separation, his awful estrangement, his terrible sinfulness? Thus it is that I can urge men to obey the 1954 decision of the Supreme Court, for it is morally right; and I can urge them to disobey segregation ordinances, for they are morally wrong.

Let us consider a more concrete example of just and unjust laws. An unjust law is a code that a numerical or power majority compels a minority group to obey but does not make binding on itself. This is a *difference* made legal. By the same token, a just law is a code that a majority compels a minority to follow and that it is willing to follow itself. This is *sameness* made legal.

Let me give another explanation. A law is unjust if it is inflicted on a minority that, as a result of being denied the right to vote, had no part in enacting or devising the law. Who can say that the legislature of Alabama which set up that state's segregation laws was democratically elected? Throughout Alabama all sorts of devious methods are used to prevent Negroes from becoming registered voters, and there are some counties in which, even though Negroes constitute a majority of the population, not a single Negro is registered. Can any law enacted under such circumstances be considered democratically structured?

Sometimes a law is just on its face and unjust in its application. For instance, I have been arrested on a charge of parading without a permit. Now, there is nothing wrong in having an ordinance which requires a permit for a parade. But such an ordinance becomes unjust when it is used to maintain segregation and to deny citizens the First Amendment privilege of peaceful assembly and protest.

I hope you are able to see the distinction I am trying to point out. In no sense do I advocate evading or defying the law, as would the rabid segregationist. That would lead to anarchy. One who breaks an unjust law must do so openly, lovingly, and with a willingness to accept the penalty. I submit that an individual who breaks a law that conscience tells him is unjust, and who willingly accepts the penalty of imprisonment in order to arouse the conscience of the community over its injustice, is in reality expressing the highest respect for law.

Of course there is nothing new about this kind of civil disobedience. It was evident sublimely in the refusal of Shadrach, Meshach and Abednego to obey the laws of Nebuchadnezzar, on the ground that a higher moral law was at stake. It was practiced superbly by the early Christians, who were willing to face hungry lions and the excruciating pain of chopping blocks rather than submit to certain unjust laws of the Roman Empire. To a degree, academic freedom is a reality today because Socrates practiced civil disobedience. In our own nation, the Boston Tea Party represented a massive act of civil disobedience.

We should never forget that everything Adolf Hitler did in Germany was "legal" and everything the Hungarian freedom fighters did in Hungary was "illegal." It was "illegal" to aid and comfort a Jew in Hitler's Germany. Even so, I am sure that, had I lived in Germany at the time, I would have aided and comforted my Jewish brothers. If today I lived in a Communist country where certain principles dear to the Christian faith are suppressed, I would openly advocate disobeying that country's antireligious laws.

CHAPTER 8

New Voices

It has become a cliché to say that until recently Christian theology was the exclusive preserve of white Western males. Like many clichés, it is not really true. Christianity began in the Middle East, and most of its early theologians came from Asia and Africa. Afro-Americans such as David Walker and Frederick Douglass were important figures in American Christianity over a century ago—and, for that matter, even in Egypt Athanasius' dark skin drew comment. From medieval mystics to early Quaker preachers, women have made important contributions to Christian theology.

And yet, most clichés contain an element of truth. Doing theology requires some education, and ideally some leisure to study and write. One gets a place in the history of theology only if someone writes down one's words or preserves one's manuscripts. And education, leisure, and attention have always been given primarily to the members of the privileged class or race or sex.

But in the last twenty-five years the voices of American blacks, Christians from the Third World, and women have made themselves heard in Christian theology. They speak about the relation of Christianity to non-Western cultures and the way Christianity speaks to oppressed people. Some of them find that Marxism provides helpful categories for understanding the roots of their oppression, though there are Christians living under Marxist regimes who testify that they too suffer oppression.

These new voices speak for a new and different Christian world. To cite one dramatic statistic, in 1900 about two thirds of all Christians lived in Europe and North America; by 2000 only one third will do so. If Christian theology is to reflect and shape the life of the church, it needs to notice how radically the church is changing.

James H. Cone (b. 1938)

From *Black Theology in American Religion*

Since the late 1960s James Cone's many books and his teaching at Union Theological Seminary in New York have made him the most important figure in black theology in the United States. In 1985 the American Academy of Religion asked him to reflect on the history of that theological tradition. These are excerpts from his reflections.

More than eighty years ago W. E. B. DuBois wrote in *The Souls of Black Folk* his classic statement of the paradox of black life in America.

> It is a peculiar sensation, this double-consciousness, this sense of always looking at one's self through the eyes of others, of measuring one's soul by the tape of a world that looks on in amused contempt and pity. One ever feels his twoness,—an American, a Negro; two souls, two thoughts, two unreconciled strivings; two warring ideals in one dark body, whose dogged strength alone keeps it from being torn asunder.

The "two warring ideals" that DuBois described in 1903 have been at the center of black religious thought from its origin to the present day. They are found in the heated debates about "integration" and "nationalism" and in the attempt to name the community—beginning with the word "African" and using at different times such terms as "Colored," "Negro," "Afro-American," and "Black."

In considering black religious thought in this essay, let us give clearer names to the "two warring ideals"—clearer, that is, from the point of view of religion. I shall call them "African" and "Christian." Black religious thought is not identical with the Christian theology of white Americans. Nor is it identical with traditional African beliefs, past or present. It is both—but reinterpreted for and adapted to the life-situation of black people's struggle for justice in a nation whose social, political, and economic structures are dominated by a white racist ideology. It was the "African" side of black religion that helped African-Americans to see beyond the white distortions of the gospel and to discover its true meaning as God's liberation of the oppressed from bondage. It was the "Christian" elements in black religion that helped African-Americans to reorient their African past so that it would become useful in the struggle to survive with dignity in a society that they did not make. . . .

Under the influence of Malcolm X and the political philosophy of black power, many black theologians began to advocate the necessity for the development of a black theology, and they rejected the dominant theologies of Europe and North America as heretical. For the first time in the history of black religious thought, black clergy and theologians began to recognize the need for a completely new starting point in theology, and they insisted that it must be defined by people at the bottom and not the top of the socio-economic ladder. To accomplish this task, black theologians focussed on God's liberation of the poor as the central message of the gospel.

To explicate the theological significance of the liberation motif, black theologians began to re-read the Bible through the eyes of their slave grandparents and started to speak of God's solidarity with the wretched of the earth. As the political liberation of the poor emerged as the dominant motif, justice, suffering, love, and hope were reinterpreted in its light. For the biblical meaning of liberation, black theologians turned to the *Exodus,* while the message of the *prophets* provided the theological content for the theme of justice. The *gospel story* of the life, death, and resurrection of Jesus served as the biblical foundation for a re-interpretation of love, suffering, and hope in the context of the black struggle for liberation and justice.

As black theologians have re-read the Bible in the light of the struggles of the oppressed, the idea of the "suffering God" has become important in our theological perspective. . . . [When] the poor of the North American and the Third World read the passion story of the cross, they do not view it as a theological idea but as God's suffering solidarity with the victims of the world. Jesus' cross is God's election of the poor by taking their pain and suffering upon the divine person. Black slaves expressed this theological point in such songs as "he never said a mumblin' word" and "were you there when they crucified my Lord."

> They nail my Jesus down,
> They put him on the crown of thorns,
> O see my Jesus hangin' high!
> He look so pale an' bleed so free:
> O don't you think it was a shame,
> He hung three hours in dreadful pain?

From James H. Cone, "Black Theology in American Religion," *Journal of the American Academy of Religion,* Volume 53 (December 1985), pages 755–756, 768–769. Copyright © 1985 by the American Academy of Religion. Reprinted by permission.

Gustavo Gutiérrez (b. 1928)

From *Liberation Praxis and Christian Faith*

Gustavo Gutiérrez, a Catholic priest from Peru, first drew major attention with his book A Theology of Liberation, *published in 1971. He has continued to write and live among his people; this article was originally published in 1973.*

The most recent years of Latin American history have been characterized by the discovery of the real-life world of "the other," of the poor and exploited and their compelling needs. In a social order fashioned economically, politically, and ideologically by a few for their own benefit, the "other" side has begun to make its voice heard. The lower classes of the populace, forced to live on the margins of society and oppressed since time immemorial, are beginning to speak for themselves more and more rather than relying on intermediaries. They have discovered themselves once again, and they now want the existing system to take note of their disturbing presence. They are less and less willing to be the passive objects of demagogic manipulation and social or charitable welfare in varied disguises. They want to be the active subjects of their own history and to forge a radically different society.

This discovery is made, however, only within the context of a revolutionary struggle. That struggle is calling the existing social order into question from the roots up. It insists that the people must come to power if society is to be truly free and egalitarian. In such a society private ownership of the means of production will be eliminated because it enables a few to expropriate the fruits of labor performed by the many, generates class divisions in society, and permits one class to be exploited by another. In such a reordered society the social takeover of the means of production will be accompanied by a social takeover of the reins of political power that will ensure people's liberty. Thus the way will be open to a new social awareness.

For some years now a growing number of Christians have come to participate in this revolutionary process. Through that participation they have come to discover the whole world of the exploited in Latin America. This Christian involvement and commitment constitutes the major fact in the current life of the Christian community in Latin America. . . .

For a long time, and still today in the case of many people, Latin

American Christians displayed an almost total lack of concern for temporal tasks. They were subjected to a type of religious upbringing that viewed the "hereafter" as the locale of authentic life. The present life was seen as a stage-setting where people were put to the test so that their eternal destiny might be decided. . . . Eternal life was considered to be wholly a future life. It was not thought to be actively and creatively present in our present involvement in human history as well.

Such was the restricted vision of human life that prevailed. On the surface it seemed to bear the hallmark of spiritual and religious traits, but in reality it stemmed from a seriously reductionist view of the gospel message. The good will of some of those who sought to salvage the absolute character of God's kingdom in this defective way had no impact whatsoever on objective results. The gospel message was thus rendered as innocuous as a lap dog. From such a gospel the great and powerful of this world had little to fear and much to gain. Their support and backing of it were quickly forthcoming. . . .

The new turn of events began modestly enough. . . . Social injustice began to surface as the fundamental cause of the general situation. How could one claim to be a Christian if one did not commit oneself to remedying that situation? The Christian individual felt challenged and summoned by the harsh reality, but at that time people did not see so clearly that it was society as a whole and its prevailing system of values that were being called into question from the roots up. . . .

But the existence of the poor is not fated fact; it is not neutral on the political level or innocent of ethical implications. Poor people are by-products of the system under which we live and for which we are responsible. Poor people are ones who have been shunted to the sidelines of our socio-cultural world. Poor people are those who are oppressed and exploited, who are deprived of the fruits of their labor and stripped of their life and reality as human beings. Poor people are members of the proletarian class. That is why the poverty of the poor is not a summons to alleviate their plight with acts of generosity but rather a compelling obligation to fashion an entirely different social order.

But we must consider this option carefully and notice its precise nature. When we opt for the poor in a commitment to liberation, we are forced to realize that we cannot isolate oppressed people from the social class to which they belong. If we were to do that, we would simply be sympathizing with their own individual situations. Poor and oppressed people are members of a social class which is overtly or covertly exploited by another social class. The proletariat is simply the most belligerent and clear-cut segment of this exploited social class. To opt for the poor is to opt for one social class over against another; to take cognizance of the fact of class confrontation and side with the oppressed; to enter into the milieu of the exploited social class and its associated cultural categories and values; to unite in fellowship with its interests, concerns, and struggles. . . .

We are not used to doing that. Spiritual life and experience is something we are used to viewing as apart, far removed from such impure human realities as politics. But we must now move in a different direction. Instead of looking for an encounter with the Lord through contact with poor individuals in isolation, with "nice" poor people, we must seek that encounter through contact with the oppressed, with all the members of a particular social class who are fighting valiantly for their most basic rights and for an altered society in which they can live as human beings. History is the locale where God reveals the mystery of his person. His word will reach us to the extent that we immerse ourselves in the ongoing process of history, and that history is riddled with conflict. It is filled with confrontations between opposing interests, with bitter struggles for justice, with human alienation and exploitation, and with yearnings for liberation. We turn this history into one of authentic communion when we opt for the poor and exploited classes, identify ourselves with their plight, and share their fate. There is no other way to accept the gratuitous gift of sonship. We must opt for the cross of Christ and have hope in his resurrection.

From Gustavo Gutiérrez, "Liberation Praxis and Christian Faith," translated by John Drury, in *Frontiers of Theology in Latin America,* edited by Rosino Gibellini, pages 1–4, 8–9, 16. Copyright © 1979 by Orbis Books. Reprinted by permission of Orbis Books and SCM Press.

Evgeny Barabanov (b. 1943)

From *The Schism Between the Church and the World*

Evgeny Barabanov is an art historian who lives in the Soviet Union. In 1973 he was investigated by the KGB and fired from his job for having sent unpublished essays on Russian religious life to the West. In 1974 the Russian government refused him permission to emigrate.

In our country a church is a "place for the performance of the rite of a religious community." This community is registered by the organs of the state. And state functionaries are appointed to supervise its life. This supervision consists in making the "liturgical department" as spiritually isolated as possible, harmless and even comic, from the point of view of the ideology of the state. And all the participants in the "rite," the hierarchs, the priests dependent on them, and laymen—in other words all the other elements that constitute the Church—meekly accept this situation and seem fully reconciled to their dependence. . . .

The position of the Church in a totalitarian world is indeed tragic, but this tragedy inclines us to forget that our present position is inseparably bound up with the tragedies of the past. . . . If we trace the mainstream of our history back up toward its source, will we not find, under the glitter of gilded pomp, all those so familiar features? And preserving our academic impartiality, despite the seductiveness of past eras with their majestic attempts at theocratic kingdoms and church-state "symphonies," surely we shall be obliged to acknowledge that in Byzantium and Russia ideas about the Kingdom of God and the kingdom of Caesar too often merged and became interchangeable. The subjection of the Church by the state is an old eastern tradition. The Emperors Constantine, Constantius, Theodosius and Justinian (not to mention the later period) openly interfered with the internal life of the Church, suppressing, dictating and avenging. We venerate the holiness of the Nicene Creed, but our Christian conscience will never be reconciled to the conclusion of the Council of Nicea, when the emperor exiled all the dissenters. That was not an isolated case—practically the whole historical path of Orthodoxy is peppered with them. For the state, as history has shown from the Edict of Milan* to the present, it has always been desirable to have a "tame Orthodoxy" which would serve the ends of autocratic power. . . . And when tsarism fell, the Church suddenly found itself face to face with a hostile, atheistic state which applied rather different methods from those of the Christian Emperors. . . .

There is nothing surprising in the fact that an atheistic state tries to reduce the life of the Church to the rite alone. . . . "You say you are not of this world, well then, there is nothing for you to do in this world. That is why I forbid you to 'set up benefit societies, coopera-

---

*The document by which, in 313, Emperor Constantine gave the Christian church legal existence.

tives of industrial societies; to offer material aid to your members; to organize children's and young persons' groups for prayer and other purposes, or general biblical, literary or handicraft groups for the purpose of work or religious instruction and the like, or to organize groups, circles or sections; to arrange excursions and kindergartens, open libraries and reading rooms, organize sanatoria or medical aid.' " ["Concerning religious societies," Resolution of the Central Committee, 8 April 1929, para. 17]. . . .

But the genuine hope of religion, the "good news" of Christianity about the Kingdom of God, which constitutes the basic content of the Gospel, is not limited to the world beyond the grave. The Kingdom of God which Christ taught us about "is not of this world" and will be realized in full only beyond the bounds of earthly history. But through Christ it entered this world and became its leaven. And it did not just "draw near," it "resides within us." And the beginning of this new all-embracing life is the Body of Christ, the Church. Through it God summons mankind and the world to perfection, to the fullness of absolute being. If the creative transformation of the world by man is seen as the realization of the Kingdom of God with Christ and in Christ, then the world is not only pardoned and justified, but is also being realized in the highest of its possible forms.

From Evgeny Barabanov, "The Schism Between the Church and the World," in *From Under the Rubble,* edited by Alexander Solzhenitsyn, translated by Michael Scammell et al., pages 173, 177–182. Copyright © 1974 by YMCA-Press, Paris. Translation Copyright © 1975 by Little, Brown and Company (Inc.). Used by permission of Little, Brown and Company and Collins Harvill.

John Mbiti (b. 1931)

From *The Encounter of Christian Faith and African Religion*

John Mbiti, a Kenyan, is the author of a number of books on religion in Africa and the former director of the Ecumenical Institute of the World Council of Churches. This essay was first published in 1980.

Since the Bible tells me that God is the creator of all things, his activities in the world must clearly go beyond what is recorded in the Bible. He must have been active among African peoples as he was among the Jewish people. Did he then reveal himself *only* in the line of Abraham, Isaac, Jacob, Moses, Samuel and other personalities of the Bible? Didn't our Lord let it be clearly known that "before Abraham was I am" [John 8:58]? Then was he not there in other times and in such places as Mount Fuji and Mount Kenya, as well as Mount Sinai? The decisive word here is "only." The more I peeped into African religious insights about God, the more I felt utterly unable to use the word "only" in this case. In its place there emerged the word "also." This was an extremely liberating word in my theological thinking. With it, one began to explore afresh the realm of God's revelation and other treasures of our faith. I find the traditional Western distinction between "special revelation" and "general revelation" to be inadequate and unfreeing. This is not a biblical distinction. If they are two wavelengths, they make sense only when they move toward a convergence. When this happens, then a passage such as Hebrews 1:1–3* rolls down like mighty waters, full of exciting possibilities of theological reflection. . . .

Revelation is given not in a vacuum but within particular historical experiences and reflections. When we identify the God of the Bible as the same God who is known through African religion (whatever its limitations), we must also take it that God has had a historical relationship with African peoples. God is not insensitive to the history of peoples other than Israel. Their history has a theological meaning. My interpretation of Israel's history demands a new look at the history of African peoples, among whom this same God of Abraham, Isaac, and Jacob has indeed been at work.

From John Mbiti, "The Encounter of Christian Faith and African Religion." Copyright 1980 Christian Century Foundation. Reprinted by permission from the August 27–September 3 issue of *The Christian Century*.

C. S. Song (b. 1929)

From *The Cross and the Lotus*

C. S. Song, from Taiwan, has been associate director of the secretariat of the Faith and Order Commission of the World Council of Churches. This essay comes from his book Third-Eye Theology, *published in 1979.*

---

*"When in former times God spoke to our forefathers, he spoke in fragmentary and varied fashion through the prophets. But in this the final age he has spoken to us in the Son whom he has made heir to the whole universe, and through whom he created all orders of existence: the Son who is the effulgence of God's splendour and the stamp of God's very being, and sustains the universe by his word of power" (NEB).

Suffering touches the heart of God as well as the hearts of human beings. In the suffering of humanity we see and experience the suffering of God. God and human beings are bound together in suffering. That is why theology begins with God's heartache which is caused by human suffering and pain. In the suffering every one of us has to go through at various stages of life, God suffers. Jesus Christ is the God-human in suffering. And it is this same Christ who is the love of the God-human in action. The cross, from the standpoint of Christian faith, is the supreme symbol of God's suffering love. It has not been surpassed even after two thousand years. In the cross we realize that suffering is not merely physical, institutional, impersonal, or secular. It is religious and human, and thus divine. Suffering is the cross God has to bear with all God's creation.

Another religious symbol that over the centuries has become the focus of the religious devotion and spiritual aspirations of a vast number of people under the influence of Buddhist spirituality is the lotus. The image of Buddha or Bodhisattva seated cross-legged on the lotus has been to the masses a source of comfort and peace. It stills the troubled mind and gives assurance that suffering is not the last word. It helps to maintain serenity in the midst of a turbulent life of bitterness. And it promises a life of bliss when all births cease. The lotus is to Buddhists as a religious symbol what the cross is to Christians. Radically different in every way, these two symbols point to a crucial question of human life—deliverance. . . .

The question we must now ask is: What has the cross to do with the lotus? . . . [They] seem to have little in common, at first sight at any rate. The lotus springs from the surface of the water. When the wind blows and the water moves, the lotus also moves. It seems in perfect harmony with nature around it. In short, it gives the appearance of being at peace with itself. In contrast, the cross strikes out powerfully, painfully, and defiantly from the earth. It penetrates space and is incongruous with nature. . . . The lotus distinguishes itself in gentleness, while the cross is the epitome of human brutality. The lotus beckons and the cross repels. Indeed, what has the cross to do with the lotus? . . .

In my view Christian faith should at least include a readiness to acknowledge that God somehow uses the redemptive elements outside Christianity to prevent human history from going completely bankrupt, to sustain a world that often verges on destruction through such human cruelty as we witnessed in World War II in which the "Christian" West was brutally and demonically involved. . . .

The Buddhist concept of a Bodhisattva takes on, in this connection, an important theological meaning. A Bodhisattva occupies a place of great importance in Mahayana Buddhism as a person who follows the footsteps of Buddha and for the sake of suffering humanity refuses to enter into Buddhahood. . . . The difficulty for Christians lies in the fact that a Bodhisattva is a human being. Theologically speaking, for a human being to save other human beings is a religious presumption that contradicts the basic meaning of the cross. For Christians salvation is the work of God, not of humanity. But this should not close our mind to the redemptive quality evident in a Bodhisattva, that is, the quality of putting the spiritual needs of others before our own, the readiness to enter into the suffering of our fellow human beings, and the goal toward which the human spirit should strive.

Bodhisattvas in areas under Buddhist influence perform the function of a spiritual catharsis similar to that accomplished by the prophets of ancient Israel. The crucial question is not whether Bodhisattvas are redeemers in the sense that Jesus Christ is our redeemer, for they are not. But because of them and through them people may see something of God's redemption at work in the world. Because of them and through them the world is not entirely lost. To put it positively, perhaps because of them and through them God gives hope to the world and shows a readiness to save people from destruction. . . .

A conclusion we may draw is that throughout human history there are men and women who have gone about doing the king's business without being aware that they are in the king's service. Through what they are and what they do, they bring hope to those in despair, transmit light in the midst of darkness, point to life when people are threatened with death, and bring freedom to imprisoned bodies and spirits. In so doing, they knowingly or unknowingly mediate God's redemptive power to those with whom they come into contact.

From C. S. Song, *Third-Eye Theology,* copyright © 1979 by Orbis Books. Reprinted with permission of Orbis Books and Lutterworth Press from *Third World Liberation Theologies,* edited by Deane William Ferm (Maryknoll, N.Y.: Orbis Books, 1986), pages 300–301, 308–309, 316–317.

Rosemary Radford Ruether (b. 1936)

From *Mother Earth and the Megamachine*

Rosemary Radford Ruether currently teaches at Garrett Evangelical Theological Seminary. Her many books and articles have made her one of the leading figures in feminist theology. This essay was originally published in 1971.

Christianity, as the heir of both classical Neo-Platonism and apocalyptic Judaism, combines the image of a male warrior God with the exaltation of the intellect over the body. The Classical doctrine of Christ, which fused the vision of the heavenly messianic king with the transcendent *logos* of immutable Being, was a synthesis of the religious impulses of late antique religious consciousness, but precisely in their alienated state of development. These world-negative religions carried a set of dualities that still profoundly condition the modern worldview.

All the basic dualities—the alienation of the mind from the body; the alienation of the subjective self from the objective world; the subjective retreat of the individual, alienated from the social community; the domination or rejection of nature by spirit—these all have roots in the apocalyptic-Platonic religious heritage of Classical Christianity. But the alienation of the masculine from the feminine is the primary sexual symbolism that sums up all these alienations. The psychic traits of intellectuality, transcendent spirit, and autonomous will that were identified with the male left the woman with the contrary traits of bodiliness, sensuality, and subjugation. Society, through the centuries, has in every way profoundly conditioned men and women to play out their lives and find their capacities within this basic antithesis.

This antithesis has also shaped the modern technological environment. The plan of our cities is made in this image: The sphere of domesticity, rest, and child-rearing where women are segregated is clearly separated from those corridors down which men advance in assault upon the world of "work." The woman who tries to break out of the female sphere into the masculine finds not only psychic conditioning and social attitudes but the structure of social reality itself ranged against her. . . .

The psycho-social history of the domination of women has not been explored with any consistency, so the effort to trace its genesis and development here can only be very general. However, it appears that in agricultural societies sexist and class polarization did not immediately reshape the religious worldview. For the first two millennia of recorded history, religious culture continued to reflect the more holistic view of society of the neolithic village, where the individual and the community, nature and society, male and female, earth goddess and sky god were seen in a total perspective of world renewal. The salvation of the individual was not split off from that of the community; the salvation of society was one with the renewal of the earth; male and female played their complementary roles in the salvation of the world. This primitive democracy of the neolithic village persisted in the divine pantheons of Babylonia, despite the social class stratification that now appeared. . . .

Somewhere in the first millennium B.C., however, this communal worldview of humanity and nature, male and female, carried over from tribal society started to break down, and the alienations of civilization began to reshape the religious world picture. This change was partly aggravated by the history of imperial conquest that swept the people of the Mediterranean into larger and larger social conglomerates where they no longer felt the same unity with the king, the soil or the society.

The old religions of the earth became private cults for the individual, no longer anticipating the renewal of the earth and society but rather expecting an otherworldly salvation of the individual soul after death. Nature itself came to be seen as an alien reality, and men now visualized their own bodies as foreign to their true selves, longing for a heavenly home to release them from their enslavement within the physical cosmos. Finally, earth ceased to be seen as man's true home. . . .

Christianity brought together both of these myths—the myth of world cataclysm and the myth of the flight of the soul to heaven. It also struggled to correct the more extreme implications of this body-negating spirituality with a more positive doctrine of creation and incarnation. It even reinstated, in covert form, the old myths of the year cult and the virgin-mother goddess.

But the dominant spirituality of the fathers of the Church finally accepted the antibody, antifeminine view of late antique religious culture. Recent proponents of ecology have, therefore, pointed the finger at Christianity, as the originator of this debased view of nature, as the religious sanction for modern technological exploitation of the earth.

But Christianity did not originate this view. Rather, it appears to correspond to a stage of development of human consciousness that coincided with ripening Classical civilization. Christianity took over this alienated worldview of late Classical civilization, but its oppressive dualities express the basic alienations at work in the psycho-social channelization of human energy since the breakup of the communal life of earlier tribal society. . . .

Today, both in the West and among insurgent Third World peoples, we are seeing a new intensification of this Western mode of abstractionism and revolution. Many are convinced that the problems created by man's ravaging of nature can be solved only by a great deal more technological manipulation. . . . Yet at the same time . . . the alienated members of the dominant society are seeking new communal, egalitarian life-styles, ecological living patterns, and the redirection of psychic energy toward reconciliation with the body. But these human potential movements remain elitist, privatistic, aesthetic and devoid of a profound covenant with the poor and oppressed of the earth. . . .

We are now approaching the denouement of this dialectic. The ethic of competitiveness and technological mastery has created a world divided by penis-missiles and counter-missiles that could destroy all humanity a hundred times over. Yet the ethic of reconciliation with the earth has yet to break out of its snug corners of affluence and find meaningful cohesion with the revolutions of insurgent peoples. . . .

Women must be the spokesmen for a new humanity arising out of the reconciliation of spirit and body. This does not mean selling short our rights to the powers of independent personhood. Autonomy, world-transcending spirit, separatism as the power of consciousness-raising, and liberation from an untamed nature and from subjugation by the rocket-ship male—all these revolutions are still vital to women's achievement of integral personhood. But we have to look beyond our own liberation from oppression to the liberation of the oppressor as well. Women should not buy into the masculine ethic of competitiveness that sees the triumph of the self as predicated upon the subjugation of the other. Unlike men, women have traditionally cultivated a communal personhood that could participate in the successes of others rather than seeing these as merely a threat to one's own success. . . .

The new earth must be one where people are reconciled with their labor, abolishing the alienation of the megamachine while inheriting its productive power to free men for unalienated creativity. It will be a world where people are reconciled to their own finitude, where the last enemy, death, is conquered, not by a flight into eternity, but in that spirit of St. Francis that greets "Brother Death" as a friend that completes the proper cycle of the human soul.

From *Christianity and Crisis,* December 13, 1971, pages 267, 269–272. Copyright © 1971, Christianity & Crisis, 537 West 121st Street, New York, NY 10027. Reprinted with permission.

Suggestions for Further Reading

There are thick volumes devoted to the secondary literature on specific periods, topics, and even individual theologians; a brief list of readings over the whole history of theology can only point the interested reader in some useful directions. Many of the books listed here have extended bibliographies that can lead on to further reading.

General

Some reference works

Eerdmans' Handbook to the History of Christianity, ed. by Tim Dowley. Grand Rapids: Wm. B. Eerdmans Publishing Co., 1977. This work is theologically quite conservative but attractively illustrated and accessible in style and layout.

The Oxford Dictionary of the Christian Church, 2nd ed., ed. by F. L. Cross and Elizabeth A. Livingstone. Oxford: Oxford University Press, 1974.

The Westminster Dictionary of Church History, ed. by Jerald C. Brauer. Philadelphia: Westminster Press, 1971.

General histories of Christianity

Paul Johnson, *A History of Christianity.* New York: Atheneum Publishers, 1976. A somewhat polemic history by a gifted British journalist.

Martin E. Marty, *A Short History of Christianity.* Cleveland: World Publishing Co./Meridian Books, 1959. Well written and on an introductory level.

James H. Nichols, *History of Christianity 1650–1950.* New York: Ronald Press Co., 1956.

Williston Walker, *A History of the Christian Church,* 4th ed. New York: Charles Scribner's Sons, 1985. Updated since its original publication many years ago, and perhaps still the standard source.

Histories of theology

Hubert Cunliffe-Jones and Benjamin Drewery, eds., *A History of Christian Doctrine.* Philadelphia: Fortress Press, 1980. A collection of chapters by leading scholars in various fields, this is somewhat more advanced than the other books listed.

Jaroslav Pelikan, *Jesus Through the Centuries.* New York: Harper & Row, 1985. Not exactly a survey history, but wonderfully readable and in a class by itself as an intellectual tour de force.

William C. Placher, *A History of Christian Theology.* Philadelphia: Westminster Press, 1983.

Linwood Urban, *A Short History of Christian Thought.* New York: Oxford University Press, 1986.

Collections of readings

Colman J. Barry, ed., *Readings in Church History,* 3 vols. in 1. Westminster, Md.: Christian Classics, 1985. An anthology that focuses more on institutional history than this book does.

The many volumes of the *Library of Christian Classics,* published by The Westminster Press, and the *Classics of Western Spirituality,* now being published by Paulist Press, represent the best general collections of readings in primary sources.

The Reformation

General histories

Owen Chadwick, *The Reformation.* Baltimore: Penguin Books, 1964.

Steven Ozment, *The Age of Reform, 1250–1550.* New Haven, Conn.: Yale University Press, 1980.

Jaroslav Pelikan, *Reformation of Church and Dogma.* Chicago: University of Chicago Press, 1983.

Bernard M. G. Reardon, *Religious Thought in the Reformation.* Harlow, Essex: Longman, 1981.

Lewis W. Spitz, *The Protestant Reformation 1517–1559.* New York: Harper & Row, 1985.

Anthologies

Hans J. Hillerbrand, *The Reformation in Its Own Words.* London: SCM Press, 1964.

Lewis W. Spitz, *The Protestant Reformation.* Englewood Cliffs, N.J.: Prentice-Hall, 1966.

Luther and Zwingli

Roland Bainton, *Here I Stand: A Life of Martin Luther.* Nashville: Abingdon-Cokesbury Press, 1950. Still marvelously readable.

Heinrich Bornkamm, *Luther in Mid-Career,* tr. by E. Theodore Bachmann. Philadelphia: Fortress Press, 1983. The last book, published posthumously, of a great Luther scholar.

G. R. Potter, *Zwingli.* London: Cambridge University Press, 1977.

John Todd, *Luther: A Life.* New York: Crossroad Publishing Co., 1982. A recent good biography.

The Radical Reformation

Franklin H. Littell, *The Origins of Sectarian Protestantism.* New York: Macmillan Co., 1964.

George Huntston Williams, *The Radical Reformation.* Philadelphia: Westminster Press, 1962. The most comprehensive survey.

The Catholic Reformation

A. G. Dickens, *The Counter Reformation.* New York: Harcourt, Brace & World, 1969. The best introduction.

Michael Foss, *The Founding of the Jesuits.* London: Hamish Hamilton, 1969.

Pierre Janelle, *The Catholic Reformation.* Milwaukee: Bruce Publishing Co., 1963.

Calvin

John T. McNeill, *The History and Character of Calvinism.* New York: Oxford University Press, 1967.

T. H. L. Parker, *John Calvin: A Biography.* Philadelphia: Westminster Press, 1975.

François Wendel, *Calvin,* tr. by Philip Mairet. New York: Harper & Row, 1963.

The English Reformation

A. G. Dickens, *The English Reformation.* New York: Schocken Books, 1964.

Michael Walzer, *The Revolution of the Saints.* New York: Atheneum Publishers, 1972. On the Puritans.

The Age of Reason

Henry E. Allison, *Lessing and the Enlightenment.* Ann Arbor, Mich.: University of Michigan Press, 1966.

Gerald R. Cragg, *The Church and the Age of Reason.* Baltimore: Penguin Books, 1960.

Peter Gay, *Deism.* New York: D. Van Nostrand, 1968. An anthology of readings, with introductions.

————, *The Enlightenment, vol. 1: The Rise of Modern Paganism.* New York: Alfred A. Knopf, 1966.

John Pudney, *John Wesley and His World.* New York: Charles Scribner's Sons, 1978. A good introductory biography.

F. Ernest Stoeffler, *The Rise of Evangelical Pietism.* Leiden: E. J. Brill, 1965.

————, *Pietism During the Eighteenth Century.* Leiden: E. J. Brill, 1973.

Allen W. Wood, *Kant's Moral Religion.* Ithaca, N.Y.: Cornell University Press, 1966.

The United States

Sydney E. Ahlstrom, *A Religious History of the American People.* New Haven, Conn.: Yale University Press, 1972. A masterpiece.

Winthrop S. Hudson, *Religion in America,* 3rd ed. New York: Charles Scribner's Sons, 1981.

Martin E. Marty, *Righteous Empire.* New York: Dial Press, 1970.

As a useful reference work, *Eerdman's Handbook to Christianity in America.* Grand Rapids: Wm. B. Eerdmans Publishing Co., 1983.

The Nineteenth Century

Karl Barth, *Protestant Theology in the Nineteenth Century,* tr. by Brian Cozens and John Bowden. London: SCM Press, 1972. Not always fair but wonderfully insightful when at its best.

Mark Schoof, *A Survey of Catholic Theology 1800–1970,* tr. by N. D. Smith. New York: Paulist/Newman Press, 1970.

Ninian Smart, John Clayton, Steven Katz, and Patrick Sherry, eds., *Nineteenth Century Religious Thought in the West,* 3 vols. Cambridge: Cambridge University Press, 1985. The first volume is especially good.

Alec R. Vidler, *The Church in an Age of Revolution.* Baltimore: Penguin Books, 1961.

Claude Welch, *Protestant Thought in the Nineteenth Century,* 2 vols. New Haven, Conn.: Yale University Press, 1972, 1985. The standard scholarly work at this time.

The Twentieth Century

John B. Cobb, *Living Options in Protestant Theology*. Philadelphia: Westminster Press, 1962.

Deane William Ferm, *Contemporary American Theologies*. New York: Seabury Press, 1981.

Alasdair I. C. Heron, *A Century of Protestant Theology*. Philadelphia: Westminster Press, 1980.

William E. Hordern, *A Layman's Guide to Protestant Theology,* rev. ed. New York: Macmillan Co., 1968. An introductory work.

John Macquarrie, *Twentieth Century Religious Thought*. New York: Harper & Row, 1963.

Index